TURNING RIGHT
Inspire the Magic

Praise for *Turning Right – Inspire the Magic*

"Kay uses his great storytelling ability to relate how his life changed when he started turning right. His running and racing is such a perfect metaphor for life and work, and something that is very relatable. Both entertaining and inspiring, he dives into the ebbs and flows ultra runners experience in every race by grappling with his own vulnerability, with honesty and a driving curiosity of how to solve the problems presented to him at any given moment. He uses those experiences in his role as a leader in his work. I highly recommend this uplifting and fun read!"

Meghan Canfield, ultramarathon coach and nine-time US-representative at the 100-km world championships and ten-time top-ten-finisher at Western States 100 Mile Endurance Run

"For sure, this is a must-read. *Turning Right* offers the reader very personal insights into how to see all the options life has to offer. There is much more to life than the daily hamster wheel. *Turning Right* inspires you to explore all the possibilities your life has to offer! You have to dare to read it."

Dr Harald Fanderl, Senior Partner at McKinsey & Company

"One of the insights from Kay's book is: 'Many things in the world we can't control, but we can choose our attitude and mindset.'

"This is a deeply personal account of how a highly intelligent man has challenged his own mindset and attitude to achieve results that were almost impossible, for example winning the Big Red Run. He has disciplined his very rational mind not to focus on the fear of failure but on how to achieve success. His key is to embrace perceived uncertainty and challenges, and then develop the resilience to bounce back from adversity – 'time to fly'. Spontaneously following your intuition leads to the magic happening! This book is really mind training for success in whatever field you choose."

Peter Kirby, former Global CEO of CSR Limited and ICI Paints PLC (UK), former Chair of Dulux Group Limited and Medibank Private, and Board member of Macquarie Bank Limited

"Kay shares a true example that absolutely anything is possible, when you put your mind to it... The book that keeps you thinking long after you've put it down... Inspiring... A true self-reflection of lessons learnt when racing doesn't go to plan."

Kirstin Bull, 100-km world champion 2016

"*Turning Right* is a detailed, entertaining and truly transformative book. It offers every reader, no matter where you are on your journey, a blueprint for greatness. Kay is a high achiever in the academic world, business world and athletic world. His insights will take you from zero to hero using tangible and achievable techniques to transform your world. All you need to do is TURN RIGHT!"

Joe Ward, champion ultra runner, and head coach and founder of Manly Beach Running Club

"Whilst I read this book over a few weeks, it has directly impacted my life throughout the months since. I have learned to stop at the crossroad of opportunity and look left to observe but turn right to thrive. I think this book can help anyone and everyone, and its lessons will stay with you years after turning its pages."

Lucy Bartholomew, elite ultra runner

TURNING RIGHT

INSPIRE THE MAGIC

KAY BRETZ

This book is dedicated to my mentors.

The perception of glory is a rare occurrence in our lives. We fail to wonder, we fail to respond to the presence ... Life is routine and routine is resistance to wonder.

—Abraham Heschel

First published in 2021 by Major Street Publishing Pty Ltd
E: info@majorstreet.com.au W: majorstreet.com.au M: +61 421 707 983

Quantity sales. Special discounts are available on quantity purchases by corporations, associations and others. For more information, contact Lesley Williams using the details above.

Individual sales. Major Street publications are available through most bookstores and can also be ordered directly from Major Street at www.majorstreet.com.au.

Orders for university textbook or course adoption use. For orders of this nature, please contact Lesley Williams using the details above.

© Kay Bretz 2021
The moral rights of the author have been asserted.

A catalogue record for this book is available from the National Library of Australia

Printed book ISBN: 978-0-6489803-2-2
Ebook ISBN: 978-0-6489803-3-9

All rights reserved. Except as permitted under *The Australian Copyright Act 1968* (for example, a fair dealing for the purposes of study, research, criticism or review), no part of this book may be reproduced, stored in a retrieval system, communicated or transmitted in any form or by any means without prior written permission. All inquiries should be made to the publisher.

Cover design by Tess McCabe
Cover image reproduced with kind permission from EYE SEE IMAGES — Patrick O'Kane
Internal design by Production Works

10 9 8 7 6 5 4 3 2 1

Disclaimer: The material in this publication is in the nature of general comment only, and neither purports nor intends to be advice. Readers should not act on the basis of any matter in this publication without considering (and if appropriate taking) professional advice with due regard to their own particular circumstances. The author and publisher expressly disclaim all and any liability to any person, whether a purchaser of this publication or not, in respect of anything and the consequences of anything done or omitted to be done by any such person in reliance, whether whole or partial, upon the whole or any part of the contents of this publication.

CONTENTS

Foreword	Finding a new path	xi
Prologue	Discovering our inner magic	xv
ACT I	**SEEKING THE MAGIC—**	
	EMBARKING INTO THE UNKNOWN	**1**
Chapter 1	Turning right at the garden gate	3
Chapter 2	Turning right beyond the garden gate	17
Chapter 3	Turning right into new territory	39
ACT II	**EXPLORING THE MAGIC—**	
	FAMILIARISING THE UNEXPECTED	**55**
Chapter 4	Turning right to prepare for the desert	57
Chapter 5	Turning right towards the desert	73
Chapter 6	Turning right through the desert	81
Chapter 7	Turning right onto shaky ground	109
Chapter 8	Turning right at the end of the world	127
Chapter 9	Turning right to new heights	141
Chapter 10	Turning right to extreme heights	159
Chapter 11	Turning right to become delirious	175
Chapter 12	Turning right until delirious	189

ACT III	INSPIRING THE MAGIC—	
	RAISING CONSCIOUSNESS	211

Chapter 13	Turning right to look into the past	213
Chapter 14	Turning right to look into the future	229
Chapter 15	Turning right to get ready for the worlds	247
Chapter 16	Turning right with the rest of the world	263
Epilogue	Navigating our turns ahead	283
Acknowledgements		291
About the author		295
Contact us		297
References		299
Index		303

FOREWORD

FINDING A NEW PATH

It's after midnight, I've been running for over 17 hours, and I'm not even at the halfway mark of the race — a 350-kilometre non-stop ultramarathon. The race is aptly named the 'Delirious W.E.S.T.', which is the race organisers' attempt at humour, mixed with the sadistic reality of a point-to-point slog along the Bibbulmun Track in Western Australia that will leave all of us runners not only 'delirious' but also at the point of exhaustion like no other race in the country.

I'm pushing myself hard as I run through the undulating sand dunes rising up next to the Great Australian Bight. Along with poisonous snakes crawling in front of me, I'm dodging cobwebs and spiders every few metres that are at face level. I'm purposely leaving them for the runner behind me whose head torch lights I keep seeing bobbing away in the distance.

The runner behind me is a guy called Kay Bretz, someone I'd never heard of before and someone who had never run this length of race. We had briefly met at the race meeting the day before, and he'd asked me how best to run this race distance as I'd run three 200-mile-plus races previously. As we chatted, I could see Kay was positive about the challenge ahead and that he had the determination to do whatever it took to finish, while still being under no illusion of the difficulty of this lengthy distance.

I had told Kay to run his own race, have a sleep plan and, most of all, enjoy the adventure into the physical and mental unknown. Now I was thinking to myself, *How can this relatively inexperienced runner be pushing me so fiercely?* No matter what I did, it felt like he was just over my shoulder and always gaining. The drive, determination and sense of purpose Kay showed to push to the limits in what was for him an unknown race distance made me want to get to know Kay once the race was over. For now, as we were both battling for the lead, I was fully focused on just trying to keep everything together and not be overtaken by him.

In the days after the race had ended, I spoke with Kay about what had unfolded on the track, and he said to me, 'There are so many things in the world that we can't control, but we can choose our attitude and mindset.' Kay had this unique ability to stick to his race plan under pressure and remain in control of the process, not the outcome of the race. He told me a story about how one day 'turning right' changed his life forever. After years of pre-programming himself to always turn left as he left his house, one moment of deciding to turn right took him on a completely new journey and one that would change his life and mindset, forever.

Just a few months after finishing the 350-kilometre race in Western Australia, Kay's decision to always challenge himself to look for new horizons by 'turning right' would lead to Kay becoming the fastest ever Australian runner at the 24-hour world championships, and he would go on to be awarded the Australian Ultra Performance of the Year. All this came from one simple life-changing moment — one moment that we can all take.

What happens, though, when you don't have the courage or confidence to turn right, and you're missing out on those opportunities that life presents you, by sticking to the daily grind and not challenging yourself to look for new horizons? In 2016, as I was running a 250-kilometre race across the Gobi Desert, I was competing for the win when something peculiar happened to me: I stopped mid-race to help a stray dog across a large river crossing. This was my own 'turning right' moment. It changed my life forever. I think about that moment with everything I do now. If I hadn't taken that decision to do the opposite of what I would normally have done, I wouldn't be writing this foreword, for one thing.

Ultra running has taught me many things about myself, made me stronger and made me learn how to be adaptable under extreme pressure. These life lessons are not only useful in sport but also relatable to life and leadership. If you want to become the best version of yourself, whether that's in day-to-day life, leadership, business or as an athlete, *Turning Right — Inspire the Magic* can guide you to achieve more than you ever thought possible.

Dion Leonard
International bestselling author of *Finding Gobi*

PROLOGUE

DISCOVERING OUR INNER MAGIC

> We tend to think of Sisyphus as a tragic hero, condemned by the gods to shoulder his rock sweatily up the mountain … He doesn't realize that at any moment he is permitted to step aside, let the rock hurtle to the bottom, and go home.
>
> —Stephen Mitchell

My wet clothes were stuck to my body, I was shivering, and it was almost midnight. I didn't have to open my eyes to realise that my worst nightmare was coming true. 'Everything okay?' one of the boys asked. Nothing was okay. This was a disaster, and I was on my own.

I was so close; it was the last night of school camp. All I could do now, however, was escape to the bathroom. I got out of bed to leave the dorm, pretending nothing had happened. But, as I stepped out of the puddle of my own wee, I sensed several pairs of eyes staring at me. Had they noticed that my light blue PJs had dark patches? Hopefully, it was too dark to notice.

When I got back to the room, nobody said a word. All I could do was not stir up any suspicion. For the rest of the night, I lay awake, ashamed and frustrated, in my own sticky mess. Everybody else at the age of almost 13 had learned how to regulate their basic bodily functions. And now this. It could not be worse. At our age, there was no room for any weaknesses. Judith, one of the girls in our class, had been bullied the entire week once somebody discovered she didn't use deodorant. We kids had become brutal, and I would be the next victim.

When we all got up in the morning, I was dreading the announcement — something along the lines of, 'Smartest guy in the class wees himself'. But nobody said anything. I could feel my classmates observing me; they had huddled in little groups and were whispering. Maybe they'd even told the teachers? If I could have, I'd have run away to save myself. Instead, I waited, impatient, and avoided looking at them. When we finally hopped onto the bus home, the public flogging had still not started. Nobody said anything that day.

Nobody said anything the week after, either. Only after several weeks did I realise I had, miraculously, escaped the worst humiliation I could imagine. My frustration with myself, however, only grew. Every few nights I needed to change into dry gear. Nobody could help. Comments such as 'Time will heal everything' from the doctors had been a lie. To add insult to injury, my father didn't stop taunting me. Declaring, 'Kay, you will wake up in a wet bed on your wedding night' was funny to him.

A few months after school camp, I was in bed reading about a little boy who was dying from an incurable cancer. While his situation was significantly more serious than mine, I could imagine how he must have felt. Being stuck in a hopeless situation was lonely. The moment would come when you just had to give up.

That was not what that boy did. Instead, according to the story, he invented a mind game in which he commanded an imaginary miniature spaceship. He navigated this spaceship through his body, destroying every cancerous cell it encountered. He made this game a nightly routine, similar to brushing his teeth, and every evening before going to sleep his spaceship slaughtered cancer cells. One day, the doctors brought him the unexpected news that his tumour was getting smaller. Within months, he was cured.

That was the answer. If this boy could cure himself with only the power of his mind, I could do the same. If my mind was creating the problem in the first place, my mind could fix it. This was clearly the path out of my misery, and I was determined. 'I will no longer wee in my bed. Never again.' Trust was the answer. With trust in myself, I could achieve anything.

My solemn vow was, almost instantly, countered by my cynicism and the small voice asking, 'What if that boy never existed? What if the writer had made the story up? What if his cure wasn't because of his mind game?' Those were reasonable objections, and they started to convince me. It wasn't going to work. My high-flying hopes were deflating.

But I was so sick of my misery that I was prepared to even trust an approach that sounded silly. I intuitively knew what I had to do: I needed to take my frightened self and begin a journey. 'Maybe we won't succeed straightaway,' I told myself. 'And, if we wake up again in a puddle, we won't panic. It might take a bit of practice. Hang in there. We can do this.' That would become my daily encouragement.

Night after night, I was dry. Each day I'd recite the promise in my mind. Nights turned into weeks. Until, finally, I had overcome my embarrassing habit.

My entire outlook shifted, and not only in relation to my wedding night. I'd seen a glimpse of the immense power I had. I could not unsee it and, more importantly, it became the spark to finding out what else was possible if I put my mind to it. And the emerging question went deeper than asking what else I could achieve. It was about who I could become, and maybe even who I was.

My epiphany was that for all those years I'd been searching in the wrong spot. I was looking for external help or trying to get different skills to make my problem disappear. Instead, I had to shift to a new identity. There was nothing to learn and only things to unlearn. I had to transform — like a caterpillar into a butterfly — but to do that, I had to drop my self-doubt. For once, I had to trust myself and know I was no longer a victim.

I felt relief, but also anger. Why had nobody told me about the powers we hold inside? What I had experienced went beyond the mental processing powers I was developing. I couldn't even speak to anyone and find out whose voice had come from deep within me. I was far too ashamed to tell anybody about the miracle.

Before long, the memory started to fade away. The adult world I grew into had no place for magical encounters or 'miracles'. Success became the mature version of childish magic. Thus, I became good at being successful. I was awarded a doctorate in record time and travelled the world as a top management consultant for global firm McKinsey. The half-life of success got shorter and shorter, however, and what grew was my desire to reignite the magic I had experienced and share it with others.

Through a succession of crazy running adventures (which I outline in this book), I embarked on an inner journey and learned how to nurture that inner voice that had saved me when I was an insecure kid — my intuition. I was passionate about exploring the depths of the mysterious forces I had once seen. I wanted to leave behind the limitations I placed on myself, this time for good. What followed was a scary journey, where I left behind the part of me that had made me a successful runner and executive. This same part had ultimately prevented me from reaching my dreams. My entire perspective on what we are all capable of shifted when I transformed from a recreational marathon runner into one of the best ultramarathon athletes in the world.

But this book is not about athletics or super-human performance. When we face seemingly unsolvable challenges, having additional skills or taking advantage of more favourable circumstances are rarely sufficient to cut through. The solution is not external; it is within us. The path requires us to leave the world we are familiar with and embrace the unknown. The key step is that first one — crossing the threshold into the unknown. That is when we allow transformation to take place.

My quest is around transforming who we think we are to reach our highest aspirations. This book is all about helping you unlock both your biggest challenges and your innermost dreams by revolutionising your inner game and undergoing vertical development — step-changing your personal growth and accessing a new level of awareness.

I've written *Turning Right — Inspire the Magic* in three 'acts'. The first act of the book focuses on the possibilities that open up when you take fate into your own hands and change your trajectory. Both as a manager and a marathon runner, I was disillusioned by life.

A seemingly random right turn led me outside of my comfort zone and challenged my identification with success. My journey was no longer built on a yearning for greatness; it was the start of an expedition to explore the magic.

The second act of the book sheds light on what it takes to unleash the magic within you and reach new heights. For me, a series of growing running adventures, culminating in a 350-kilometre race, challenged me to deal more effectively with the unexpected.

In the final act, I hope to answer my question, 'How do we make the magic accessible in the whole of our life?' Our volatile world is asking for accelerated leadership development and cultural transformation in organisations. By raising your consciousness, you can become better equipped to deal with what's thrown at you, knowing you can reach your highest aspirations.

Turning Right — Inspire the Magic is for people who, like me, desire more from their existence and have the courage to lead a life where they shine brightly. To help with your own transformational journey, I've included 'self check-in' questions at the end of each chapter to help you reflect on the journey and focus on this course.

I'm curious — what magic is waiting to emerge from within you? Over and over again, I have experienced the joy of leaving behind what seems reasonable and logical. And, over and over again, I have seen how doing so can unleash something extraordinary in us. I hope this book inspires you to encounter what you're seeking in life and unleash the extraordinary within you.

ACT I

SEEKING THE MAGIC

EMBARKING INTO THE UNKNOWN

Two roads diverged in a wood, and I —
I took the one less traveled by,
And that has made all the difference.

—Robert Frost

CHAPTER 1

TURNING RIGHT AT THE GARDEN GATE

> *Sadly, developing our leadership effectiveness often gets side-lined because we resist the vulnerability of learning and changing.*
>
> —Robert Anderson and William Adams

I had sneaked out while it was pitch black, before anybody else was awake. I was getting absolutely drenched, which I hated, but at least I'd gotten used to the darkness. Running through these hilly, unfamiliar streets in heavy rain was no fun. Yet, in six months' time, I had to be in the shape of my life.

The upcoming trip back home to Germany after two years of not having seen my family would be special, but the icing on the cake would be to run the Berlin marathon and pass through the Brandenburg Gate as countless spectators cheered me to the finish line. I've loved running marathons since high school, and I'd missed it keenly when I worked as a management consultant. Here was an opportunity to not only run another personal best but also do it at home.

My work weeks of up to 100 hours and seemingly constant jetlag at McKinsey had put a hold on my passion. I knew all this time had been an investment in securing a decent career, and it had opened surprising doors. When I left Germany, my experience had catapulted me into a senior position with a major supermarket in Melbourne, Australia — the other side of the world. I no longer worked the crazy hours of a consultant and thrived on getting back to my love for running. It kept me sane. I loved the freedom of those early morning runs, and they became a non-negotiable in my daily routine — that is, until the reality of running my department kicked in.

Colleagues had often asked me how I found the time to run as much as I did. Not being in a relationship certainly helped, I answered, but there was more to it. Running was not a time-drainer for me; on the contrary, I couldn't afford not to run. When I did give myself the occasional rest day, I got significantly less done than on the days I ran. Even my team noticed that lack of balance. The more I ran, the more the other areas of my life just fell into place.

Once again, I had lost myself in thoughts during my run in the dark and rain and, as my morning exercise was coming to an end, I saw I had only to make it up one last hill. My enthusiasm for hills was not far off from my hate for running in the rain. Hills sucked.

For the entire week, I'd had no choice but to run hills. I was looking forward to getting back into my usual routine, but for a couple more days I was locked away with a bunch of work colleagues for an offsite training course. 'Inspiring the Magic' was the theme for the course, elegantly summing up my employer's next grand vision.

I couldn't make up my mind whether the course was great or a waste of time. While a multi-year turnaround had significantly improved my employer's market performance, the company culture seemed to have been sacrificed along the way. For me, work was anything but inspirational, and I felt only a massive portion of magic would fix the overall sentiment and team engagement. Most of our energy was drained by meetings, and the level of aggression among colleagues seemed to rise with the rank of the attendees.

One of the worst experiences for any employee was to be invited into the boardroom and witness an episode of yelling and fists banging on the table. The most obvious indicator that the state of tension was rising was when a leader pushed the button for the creeping frost on the boardroom's big glass walls. From one moment to the next, the transparent fishbowl turned into an opaque hideout. Nobody in the open-plan office could witness the scene, but everyone knew what was happening.

The experience reminded me of my dad's regular outbursts and mum racing to shut all the windows, so the family shame was not shared with the entire neighbourhood. By this time in my life, I'd hoped to have closed the chapter on being an abuse victim, but there it was — an appalling show of autocratic behaviour that I hadn't thought would be tolerated by grown-up executives. As a teenager, I had learned that making myself small was the wrong strategy. Once I stood up for both my mother and myself, my dad stopped his aggressions.

INSPIRING THE MAGIC

If we did not find a way to fix our company culture, we would regress into darker times. The largely dictatorial management style might, in the short term, have helped accelerate decision-making and fix business fundamentals. Now, though, the high turnover of employees and our fear, or inability, to express our opinions did very little to foster the sustainable upward trajectory the board expected from us. To lead the company into the next transformative phase, the entire leadership team needed to learn how to bring out their 'X-factor'. To date, all directors had participated in the 'Inspiring the Magic' course. So far, however, I hadn't really seen many of them shift their behaviours. Now, all expectations lay on us, the levels below.

The content of the course was promising. But without role-modelling from the very top, the program was doomed to fail. I certainly wasn't going to endure the toxic environment forever. Not only was the business in desperate need of change, but so was I. I felt stuck. I was responsible for pricing and offering great customer value in the middle of a price war and, while it was never going to be an easy task, I was too familiar with the topic to have sleepless nights over it. My personal learning curve had flattened out — I had no proper challenge and, for the first time in my life, was barely being stretched.

I was craving more 'oomph'. Finding that feeling of being on top of the world was becoming harder and harder. My colleagues would have said that I was expecting too much from life. What else did I need apart from doing a great job, being backed by the leadership team and receiving a good salary? Wasn't my success sufficient? I even carved out enough time for daily sports. I should be happy, was the implication.

Still, I did have a predicament. I didn't feel satisfied with my achievements, and any acknowledgement of them faded almost instantly. I had success, but I lacked fulfilment. Every time I reached a higher peak, I realised it wasn't what I was looking for in the first place.

Yet, what was the alternative to pushing myself in work and sports? *No*, I thought and doubled down on my efforts; perhaps the next peak would be more fulfilling. Some light was better than no light at all, and I didn't know of any other way to reignite the magic in my life.

Once again, I had gotten so lost in my own head that I hadn't even noticed I'd conquered the final hill of my run. I had to park my biggest challenge for another time. Now, back at the conference centre, I had just enough time for a quick shower and to inhale some breakfast before our day started. The agenda looked promising — with a stimulating guest speaker who would be the highlight of the week.

Gavin Freeman's credentials were most impressive. Apart from working as a business coach, he had been a sports psychologist for the Australian team at Summer Olympics, Winter Olympics and Paralympics. Particularly notable was that he had been responsible for the mental training of the archery team leading into the 2000 Sydney Olympics, which culminated in Simon Fairweather's gold medal.

The memories came back about how I, always a sports enthusiast, changed my sleeping routine over weeks to follow the Sydney games live on TV from Germany, where I lived at the time. I remembered jumping up and down in my living room, cheering for middle-distance runner Nils Schumann, who surprised with a gold medal in the 800-metre race. Now, I was intrigued to discover what it took to win a gold medal for your country, with thousands of spectators cheering in the stadium and millions following on TV. Managing that level of pressure was beyond my comprehension. Mastering such a skill would be handy, regardless whether I was running marathons or a department.

The first few morning sessions of the course were not overly exciting. Finally, after a few hours, Gavin Freeman stood in front of us.

He covered health and wellbeing, and we discussed how to enhance our leadership by leading ourselves better. The suggested solution, however, barely required anybody of his calibre. In a nutshell, his recommendations included getting sufficient sleep, doing some exercise and eating a balanced diet. I agreed completely, but the session did not teach me anything new. Those were basics even non-athletes knew. Impatiently, I looked at the clock. Gavin had turned into the man who stood between us and our lunch break.

Thinking about lunch helped me see the irony of the situation. Here we were talking about healthy food, and what was waiting for us next door? A platter of mostly unhealthy sandwiches, spread with uninspired ingredients packed with mayonnaise — one ingredient I would not touch with a barge pole. The other meals of the day were not much healthier, but at least they were tasty. I imagined how great it would be to see my favourite lunch waiting for me: a large plate of pasta with cheese. Even though I ate it every single day, I never got sick of it.

'Kay, are you with us?' No longer did the facilitator pronounce my first name as if it were a girl's name, rhyming with day. By now he knew it was pronounced 'Kai' and rhymed with sky. My German parents could never have foreseen that giving me this boy's name would lead to regular confusion once their son lived in an English-speaking country. Over the years, I'd gotten used to it.

The facilitator took a step towards me and asked, 'Do you have a question for Gavin?' My silence went on for so long that the room buzzed. Luckily, a colleague stepped in. She asked Gavin what made the difference between winning and losing at the Olympics. Why did some favourites choke on competition day? Instantly, Gavin was in his element. I could sense this was his world. Probably, he was as bored talking about the basics of wellbeing as it had come across. Suddenly, he was full of energy, and his entire body was radiating the glory of the Olympics. Finally, Gavin demonstrated that he was worth his money.

He explained how the difference in the competitors' mindsets determined their results. Each one of us could be motivated along a spectrum of two extremes. On the one hand, we could strive to overcome challenges, focus on the process and give our best. With that mindset, anything was possible. He called it 'motivation to succeed'. On the other hand, we could spend our energy avoiding a negative outcome. This was 'motivation to avoid failure'. Whenever people with a similar skill level competed against each other, their mindset made the difference. When we witnessed favourites choke, they were typically driven by their fears. They were motivated to not fail, rather than motivated to succeed. In summary, Gavin concluded, the key difference between good and great was the ability to perform consistently under pressure.

Gavin triggered something in me that I had not felt for a long time. For a moment, I had the privilege of seeing life from a completely fresh perspective. Instead of being caught in the settled life I was leading, I could smell adventure in the air. Those elite athletes were working hard on themselves to overcome enormous challenges. How I wished to be one of them. Delayed gratification is not everyone's cup of tea, but I had come to terms with the reality that the reward was all the sweeter when it followed the upfront hardships. But how was I motivated? To succeed or to avoid failure? Colleagues and friends considered me a positive guy. Therefore, surely, I was mainly motivated to succeed?

Gavin had referred to a magical feeling where anything seemed possible. I knew that feeling of being invincible, without being restrained by the usual limitations. The more Gavin explained the concept, the more it dawned on me that my mindset had shifted over time. Initially, when marathons were new to me, I wanted to expand my limits. Nowadays, running mainly served the purpose of stilling my hunger for another personal best. There was little room for error. Everything needed to be perfect: my training plan, my discipline, the course profile and the conditions on race day. Nothing could be left to chance; I needed to manage any detail I could think of. I realised my focus was all about not stuffing up, not failing.

In a recent marathon everything had come together to run another personal best. The following day, a colleague brushed away my achievement with a cold, 'All of that effort for a meagre nine seconds?' He disregarded sports being more about the journey than the outcome, and I wanted to be clear — a win was a win. I was disappointed he wouldn't acknowledge my mental toughness, fighting to the final metres of the race. Whereas the race result might not have a life beyond the race itself, I thought that I could bring the mindset that achieved it anywhere, including to work. Where he had a point was that my talent was limited and, soon, I could not expect any more improvements. I was terrified about reaching the imminent plateau. Was it possible that I was motivated not to fail? After all my efforts, maybe I just didn't have what it took to be great?

Luckily, the session concluded and, with it, my dark thoughts disappeared. Once everyone had sprinted off to lunch, I introduced myself to Gavin, and we had a short chat about sports. I told him I was training for the Berlin marathon and that I was intrigued by the idea of working on the mental side of things and shifting my mindset. I had never, either in sports or at work, come across anybody who had put any effort into this area. He affirmed I had to work on it if I wanted to become great.

To get me started, he promised to send me his book *The Business Olympian*, in which he transferred lessons from elite athletes into management. If I had any questions, I could always reach out to him. What a generous offer. Not a wasted morning after all, I had to acknowledge. Maybe his book would reveal some secrets to becoming a faster runner. It took me by surprise to notice that potential business improvements excited me significantly less.

EMBRACING THE MYSTERY

Suddenly, momentum was pumped back into my life. Everything happened quickly from there. Before I got home from the workshop, Gavin sent me a PDF version of his book, along with an invitation for a coffee catch-up. Luckily, I could spend the weekend reading his book in preparation. I did not read it; I inhaled it. I sensed an entirely new world opening up in front of me. Everything was so different from what I knew — so much so I even had to re-read the book to grasp its richness.

A week later, I sneaked out of work early to meet Gavin in a café. The afternoon wind had picked up, and I was chilly sitting outside just in my shirt. I wished Gavin had picked a quieter place. Hordes of school children streamed out of the nearby train station, and several kids bumped into our table as they passed by. The café staff weren't welcoming either, announcing that we could only squeeze in a quick coffee before they shut.

Nothing happening around us seemed to bother Gavin, however. He was interested in who I was and why a manager like me was so obsessed with marathons. My passion for sports must have come across, because only a few minutes into our conversation Gavin suddenly offered to mentor me for the upcoming event in Berlin. He would help me experience the difference between good and great. I would learn what he had taught Olympians and become a master of pressure situations.

I had just hit the jackpot. An expert in his field was taking an interest in my passion. With his help, I would easily run another personal best in Berlin. To my surprise, Gavin did not even want to charge me for his support. He only said, 'Sometimes you have to pay it forward. What goes around comes around.' He had worked with many elite athletes aspiring to become business people. Why not the other way around, work with a manager on his athletic efforts? All I had to do was put my approach on paper, so that he could build on it. That assignment was straight down my alley. If I was good at something, it was communicating a plan.

I was riding a wave of excitement and, by the end of the following weekend, Gavin had my detailed 12-page plan in his inbox. It was a masterpiece I was proud of. Similar to a child waiting for Christmas, I was desperate to receive his reply. From there onwards, things turned fast. Gavin sent me a text a few days later, which brought me back down to earth. He sounded way less excited than I had been and just stated, 'Kay, we better catch up in person. I do not want you to misunderstand me.' Oh dear. It sounded like I was going to hear some uncomfortable news.

As much as I tried, I could not find any flaws in my plan. Impatiently, I waited for our next catch-up, this time over an early breakfast before going to work. It was our first breakfast meeting at The Merchants Guild, which was about to turn into our headquarters. We had much more privacy for meaningful conversations, and the food menu was original. The superfood breakfast was a winner and so was the freshly brewed chai latte.

Gavin was still half asleep and looked as if he had just rolled out of bed. Even after a strong long black, he couldn't give me the answers I was hoping for. I heard what he was saying but didn't understand a single word. Nothing made sense to me. 'You're too planned and don't leave anything to chance' was his verdict. Apparently, my plan was very diligent and would be great for anyone else. *Perfect*, I thought. Not for me, though. Gavin had a gut feeling that my plan was not giving me room to deal with the unexpected. While road marathons didn't throw up many unknown variables, in his experience, something always went off plan in any challenge. He suspected that I was not good at dealing with curve balls, in sports or in business.

Gavin was aware that he could hardly explain what he was trying to convey. With no further explanations, he asked me to just trust him and his intuition.

Too planned? What? My plans had gotten me to where I was now. I was a fast marathon runner due to my planning and disciplined execution. And now he expected me to trust him, when he could not even explain his point of view? Surely, the Olympians he had coached had received better explanations than what he'd given me. I had no time to dwell on this trust matter, however, because our conversation was about to get worse.

Gavin didn't waste a single further word on how we could save my plan. He ignored it altogether. Apparently, it was not worth the paper it was written on — not if the aim was to lift me from good to great. I was hoping to find another edge, but Gavin was not interested in tempo sessions, interval efforts or long runs. Running training, he said, was just a ticket to the game, purely the basics that needed to be done and, therefore, my responsibility. He'd support me through my mental training. Then, suddenly, he got excited and for the first time that morning appeared awake. 'Kay, you have to do runs, but you cannot foresee what they are about.'

Clever, Sherlock. How should I plan to do something unplanned? Gavin was still going on about this risk of something unexpected happening in the race and me not being able to cope with it effectively. My urge to control could be my downfall. He kept repeating himself, until he said, 'Why don't you ask a friend to lead a running session, without telling you what it is? All you do is follow him and do whatever he does.'

My face must have gone white and, in shock, the only answer I could get out was, 'Do you mean a mystery run?' That was exactly what he meant. Within a few minutes his idea had gained shape. I just had to run. If the pace increased, I would run faster until my friend slowed down again, whenever that might be and for however long the session would last. Anything between a walk and a sprint was possible. A session might finish after five minutes or last for several hours. I would not be able to figure out what I was in for the entire way. No control. It sounded like torture.

The more excited Gavin got, the more my curiosity was replaced by sheer terror. I knew my friend Corey was the ideal partner for this mystery run. We were best friends and already trained together on weekends. My mistake was that I called Corey straight after breakfast and told him all about Gavin's suggestion. It was no surprise that he loved the idea, and I had lost my chance to get off the hook. That morning, I had made two gentlemen very happy. The first, Gavin, was content with his plan and wished me good luck for the mystery run, saying farewell with a massive grin on his face. The second, Corey, laughed at the prospect of making me suffer. I got tricked and missed my chance to stay in control.

When I had arrived in Australia, I had been warned of the 'tall poppy syndrome': stick out your neck too high, and you will be chopped back to size. My brain was already racing, and I tried to figure out how I could survive those sessions.

While I might have been better at marathons, Corey had a middle-distance running background and was much faster than me. Both of us knew that he could 'break' me whenever he chose to do so. At no point during the mystery run would I know for how much longer I had to hang in to find relief. Naturally, my key concern was when it would be fair to give up. Asking Gavin for help was clearly a mistake. Relying on Corey was another mistake; he just wanted to see me suffer. I was on a path to disaster. Mystery runs sounded like hell and, in the end, I was probably wasting precious time to train for a faster marathon. I had just lost ownership over my training and potentially even the prospect of a successful race altogether. Calling off the mystery run would be for the best.

Pure pride probably prevented me from chickening out; I'd have to admit to Corey that I was terrified. Maybe, deep down, I was curious to see what Gavin had in mind. In the few days leading into the first mystery run, I tried to get ready as best as I could. I read Gavin's book for a third time and found it made absolutely no reference to mystery runs. He apparently let Olympians off the hook way easier than me. Even worse was the fact that he had not given me a single clue how to prepare myself. When Corey picked me up at my house in Albert Park, on the south side of Melbourne, I was tense and nervous. The grin on his face was at least as big as Gavin's when we'd said goodbye after breakfast. These guys were having far too much fun at my expense.

Without doubt, my sole motivation was to avoid failure. My thoughts were spinning around the level of discomfort at which I had the right to give up. I felt like I'd just gotten on a roller-coaster, with the suspense building up as I slowly crept up that first climb. Only this was not going to be any fun. Corey dropped his belongings in my kitchen and led the way out — no more time to say any prayers. The mystery session was on. He opened the front door and then the flyscreen, crossed the little front garden, went through the garden gate and turned right. Corey turned right and so did I.

SELF CHECK-IN

- What brings you joy and revitalises you?
- To what extent do you seek this joy out, or feel you should try to be happy with what you already have?
- What are you dreaming of in your life?
- When did you last challenge yourself way outside of your comfort zone?

CHAPTER 2

TURNING RIGHT BEYOND THE GARDEN GATE

Messy disruptions will be most powerful when combined with creative skill.
—Tim Harford

I had lived in Albert Park for almost three years and ran daily. Yet, I had never come out of my front yard and turned right. Every single time I had left my house, I had turned left at my garden gate. I didn't even have a reason for it. My street was parallel to the beach, so I did two left turns to get to Beach Road. Instead, I could have done two right turns to get there. That was what Corey did. It had just never occurred to me.

I had no time to further ponder our choice of direction. We were only a few minutes into the run, and my concerns were growing. This felt wrong and uncomfortable. Corey was on a mission and, once we heard the first kilometre beep of his GPS watch, he increased the pace. This was a very different Corey from the one I normally trained with. It always took him forever to get moving in the mornings. Now, we were only five minutes into the run and he was running at marathon pace. And so was I. My thoughts were racing: How long would he be doing this? Why was he doing this to me? I should have known better and not said yes to this mystery run. Silly me. Maybe there was a way out of this? Maybe cut it short. Or even better, stop now.

Before I could pull the pin, I unexpectedly got a bit of time to breathe. After only one kilometre of this faster pace, Corey slowed down and took a very unusual route through St Kilda, passing shops and some random, unfamiliar residential streets. He was clearly taking me on an emotional roller-coaster, shaking me up in a scary ride, oscillating between hope and despair. We were about to hit the next bumpy section and accelerate. Corey took us on to a footy oval, where he picked up the pace to almost a sprint. Huffing and puffing, I managed to finish the first lap. No stop, no rest, onto our second lap. 'Corey! Don't break me!' I said, but he didn't hear. The cries for help were happening in my head. I didn't have enough air to scream out loud. Again, it must have been my pride that prevented me from giving up. Soon, though, I would have spent the last drop of it. My breaking point was close.

Luckily, we left the oval after just two laps. After not even 10 kilometres we were on our way back towards Albert Park. Less than an hour had passed since we had left my home, and I was grateful to have survived the first session.

Corey looked at me and, smiling, mentioned he'd signed up for a triathlon the following day. That explained why we were easing into these mystery runs. I quickly learned it was a mistake to assume anything, however. Corey waved in the direction of my house, laughed and picked up the pace again. The session was far from over. We kept on going towards Port Melbourne.

This time, he was not going to let me off the hook, and we did the next two kilometres at a punishingly fast pace. Corey was clearly relishing his power over me. The struggle for me was not the speed. I was keeping up. The issue was the next edition of the narrative unfolding in my head. I was thinking through the worst-case scenario, still unsure when to give up. Normally, the idea of approaching a fixed finish line got me through to the end. My self-talk could be, 'I'm exhausted now, but I can hang on for another kilometre. Then it will be over. Now, only 500 metres left. I can see the finish line; 200 metres to go. Done.'

But now, how could I unlock those last reserves and push through if I couldn't make any assumptions? I felt helpless and stripped of any comfort by this man, Corey, who was no longer pretending to be a friend.

Luckily, he didn't try to 'break' me and, after 17 kilometres, we reached home. I was still alive. Instantly, I played down the discomfort and fear. The run itself had not been as hard as expected. I wasn't sure I enjoyed the run — it was different from anything I had ever done before — but I appreciated that we'd eased into it. As I reflected, I realised that the most intriguing aspect had occurred at my garden gate, before we actually got started — I had turned right.

EXPLORING RIGHT TURNS

I tried to figure out what turning right meant. Every time I left my house, I turned the same way. Over time, I had become rigid and was acting on my conditioned reflexes. Although I constantly had a choice to explore the alternative option, I repetitively chose the predictable outcome and turned the way I knew inside out. In the moment of turning right, I felt I had stumbled over something very important; however, now, with a bit of distance, I could not see any benefit. Reviewing it rationally, nothing seemed to be wrong with turning left. It had helped me gain numerous successes. How would turning right make me a faster runner? It didn't make any sense. The more urgent question was, what did I need to do next?

When I reported back to Gavin, he was very pleased and almost surprised how little time it had taken to get to a breakthrough. He was exaggerating. All that had happened was Corey had messed with my routine. I was desperate for explanations but, for a second time, Gavin refused to provide them. The mission we were on was to get me from good to great, and that meant further developing my ability to perform under pressure and to do it consistently. Rationalising would hamper further progress, and Gavin prescribed another mystery run with Corey. 'Just see what happens,' were Gavin's wise words before he hung up the phone.

Two weeks later, on Good Friday, Corey was on mystery-run duties again. He was creative and took me to a place I had never been before. We drove for about 40 minutes to get to Lysterfield Park, in the foothills of the Dandenong Ranges, with its network of running and mountain biking tracks. He knew that trail running was new to me, so why not get off the roads for a session? I had no expectation that he'd be letting me off the hook as easily as the first time. We had a long weekend ahead of us, and Corey didn't have a triathlon scheduled that he needed to save his energy for. I did not expect any mercy and was waiting for the crucifixion to begin — and I didn't have to wait for long. After a warm-up and a few shorter surges, Corey got serious.

We got to the bottom of a nasty hill, only a few hundred metres long but extremely steep. I had almost stumbled when we'd run it in the downhill direction during our warm-up. Now we were about to go up. Corey's shuffle turned into a sprint. My brief was to keep up with him. We were both moving at pace, climbing quickly and breathing heavily. I kept up pretty well and then suddenly noticed I was accelerating even more. I was now a step ahead of Corey and could hear him breathing into my neck. We probably had another 100 metres to go. My muscles started to burn. But I was not giving in to the pain. I was pulling away from Corey even further. I reached the top first and felt like I had just conquered Mount Everest. My heart was racing and I could barely breathe, but I was on top of the world.

Now this was a breakthrough. Well, it was significantly more than a breakthrough — it was a miracle. It was another right turn. Even though I didn't understand what it meant exactly, I knew it was true. Again, I had entered unchartered territory. Compared to me, Corey was a middle-distance specialist. In none of the cross-country and road races we'd participated in did I ever have a chance of keeping up with him. I had never out-sprinted him either. The only distance I was faster at was over a full marathon.

This run had only been over a few hundred metres, and I was far from a hill expert. On the contrary, I sucked at running hills. In my first race in Australia, a half-marathon event in Melbourne, I had to run a small elevation on each of the two laps. I had been breathing heavily when another competitor passed me, looked over his shoulder and noted, 'You don't like hills, do you?'

Being faster than Corey was surprising enough. Even more remarkable was that I hadn't made a conscious decision to increase my pace and overtake him. I had just followed my gut. That was acting outside of character. My default would have been to not even give it a go, because I 'knew' that Corey was the faster runner. This time, however, my competitive drive and my intuition had taken over. There had been no self-talk, no assessment of whether it would be a smart thing to do and, most importantly, no fear of being overtaken again. The result was a surprise my rational brain had been unable to predict. I had just focused on the task at hand, allowed the miracle to unfold and almost felt like a spectator as it did.

Corey tried to redeem himself on two other hills that morning, but I had smelled blood and was relentless each time — until Corey crowned me the mountain goat. After only two mystery runs, I was entering the new world Gavin had sketched in *The Business Olympian*. That sensation that anything was possible was a force kicking in, propelling me to a different level. I had re-encountered that magical feeling of achieving something way beyond my imagination. I was not any fitter when I sprinted up that hill in Lysterfield Park. The secret was not in my legs. I had unlocked something in my mind. A link existed between turning right and this magic, but I still could not figure it out. All I knew was that this second mystery run had rattled my belief about what I was capable of. If I could outrun Corey, what else could I do?

Gavin owed me some explanations. Over the following weeks, however, Gavin made himself scarce, so all I could do was see what else would happen. One Monday night after work, I went to a training session with my running buddies from South Melbourne Athletics and the Crosbie Crew. We did 10 intervals of 400 metres with a short recovery in between sets. I dreaded tough track sessions like this one. Not even halfway through, I always asked myself how I was going to get to the last set. That night was no different until I completed the set of 10. As always, I felt a big weight lift off my shoulders when the last lap was done and dusted. I had given it my all and was pleased with the session.

The coach approached me and asked me to join another runner on her last set. She had arrived late and so was 400 metres behind everyone else. Without even questioning, I did lap number 11. No arguments; no thinking it had not been the plan. I just did an additional 400 metres. This might not have been a big deal for many, but for me it was. Usually, I would have refused, arguing I was exhausted. It was an unfair expectation. It was not part of the deal. I would probably even accompanied this with some swear words. That night, though, I confirmed that something was shifting in me. I was, again, turning right.

Even Corey started pointing out that I was turning right more often. He used the term whenever I acted out of character or when I was not being 'myself'. One Sunday, after a massive training week for me, the two of us went for an easy long run. Given that my legs were tired from a big week, we agreed to not do a mystery run and instead just run slowly for about 25 kilometres and chat along the way. To my surprise, at around halfway, Corey threw the gentlemen's agreement out the window and suddenly increased the pace. With a cheeky grin, he demanded I do the same. It was time for another right turn. I resisted and got angry. He wasn't sticking to the plan. I got even angrier when he pointed out that I hadn't learned my lessons from the previous mystery runs.

Corey stormed off, and I continued at my slower pace, also storming. He couldn't just introduce a mystery run whenever he wanted to and make me his puppet. I was dwelling on how heavy my legs felt and stayed annoyed at him. Yet, before long it dawned on me that perhaps he had a point. Was I falling back into old habits and just following what I deemed the smart thing to do? What if I just picked up the pace?

I dropped my pride and caught up with Corey. We moved faster and faster, with Corey pushing the pace and me hanging in. Jointly, we were flying along Beach Road. No words were required; we both understood that this had become competitive. The session had morphed from a casual chat to a battle between two competitive adults, who behaved like immature adolescents. Neither of us gave the other the satisfaction of giving up first. We both raced until we got back to where we started.

In hindsight, it turned out to be the most valuable training session, getting me into race mode for Berlin.

My departure to Berlin was approaching, and I finally got to catch up with Gavin again. When he entered The Merchants Guild for our next breakfast catch-up, he seemed more awake than the previous time and his expression mirrored my excitement. Times had changed since the prescription of my mystery runs — finally, Gavin was going to shed some light on what had been happening.

Through the mystery runs, my model of the world had been shattered. I had always been very disciplined and, with that, had become a faster runner. Yet, due to the law of diminishing returns, the efficiency gains were getting smaller and smaller. Trying harder had its limits, and I had reached a plateau. What got me to this point was not getting me much further. Nonetheless, I kept on clinging to old ways of working and missed the point that their usefulness had expired. The less I saw them working, the more my motivation to avoid failure grew.

My self-control, which once had been my strength and had gotten me to where I was, was now limiting me. I had over-extended my gifts.

Gavin had taken away my ability to play out my default behaviour and conditioned reflexes. No longer could I be planned, disciplined and well considered. I didn't know what Corey was going to do next, so I had to wing it. The trick was to not listen to my seductive voice of reason, which was also full of self-criticism, judgements and set expectations. When I stopped thinking altogether, I went beyond what I believed to be possible. As a consequence, I experienced a completely different approach — getting me to unexpected heights.

Gavin hadn't finished, and I was astonished how complex the inner game was. To reset my beliefs, I needed to experience first-hand that my autopilot had flaws. Using a rational argument about changing my beliefs regarding training would not have convinced me. Therefore, Gavin had refrained from explaining anything.

Instead, my experiences opened up the possibility for transformation. And, in turn, I discovered that the key was to embrace uncertainty. I had to leave my comfort zone and deal with discomfort for anything to become possible. I had turned right at my garden gate into unknown territory in my first mystery run, disrupting engrained behaviour. Subsequently, metaphorically speaking, I turned right more often. It did not even matter whether I turned right coincidently or intentionally. Each right turn was nothing more than crossing the threshold into unknown territory. I perceived uncertainty as danger and, therefore, needed courage to keep going. The reward was a significant shift in my perspective, perhaps even a paradigm shift.

I thought back to when I raced Corey on the hill in Lysterfield. I had never previously challenged him, because I 'knew' that he was faster. My rational mind told me that failure was inevitable. Spontaneously racing him and following my intuition was a move out of character. The nature of turning right meant I couldn't predict the result. By letting go of conditioned behaviour, I opened myself up to unknown possibilities. Instead of securing predictable results, I embarked on an adventure with uncertain outcomes. When I fully immersed myself in the unknown, suspending my thinking, surprising solutions presented themselves and could lead to unexpected outcomes. This discovery surely could have consequences for mindset shifts in any of us, allowing us to let go of rigidity, predictability and fear, and instead become curious, courageous and full of energy. When you stop thinking and your intuition takes over, solutions present themselves effortlessly, which could lead to unexpected performance and growth.

I had a lot to take in. If there was a simple message, it was this: I was my own worst enemy. My head was getting in the way of extraordinary experiences. To see more of the magic unfold, I had to turn right more often. The price to pay was to overcome discomfort and fear. Courage was key. My primary objective had been to avoid disappointments, and I had gotten stuck in the reactive habits and patterns I had developed consequently.

Instead of reacting to problems from a state of fear, I had to learn to embrace challenges, driven by my aspirations. For Gavin, my results so far confirmed we were on the right path. I got the impression that turning right granted access to a new territory, way beyond the journey from turning good into great. The magic had a different quality to greatness.

DEALING WITH THE UNEXPECTED

Suddenly, Gavin's face turned serious. He reminded me that the biggest challenge still lay ahead. I should not forget that eventually we were here to make the shift from good to great. The test would be whether I could perform consistently under pressure in Berlin, where I should expect to fight a mental battle. While I could sense the pressure rising, Gavin changed tack yet again and had another surprise for me.

He demanded I drop my goal finishing time. First, he'd insisted on no structured plan, then messed with my routines and now wanted me to not have clarity of what goal I was supposed to chase. Gavin asked me to just set the intention to allow the impossible to eventuate. His challenge was that any goal was arbitrary and most likely restricting me. Goals had their place but also their limits. I was a master at setting realistic goals but inexperienced in allowing whatever was possible to unfold.

Next, Gavin put on a solemn voice and handed me a cheap rubber band, the kind most people dump in their kitchen drawers. Before I could make fun of the generous gift, he explained its value. I was to wear it around my wrist during the race. If I started running into serious trouble, I just had to flick it, and I would run well again. No black magic was involved. Psychologically, the light pain inflicted by the rubber hitting my skin would trigger an effect called 'thought stoppage'. Instead of getting caught up by my mental drama, I would leave negativity behind and get back on track.

I left the catch-up with a final piece of advice from Gavin and, as always, he wanted to shake things up. He recommended I have a few runs with no other purpose in mind than to have fun. My GPS watch allowed me to see the route I had taken on a map once I completed a run. Gavin's idea was for my route on the map to spell the name of my employer. He wanted me to be artistic and take the seriousness out of running for once. It sounded pretty stupid to me.

Therefore, I used my artistic freedom to only take on the spirit of his idea.

I chose a section of my neighbourhood and ran through every single street at least once. On the map it looked like I had coloured in the block. How I hated painting. But I was very proud of my work and sent him a screenshot of my first 'Picasso run'. After repeating the session twice more in other sections of my neighbourhood, it was time to pack for Europe. Whatever was ahead of me was going to be way more serious.

It was great to fly back to Germany and hug my mum, after not seeing her for a few years. When I was five years old, I would routinely jump on my parents' bed as if it were a trampoline and fly into her arms. I would not only tell her how much I loved her but also clumsily indicate with my little arms how big my love for her was.

Despite all the time that had elapsed since we'd seen each other, I could still count on my mum's moral support and hoped to spot her along the course while I was racing the Berlin marathon. Of course, for the majority of the event, I'd have to fight it out on my own.

When I checked in to my hotel in Berlin, I was informed that breakfast wasn't available at the ungodly hour when I needed it before the start of the race. If I had learned one thing in the months working with Gavin, it was adaptability. Not having breakfast was not an option. Instead, I convinced the hotel staff to lend me a microwave so I could make my own porridge in the morning.

After picking up the race bib, I had to complete two more important tasks. One was to practise catching the train to the start line. Gavin had told me to practise any race-morning procedures to avoid unnecessary stress — and I was glad I took the train to the start area the afternoon before, because I learned about maintenance works and how to navigate the diversion. Finally, I had found a role for my discipline.

The last activity before going to bed was to meditate, which I was relatively new to. While I found it challenging to just sit and pay attention to my breath, I welcomed its calming benefits. I had worked hard for this race, and I couldn't deny that I felt the pressure building up. Gavin had freely offered his help; it was on me to ensure his generosity had been worthwhile.

I had never participated in a sporting event as big as the Berlin marathon, and the atmosphere at the start line was worth all the early wake-up calls for training before going to work. I had the privilege of starting right behind the elite runners and was only metres away from a bunch of Kenyan competitors. Before I knew it, we were off — and I was just loving it.

Surrounded by 40,000 fellow athletes, I glided through the streets of the German capital, which were packed with spectators. I was experienced enough to know that a marathon did not start before the 30-kilometre mark. Anywhere from there onwards, I expected to have to dig deep.

Gavin had warned me of the chance of something completely unexpected happening. Disaster struck even before halfway. Only 18 kilometres into the race, out of nowhere, it felt like someone had punched me in my chest. The pain was excruciating, and I could hardly breathe. What was happening? I had never experienced this pain before. It frightened me. Was something dangerous happening? I was concerned about my health.

The pain forced me to slow down. A few strides later, I even had to walk. I lacked the oxygen to run. My fears grew. Did I have to write off my ambitions and give up my race? I could not carry on like this. Was this where my journey with Gavin was coming to an end?

Runners were passing me right, left and centre. I tried to breathe deeply to ease the heaviness on my chest. Then I remembered the rubber band Gavin had given me. For a second, I was not paying attention to my chest but to my wrist. What a relief that short, sharp pain was. It did not stick around but went with the same speed with which it came. And as it went, it took away the chest pain. Flicking the rubber worked. I regained my rhythm and with it my hope. The chest pain eased as mysteriously as it had appeared. Within a hundred metres, I was back on track. It seemed like my mind was playing tricks on me, but I had no further time to look back. My dream had resurrected, and the next 24 kilometres required my full focus.

It was a long way to the finish line, and I had to fight every single remaining metre. I certainly had run easier marathons in the past. Then, the Brandenburg Gate came into sight. Shortly after, I completed my fastest marathon ever, improving my personal best by two minutes to 2 hours and 44 minutes.

I felt weird. On the one hand, I was happy and proud. I had achieved my biggest improvement for the last few years. I had stepped up from good to great and testified that I could perform consistently under pressure. On the other hand, some dark thoughts lingered in my head. The Berlin marathon hadn't been the extraordinary breakthrough I had secretly hoped for.

It was Mum who lifted my spirits. Being with her reminded me of the uncountable instances during my childhood when I had been confined to my bed due to yet another mid-ear infection. She was my rock, giving me comfort and strength in the good and the bad times.

After the race, we had pasta for lunch in a quirky Berlin restaurant. My mother reminded me of what the statistics didn't capture, and that personal development was much more rewarding and sustainable than success. She pointed out that I was thriving on finding growth through challenging myself. My mother was right; the journey itself had been worth more than the finisher medal. Turning right had taught me a lot more than becoming consistent under pressure. What had made the difference was a new choice of direction at a well-known junction. I was on an amazing trajectory. My mindset was shifting, even though I could not fully put my finger on where the journey was going.

Thanks to Gavin and Corey, I had experienced miracles right in front of my doorstep. It started with a small dent in my belief in routines and ended up with opening the floodgates for unknown possibilities. I had embarked on an adventure far outside of my comfort zone and seen snippets of what was possible when I connected with my gut feeling. Once I stopped confining myself, something much more immense was within me wanting to manifest itself. The question which emerged was, who would I become if I continued on the path of turning right?

EMBEDDING THE MAGIC

I would have loved to stay longer in Europe, but my boss had only approved a two-week break. In no time, I was back at work and the memories of Berlin were fading. While the 'Inspiring the Magic' course had a significant impact on me personally, it seemed to have failed in its original purpose to turn around the company culture. Directors saw it as a skill-improvement project, instead of a journey to upgrade our collective identity. What had started as a transformational program was reduced to a bundle of change initiatives of the outer game; the idea or ideal of advancing our inner game was neglected. With several changes at the top, the ways of working deteriorated even further.

I was convinced that all we needed was the top management to turn right as well. But they were as stuck in their old ways as I had been. Their own cultural transformation program had failed. Was transforming someone who did not want to change ever going to be possible?

I tried to resist the daily routine getting its claws back into me again. With work tumbling further into darkness, however, that was almost an impossible task. How I would have loved to trigger the change we desperately needed. Broader inspiration in the work context was too much for me to chew off. Yet, I was determined not to let go of the magic I had encountered. I could start small by inspiring the magic in my own team and double down on running. Turning right was much more powerful than to just be used for running a personal best. What had started with Gavin's call to strive for greatness had evolved into the pursuit of magic. I sensed that I could allow its full glory to flourish but, to do so, I needed to find out how to broaden its application.

I was aware that, throughout my life, magical moments had never stuck for long. The risk of reverting to old habits was high. I was under no illusions — my inner demons, who craved control, had by no means been crushed. They were waiting for their comeback. I sensed that I urgently needed Gavin's advice.

I was surprised to feel sad driving to our next breakfast catch-up at The Merchants Guild. Then I realised it was because the best adventure of my life had come to an end. This was it. From here, I was on my own again. All that remained was a final review with Gavin and, hopefully, some wise words before saying goodbye.

With mixed feelings, I handed Gavin my parting gift, an official t-shirt from the Berlin marathon. We were both looking at some race photos online when Gavin asked me whether anything unforeseen had occurred during the race, reminding me that his suspicion that I wouldn't be able to cope with the unexpected had been the genesis of the mystery runs and our turning right adventure.

Now it was me with a grin on his face. I confirmed that he had been spot-on and told him the story of my sudden chest pain and how I got past it with help of his rubber band. To my surprise, Gavin wasn't listening, though. One of the photos had grabbed his full attention, and he asked me why I was running next to a car.

I had completely forgotten about the ominous vehicle on the course, which had appeared relatively early on in the race. Now, it all came back. It must have been at the German parliament. I had just found my rhythm when a white BMW suddenly came from behind, moving through the field of runners. It overtook me, but I caught up with it again a few kilometres later as it was slowing down. I overtook it, only to be overtaken again shortly after. Having to deal with traffic was actually even more unexpected than the chest pain that struck a bit later. Yet, the car hadn't disturbed my concentration. I had not only locked it out of my focus while it was happening, but also erased it from my memory.

I could see deep satisfaction on Gavin's face. This story was worth more to him than the t-shirt I had given him — it was the ultimate proof I had come a long way. Previously, such an incident would have hijacked my attention and quite likely destroyed the entire race. It would have made me angry and frustrated. A car had no right to be there, and driving through runners was not what was supposed to happen during a marathon. But, instead of trying to make the situation what I wanted it to be, I dealt with what was happening. And the purpose of the mysterious car revealed itself later in the race — it picked up the elite pacers, who dropped out of the race. Their role was to help the Kenyan winner Dennis Kimetto stay on course for a new world record.

I picked this moment with Gavin as my opportunity to share my concern that I would lose touch with the magic again. If I were a better athlete and able to make a living with running, I would have been prepared to switch careers. Unfortunately, that was an unrealistic scenario. My place was in the corporate world. While I was dwelling in my self-pity, Gavin was in charge again. He confirmed that I needed to consolidate the new mindset, because the risk of reverting back into old patterns was indeed high. To do so, I had to take two actions. The first task was straightforward: I had to transfer the insights into the work context. Jointly, we would hold a workshop with my team and any interested colleagues to share our journey and discuss its relevance for them.

The second task was to 'change the language'. This was similar to a final exam, Gavin pointed out. I was letting go of old worldviews and coming to a new conclusion of who I thought I was. My development was as profound as the metamorphosis of a caterpillar to a butterfly. I was in the process of finding a new identity, but my transformation would not be complete until I used new terminology for the new mindset. This somehow made sense to me: once a caterpillar turned into a butterfly, it substituted 'crawling' for 'flying'. It couldn't express the new activity by referencing old habits. But I had no idea what that meant in my case. What was the new creative language around turning right? And how was it different from the old reactive language around 'being in control'?

I went around in circles and did not get to a satisfactory solution for what the new language could be. And I couldn't endlessly dwell on this task, because the workshop with my team was approaching and had to be prepared. I loved the fact that this assignment unexpectedly extended the time I could work with Gavin, as we jointly outlined how we would run the workshop. A few weeks later, about 40 team members came together to discuss what shifting from good to great took.

We shared our story in all its glory and all its ugliness. My team roared with laughter when Gavin painted the picture how he kicked me out of my comfort zone. The terrified look on my face had been priceless. When he mentioned that my urge to be in control was an issue, someone shouted from the back that we should have asked them. Even the metaphor of turning right resonated with them as a catalyst for the transformational journey. The room became quieter at the realisation that what got us here as a team would not get us any further. Changing successful habits, which had reached their operational limits, was one of the hardest challenges. I could see their brains working.

For the majority of the time, we explored how each one of us could become better at consistently performing under pressure. We brought to life the four areas that shaped our inner game: discipline, focus, resilience and motivation to succeed. It was fascinating to observe what captured the audience's attention.

While there was agreement on the need for discipline and focus, the energy in the room stayed relatively flat. It appeared those elements were mostly regarded as boring or were associated with frustration. Once we moved on to resilience, everybody seemed awake. Resilience was seen as extremely relevant in the work context — especially as the deteriorating culture in our company demanded a strong ability to bounce back from adversity.

The final concept of motivation to succeed versus motivation not to fail was new to most and led to significant self-reflection and many insights. The closing photo of our presentation was a shot of me running in Berlin. I seemed to hover above the ground and had given it the title 'Time to fly'. Somebody summed up beautifully their insight into this with a question: how much more might we be capable of, if only we were caught up less in our own reactivity? We pointed out that it all depended on how we navigated the junctions we were so familiar with. We could either stay on autopilot or explore the unknown path, which might lead to the magic.

The only section that did not resonate with anybody was when I shared the change from old to new language. To consolidate my transformation, I explained I needed new reference points, and that I had moved from 'Kay-the-pacer' to 'Kay-the-racer'. Pacing stood for conscious control and being overly careful, whereas racing stood for intuition and courage. Everybody looked at me in silence with blank faces. They were missing how this could be applied at work. I might as well have talked Latin to them; the new language was dead. I had failed Gavin's final exam. If he was right about its importance to ensuring the sustainability of our journey, big trouble was looming over the horizon. Familiar demons would come back and haunt me.

The workshop was received well — despite there being some discomfort and a loss of energy in the awkward section. But did it inspire anybody? Probably not. We all went back to our desks and carried on with our work. I did not feel that I had cracked how to apply turning right to the business world. I felt I had only tapped into a fraction of what it was capable of achieving.

There it was again: that underlying dissatisfaction deep within me. I had hoped for more. Probably, I had been overly aspirational expecting a magical reaction. If inspiration was my goal, I had much more to learn. At least the session served as a nice wrap-up of an extraordinary adventure with Gavin.

A few weeks later, I caught up with one of my peers who had attended the workshop. We were sitting at his desk when a piece of paper pinned to the wall caught my attention. I read three words in big capital letters: 'TIME TO FLY'.

SELF CHECK-IN

- Think of a time in your life when you 'turned right'. What happened and what struggles did you have to overcome?
- What exactly was the right turn for you, and how did it interrupt engrained behaviour?
- What growth emerged from deep within your inherent potential?

- What tightly held beliefs dissolved or did you let go of?
- What magic do you feel is waiting within you? Is now your time to fly?

CHAPTER 3

TURNING RIGHT INTO NEW TERRITORY

Playing to Win is consciously choosing to not automatically avoid situations in which we might fail, be embarrassed, or rejected.

—Larry Wilson and Hersch Wilson

Weeks had passed since the Berlin marathon, but I was still suffering the 'post-marathon blues'. I felt lethargic and flat and, with my usual sense of purpose missing, crawled to work every day. Keeping the spirits up in my own department was not particularly inspiring, and the struggle with work tumbled me further into darkness.

Berlin was such a major adventure and, for me, a massive accomplishment. Since returning, nothing seemed worth getting out of bed for.

In the past, I'd committed to the next marathon almost as soon as I'd crossed the finish line. It was a highly effective drill to bring back the energy as well as compensate for darkness in other areas of my life. Running ever-faster marathons was who I was, and I moved from one race to the next, looking for improved performance. For a short while the successes numbed my insecurities; soon, though, I was desperate for ever higher doses of success.

CHANGING DIRECTION

I'd been caught off balance this time. Understanding that chasing success was never going to be fulfilling had been a dramatic insight; but I'd even, with Gavin's help, experienced the alternative. I'd gone beyond the mere result of the race and found growth, perhaps even some deeper meaning. After being stuck for years, I had reconnected to that exhilarating state of mind where anything was possible.

On no account was I going to lose that 'oomph' by regressing to pure results-based thinking. Another personal best? Not what I needed. I was tired of running marathons and, even though I had not yet run the even faster marathon time I was capable of running, I had made up my mind. No more marathons.

But what could I do instead to embed the magic in my life?

After the workshop with my team, Gavin had casually planted the idea of my switching from running to triathlons. He had asked why I wasn't considering doing an Ironman event, trying to qualify for the world championships in Hawaii. I agreed that my marathon days were over. But why add swimming and cycling, just to get to what I really loved doing — running?

I'd always loved running. Even at the age of nine months I must have become so frustrated that I was incapable of crawling that I skipped that step completely, stood up and started walking. I developed a love for propelling myself forward on my own feet and remember the seemingly endless energy I had as a kid to run around the schoolyard.

I was good at most sports at school — although the German national sport of football (or soccer, as my Australian colleagues insisted on calling it) was the exception. I preferred being goalie or, even better, watching other kids play from the sideline. At 16, I spent a year at a Scottish boarding school, and my love for running grew. To be part of any group, I had to be good at sports; my academic success was meaningless. On the first day of school in Scotland, I had to face the new reality: I sucked at sports. The autumn/winter term was rugby season, and I had never held a rugby ball let alone knew any of the rules. After multiple forward passes I was sidelined and never returned to the field. I found my new home in the cross-country running team and did not tempt fate in subsequent terms, knowing I would have been similarly useless at hockey and cricket. Instead, I became good at running.

Yet, even after my performance at Berlin, Gavin was clearly overestimating my athletic capabilities. His idea about my participating at world championships level was unrealistic. I just didn't have that level of talent. But something was still worth doing — I just needed to find it. I needed another shock to the system.

To find that shock, it was time for another right turn. I realised what excited me was the idea of running ultramarathons. Any distance above the traditional marathon could be called an 'ultra' race, but I became interested in the ones with distances significantly longer than a marathon. Mentally and physically, they were far from 'more of the same'; they were a completely different beast from what I had ever tackled. Many of them required participants to get off paved or sealed roads onto trails and out of the major cities into nature. I was ready to dive into the deep end of the pool of ultra-distance running and set my sights on Big Red Run. When I'd first read about it, it had seemed terrifying. Now, this was exactly the kind of stretch I was after.

Big Red Run, a 250-kilometre race through the Simpson Desert in the middle of the Australian outback, had a purpose other than merely running. Through it, the organisers were raising funds for research into finding a cure for type 1 diabetes. The run started and finished outside the iconic Birdsville Hotel. Runners would be far away from so-called civilisation, surrounded mostly by sand dunes. Their only company would be thousands of flies, dedicated to finding, and attaching themselves to, any spot of moisture on their face and body.

At night, participants slept on rocky ground in tents and, unless too exhausted to care, would have a prime location to observe millions of stars. The race schedule included a marathon on each of the first three days (42 kilometres), followed by a 'sprint day' (32 kilometres). The classification would then be finalised on the 'long day', with a double-marathon (84 kilometres). The final eight kilometres on the sixth day were untimed and were instead the time for runners to celebrate their achievements together and, traditionally, finish with a beer or two. Participating would be an epic challenge and one far bigger than anything I'd done before.

This was so far outside of my comfort zone, and taking it on was probably even bordering on stupidity. Yet, such a challenge — such a call to let go of any unnecessary control — might be the price to pay for witnessing something miraculous. I'd experienced a measure of personal growth when I explored unknown territory before, and I'd even endured the discomfort that came with it. Obviously, this was a race that asked for more turning right.

Pushing my limits was the recipe for not getting stuck again. I wanted to leave behind my old, well-measured self, who only committed to safe options. I liked the vision of learning from sports and applying it across life. And, right then, I needed something that disrupted my habits; something that scared me. The best way to learn was to immerse myself in a big challenge and let the experience be my teacher.

The discovery of turning right had been the spark to make me pursue my yearning for leading my life more courageously. When I'd trained to be consistent under pressure, I'd moved from good to great. Yet, while consistency led to greatness, turning right led to something more powerful. It led to miracles. Outrunning Corey at the hill in Lysterfield Park was one of many recent examples. Turning right had catapulted me to heights beyond any measurable success, and had led to me being more spontaneous and following my intuition. It was as if I were becoming a new person. Certainly, this new approach would boost my development and bring light into my life, which, when thinking about work, was pretty grim. Maybe I would even experience more of those meaningful moments that had the potential to change my life forever.

More questions were alive. What would happen if I turned right more often? Would it really reinvigorate my life? Who would I become? I was after more of those goosebumps I got when I was vulnerable, yet stumbled my way forward anyway. I wanted to fly again. If I could keep up that motivation to succeed, nothing could stop me.

WRESTLING WITH FEAR

I had an almost romantic vision of turning right: I was going to follow the mysterious calling, leave my comfort zone, walk new paths and explore unknown territory. I would answer the call to another adventure full of excitement, mystery and fun. If Berlin was what great looked like, what did it take to go to the next level? Was it as simple as giving it a go, pushing through discomfort? And, if it were that simple, was anything possible? That was how I remembered feeling after the right turn unfolded in Berlin. So I was excited and ready to sign up for Big Red Run. Till then, it had been all self-talk and no action.

But that evening, all too soon the fears rushed in. Doubts crept out of the dark and entered my head. Whereas during the day I'd felt like a hero embarking on the next adventurous quest, when I was home that night and lying in bed, I was terrified. I twisted and turned, trying to shake off the uncomfortable feeling of being overwhelmed. I had underestimated how quickly my fears would crush my excitement. Any intellectual understanding of the expected benefits seemed irrelevant.

The warnings and put-downs yelled an unambiguous message. Even in a car, they complained, 250 kilometres was a long drive; running it was a crazy notion. Maybe I was a reasonable marathon runner, but this was out of my league. And besides the ridiculous distance, I was a road runner and not made for trails; I was made even less for running on soft sand. I then moved on to the mental side, which I knew would be even more challenging than the physical aspects. Knowing my brain, it would shout and scream once my legs became tired on the first day of the race. I would still have to run more than 200 kilometres on the following stages. No relief would be waiting on the horizon. I didn't have what it took to complete Big Red Run. It was brutal news to digest, but it was spot-on. My inner voice was right. I had forgotten to conduct a reality check.

I'd become used to being among the best at whatever I worked hard for. My mother had taught me how to be successful, role-modelling the values of excellence, determination and resilience. I was a top student and had even managed to score the highest mark in my English class in Scotland. Being smart at school and graduating from university in record time with a master's degree and then a doctorate certainly attracted a lot of envy, but I learned how to deal with some classmates' hostility. In my corporate life, I never looked back climbing up that ladder.

The prospect of leaving marathons behind opened the very door I'd avoided all my life. On the wall behind that door was written, in capital letters, FAILURE. Choosing Big Red Run was choosing the path to disaster. Being destined to fail reminded me of art lessons in primary school. Art was the only subject I was never good at, and I hated anything to do with painting — with a passion. I was 10 years old when, for the only time in my life, I earned a mark on my final report that was not 'very good' or at least 'good'. No, it was 'satisfactory', and it was my mark in art. From the day of receiving that catastrophic report, two new, highly effective golden rules took over my life. Number one, don't pursue activities where failure is likely, such as drawing and painting. Number two, put in whatever work it takes to see sunshine and avoid rain.

All the clarity I'd had during the day about signing up for Big Red Run vanished with nightfall. Undeniably, I had forgotten the sweat, the pain and the hardships I'd experienced during the training for Berlin. All the misery that formed part of my previous endeavour had been replaced by the glory of completion. Suddenly, all those struggles came back with a vengeance. The more I thought about Big Red Run, the clearer I could see that I was kidding myself. I saw a vivid picture of the worst-case scenario, and it appeared very realistic.

Why waste my time, if I could not finish the race? Instead, I could just stick with what I was good at, running marathons.

For short periods, the story of 'I can't do this!' was interrupted by a weak, hopeful voice. My inner adventurer spoke up. He was keen to travel to the centre of Australia and was excited about giving the race a go. According to him, success was an option.

Over the course of more than six months, my training could prepare me for these crazy distances. Something inside me was desperate to grow. As the same time, my confusion about which voice to follow increased. As the night wore on, I decided to review each concern individually. Would any of them stop me? I needed to regain control over the chaos in my head.

The analysis, however, only opened the floodgates for all the reasons Big Red Run was a stupid idea. How would I find the time to train like a maniac? Compromising work was not an option. What about the risk of injury? Training efforts would be in vain. What about my safety in the desert? I'd heard about a woman who did a trail race and suffered serious burns in a bushfire.

One barrier solved only led to the next stop sign. I could no longer distinguish what was a genuine concern and what was just an excuse. My thoughts were going round and round in repetitive loops. I became even more unsure about what to do.

I was afraid of having to sacrifice what I had worked for during my entire running career. At least I knew very well how to be successful at running marathons. The excitement might have palled, but at least I had certainty. Doing something new, on the other hand, was full of question marks. I could not attach any tangible value to the unknown path. So far, I had invested years and years of effort and sweat into becoming faster at marathons. Was it worth leaving all of that behind? This loud voice was coming from my inner bureaucrat, who urged me to come to my senses, to not be irrational and pursue a path doomed to fail. The call to adventure I heard came from treacherous sirens, luring me to catastrophe.

Midnight was approaching, and I was still paralysed. Every few minutes I switched on the light again, sat up and checked any information I could find on Big Red Run. It didn't get me anywhere, because I couldn't trust any of my inner voices.

'What would Gavin say?' I wondered out loud. I realised he would simply ask, 'Kay, are you motivated to succeed or not to fail?' That was the answer. I could not have both security and growth at the same time. If I dared to do something new, I'd inevitably make mistakes along the way. This was how we all learned.

But right now, I was trying to avoid slip-ups at all costs. The thrilling desire to expand had silently turned into the command to not stuff up. The challenge felt like a threat to my existence. Success was an integral part of who I was, and I had disproportionate anxiety about failing.

That was why my inner bureaucrat wanted to drag me into safe, shallow waters. By focusing on the dangers, I refrained from pushing the envelope. I tried to avoid the situation altogether and faced the risk of running ultramarathons ending up in the same drawer as painting. My fears were keeping me small and comfortable. Instead of aspiring to thrive, I was happy to merely survive.

Over the years, I had fought my battles and gained a fair share of scars. I'd matured and was 'realistic' in what to expect. Or was it only that I now selected safe situations, where the prospect of losing was never on the line? I'd worked extremely hard all those years to build the illusion that my life was under control. My recipe was working, and it had made me who I was. There was nothing wrong with clinging to my own way. Or was there?

RISKING FAILURE

Deep down, I knew that if I kept doing the same thing, nothing would change and stagnation was inevitable. I could still remember how I'd felt before the mystery runs; clinging to predictability and control and, thus, repeatedly turning the same way every day. Now, it was too costly to keep believing my old story. I had the burning desire to embark on a quest for more oomph in my life. For that, I had to stretch my imagination and embrace uncertainty.

Making lists of pros and cons kept me wrapped up in a world of thinking. My rational mind was after security, predictability and control. It gave me a very clear picture of hell, but was less able to provide a vision of heaven. But when I stopped thinking and trusted my intuition, the magic happened. My next step was clear. If I wanted any sleep, I immediately had to sign up for the race. No more overthinking. No more listening to my cynicism. I was going to drop the desire to be sensible and see for myself. I was being asked to stand tall and face my fears. I'd done this as a teenager when I'd signed up for my very first marathon.

The memories of 1998 came back. In my last year of high school, I was certainly not known for making stupid decisions. On the contrary, I thought things through from all possible angles and made sound decisions; in other words, I was a typical insecure over-achiever. But on this occasion of deciding to run my first marathon? I was terrified. Still, I was also excited. I'd outwitted the sensible decision-maker in me and instead followed my intuition. It turned out to be a stroke of genius. I was on a mission and simply announced to my friend, 'Sven, I'm going to do this.'

Let me set the scene more fully. We'd just been on our weekly run, and it was a sunny yet muggy spring afternoon. Friends from the age of six, Sven and I were now preparing for final exams and entry into university. For us, running was a great way to mix studying with a mental recharge, and we'd recently taken up 'serious' long-distance training: one run a week of about one hour. The runs helped me concentrate and feel less stressed. What fascinated me was that each run had the opposite effect on my mind than it had on my body. A run upset the body and wore me out but calmed the mind and allowed me to be more focused.

On that day, our legs were wobbly. That happened every time at the end of our runs, and I could pinpoint the moment they became shaky: exactly when the run faded out into a walk. Our bodies were just not used to the effort we asked from them. This was a particularly humid day, and we were sweating more than usual. To cool off, we stayed on the street outside my parents' house and chatted.

Nowadays, I can't be certain who started the conversation, but my bet would be on Sven. It was just not the type of idea I would have had. While we were standing there on our exhausted legs, Sven suddenly burst out, 'I bet we could run a marathon.' The idea was now out there. My reaction — as a typical adolescent — was, 'Sure we can.' Grow our confidence and point out how good we were at the same time.

'Not many in our school could run for an hour without walking. We do that every week.' One of us added, 'We might not be super-fast, but we're not slow. Today, we ran further than last week.' In that moment, we were both convinced we could do it. Nothing was stopping us. The conclusion (and conversation) was simple:

'We are going to run a marathon. Are you in?'

'Certainly, I am in.'

'Sure? Because I will run it.'

'So will I. Absolutely sure.'

Our excitement soon took an unexpected hit, however. The following moment, Sven asked me whether I had a clue how long a marathon was. The only answer I had was, 'I don't know exactly. Must be very long.' We could vaguely recall that a marathon event had been held in our hometown of Cologne the prior autumn but, in those times, marathons were not remotely popular. My parents had bought our first computer, but we didn't yet have an internet connection, so we couldn't do any research that way. Luckily, Sven had an old *Men's Health* magazine that could tell us more about marathons. He decided to cycle back home and then let me know about the specifics of what we had just committed to. In the meantime, neither of us had any particular reason to be overly concerned. 'Very long' did not sound impossible.

I had already forgotten about the marathon as I hunched back over my books later that afternoon. When I heard Sven's voice on the phone, however, I knew we were in trouble: 'Kay, it is impossible.' He explained that, at 42.195 kilometres long, we were not capable of running a marathon. I silently agreed that it sounded ridiculous. He was right. We would not be able to succeed. How, in a single race, would we run more than we usually ran in an entire month?

Up to that point, I had not said a single word. I was just listening to Sven's explanation of why we had to bury our young dream of becoming marathon runners. The vision only appealed to my under-developed adventurer; not to the bureaucrat in charge. Suddenly, I heard my own voice say, 'We have committed. Sven, I'm going to do this. Let's do it together! We are going to run a marathon.' I radiated confidence, even though this had no foundation to stand on. But I had positioned myself and did not move from there. I'm still unclear whether I was too proud to back away, overly ambitious or just foolish. The thinking came back a bit later, when Sven confirmed that he was out — and with the thinking came the worrying. But I had committed, and I signed up for the next Cologne marathon.

CROSSING INTO THE UNKNOWN

Back in Melbourne, I had made my choice and history was repeating itself. I'd sign up to Big Red Run and, in doing so, end an era of running marathons. This was precisely how I'd gotten into marathons in the first place — by setting sail without a map but still navigating the foreign waters.

The only difference was that, as an adult, I'd learned to respect my own limitations — or what I believed to be my boundaries — much more. But what if in doing so I had traded in the most precious mindset I had been gifted with — that of courageously exploring new frontiers? And what did I get in return? The feeling of being more in control coupled with the illusion of steering clear of painful failure.

It was past midnight when I searched for my credit card and entered Big Red Run. My inner bureaucrat had almost wrestled me down, but my adventurer had stood up to pursue his desires. I was in. It felt more like the challenge had chosen me rather than the reverse. Now, I could only hope for history repeating itself even further.

Almost two decades earlier, when I'd hobbled over the finish line beneath the majestic Cologne cathedral, I'd felt invincible. I was less proud of the performance itself than the fact I had tackled something that had appeared impossible.

I seemed to repeatedly arrive at similar junctures in my life. I only wished that, with time, crossing the threshold into the unknown became easier. I still struggled accepting that big adventures went hand in hand with vulnerability and uncertain outcomes. If only somebody could have told me how the story would unfold. At least, remembering the episode from my high school years helped me find the courage to follow the calling now and take on the associated risks.

Mine was not a quest for success but an inner journey to reinvigorate my life. This was not a technical challenge either, in the same way as my first ever marathon. I didn't need more skills alone but a completely different mindset. Berlin had laid the foundations. Next, I needed to evolve my capacity to deal with chaos. Not knowing the way was frightening, but it created the optimal tension for me to grow. With Big Red Run, I was facing an adaptive challenge that asked me to morph into whoever I needed to become in order to close the gap between what was required and what I was capable of.

In true Aussie style, I organised a barbecue with my friends and running buddies a couple of weeks later. Until then, I kept my expedition into the desert a secret, but I knew that telling family and friends about my next endeavour would help me be even more committed. While I wasn't going to do the race for them, by telling others, I created some external excitement that would help me through the difficult times.

My friends were surprised and very encouraging. One asked me whether I had chosen the race because I enjoyed running on sand. 'Quite the opposite,' I responded. 'I hate getting bogged down and not making any progress.' How could I explain that the reason I had chosen the race was to learn more about myself? Similar to Olympians who become amazing at what they do by understanding themselves better, I wanted to revolutionise my inner game.

Once my friends left that evening, a wave of fear crushed over me. I had taken a very bold step, without having the faintest idea what it took to get 'desert ready'. The time had come to move on to solving the 'how'. The challenge of signing up had evolved into a challenge of wayfinding.

Despite there being more than six months until the race, no time was to be wasted. I'd signed up to a challenge that seemed unachievable, so neither procrastinating nor losing my composure would serve me. I needed to channel my energy, and the conversation with my friends had revealed what I desperately needed. What better way to start getting ready than running on sand?

By the next morning, Monday, my urge to get started had faded. On Tuesday, I found another excuse to not go to the beach. I felt bad but didn't do anything about it. I was procrastinating.

But I had to bite the bullet. I set the alarm for an early Wednesday morning run to the nearby beach. At 5:30 am, with the night still dark, I started with a warm-up along the firm footpath. I was still avoiding the beach itself but, after a while, I found the next access point to the soft sand and turned right.

SELF CHECK-IN

- Do you have an inner bureaucrat (or something similar)? To what extent does their voice drain out all others?

- What would you do if you had no constraints whatsoever? If you were not afraid?

- When did you last risk all to become all that you can be?

- How could you do more of what fulfils you?

ACT II

EXPLORING THE MAGIC

EMBRACING THE UNEXPECTED

Use yourself as a laboratory to find out who you are and what you are capable of.

—Jon Kabat-Zinn

CHAPTER 4

TURNING RIGHT TO PREPARE FOR THE DESERT

Excellence is mundane. Superlative performance is really a confluence of dozens of small skills or activities ... carefully drilled into habit and then are fitted together into a synthesized whole.

—Daniel Chambliss

Running on sand was worse than expected. It was hard work, and I almost came to a halt straightaway. After about 10 minutes, I finished the session. I hadn't gotten anywhere, had to concentrate to not twist my ankle, and even a snail would have had a chance at outpacing me. Why did I leave predictability and comfort behind, just to run my own race? However, to my surprise, I didn't beat myself up for the short workout. I was just content that I'd started.

Two days later, I did my second sand run, just short of half an hour. It was awful, and it was four kilometres. So the logical question now was, if that was so awful, how would I ever run 250 kilometres?

The clock was ticking on becoming a decent desert runner. I'd signed up for a challenge, created a burning platform — and was now desperately searching for the fire extinguisher. I had no illusions about my strengths. I was more of a problem-solver, and I liked to think things through.

If I was going to run 250 kilometres through the desert, I would have to deal with the unexpected, and adapting to curve balls was not my forte, particularly under pressure. My only chance for some success was to hope that more right turns would bring the answers. Otherwise, I was in big trouble. I'd fail in the desert, and also fail to embed that magic, the light that I'd just re-encountered, when the darkness of my workplace was trying to swallow me.

An unexpected lift came in the form of an invitation from Gavin for another breakfast catch-up. He didn't yet know about my next adventure and just wanted to check in. This would be a chance to surprise him and let him know I was still walking on the exploring path and stress-testing turning right. I'd also come up with a one-page outline of how I wanted to tackle Big Red Run. I'd learned my lesson since I'd presented the over-engineered 12-page plan for the Berlin marathon — the one Gavin subsequently had ripped apart.

To master the challenge ahead, I needed more than new skills. Any adaptive challenge required a new mindset, and this was a dramatic adaptive challenge. My mindset had become too restrictive for it. Big Red Run was a chaotic environment and demanded more than I was presently capable of. So my one-pager was simple. In it, I named three principles of how I'd prepare — adaptability, holistic preparation and consistency.

'Wow, 250 kilometres through the desert?' Gavin said, genuinely surprised. But, once I spelled out my three principles, he instantly promised his full support for the whole journey of my preparation. Another six months working with Gavin! With his guidance till now, I'd experienced how our minds could either limit us or propel us to unexpected performance levels. Gavin gently pointed out that we'd barely scratched the surface, and I was about to learn how to master the inner game.

I wasn't in any doubt that the race would present similar challenges to those we face in everyday life: fears, doubts, lapses of concentration, disappointments and, almost certainly, physical pain would all emerge. It was the ideal playground for learning for life. Also, the race environment would be no different from the business world with its VUCA elements — volatile, uncertain, complex and ambiguous.

I couldn't escape dealing with the unexpected. I'd have to drop my overthinking. We both agreed, Big Red Run was the perfect adventure, and it would lead to more right turns. Turning right had, I sensed, something significantly more profound to offer than lifting good to great — and surely I could translate any lessons learnt to work. As a bonus, this was also my first breakfast meeting with Gavin where he didn't alter my approach. The Berlin experience was paying dividends.

PREPARING INSTEAD OF TRAINING

I had the crew together: Gavin mentoring me and Corey accompanying me on many training runs. Corey seemed almost more excited about my adventure than I was. We did a lot of trail running, and this was truly thrilling — particularly when we met a random fox before sunrise and regularly crossed paths with kangaroos. We also encountered some less appealing wildlife, of course. One morning on a narrow forest trail, Corey almost stepped on a two-metre eastern brown snake.

He only noticed this particularly poisonous reptile warming itself in the early morning sun at the last moment, but managed to jump over it. Straight after the incident, I took over the lead to give Corey an opportunity to process the shock. Within minutes of his lucky escape, I was running down some stairs, saw another snake, had too much momentum to stop and only just managed to miss stepping on it. But it wouldn't send me back to the safe days of running on bitumen.

I was living and breathing the three guiding principles of my preparation — adaptability, holistic preparation and consistency. Adaptability meant I did not have a detailed upfront plan to execute but would be agile and iterative in my approach. It also created room for strengthening my intuition and making further right turns. Holistic preparation expanded my focus beyond mere running training and covered the mental game, getting used to running with mandatory equipment and sorting out hydration and nutrition. Finally, I took consistency under pressure to the next level.

Apart from sand running, the most significant change I made was to meditate regularly — I was diligent about my daily 15-minute sessions, practising stillness. Even without regular practice until then, I'd already felt how powerful meditation could be — providing stronger focus, improved resilience and even a more positive outlook. Perhaps, a more positive outlook could also change negative thought patterns. Maybe even lessen my need to control, allow things to happen and be more comfortable dealing with the here and now. My thinking mind was my biggest enemy during this quest, even more dangerous than the snakes.

After those first days, training only got tougher. One weekend, I wanted to run two training marathons — fitness and more confidence were the goals. Corey led the way in the first run through Lysterfield into the Dandenong Ranges. After only 10 kilometres, disaster struck. I struggled, got slower and eventually had to walk. Neither Corey's encouragement nor his appeals to pull myself together worked. We cut the run short, and I barely made it back to the car. We'd only covered 32 kilometres. I couldn't avoid thinking about the 84 kilometres of desert on the fifth day. It was an insane distance. I came home, defeated — and the worst part was not understanding why I'd been struggling.

Nonetheless, my running shoes were back on before dinner, and I went out to finish the marathon distance for the day. I still felt miserable, but I wanted to prove I had the resilience to get back up after being thrown to the floor. Before sunset, I went to bed and, by the next morning, I felt much better. I decided to give the second marathon a go. Would it be the full distance? I couldn't say, but, strangely enough, I wasn't concerned. All I could do was to try.

I ran to Olympic Park and did laps on the athletics track. At first, I moved slowly, and then got some momentum. So much that I finished a full marathon in just over three hours. The painful experience of my disappointment on the previous day had, it seemed, driven me forward. It turned into one of the biggest confidence boosters in my entire preparation. My take on it was, even if I struggled in one race stage, the following day could still be good. It was a timely lesson not to blindly trust my rational mind. The 'logical' was not necessarily true and, with that realisation, my powerful self-limiting assumption had been transformed into a much more productive belief.

It wasn't only my training that was gaining momentum. I had, some weeks earlier, met Rebecca after she joined the group

I occasionally ran with. Rebecca managed a business unit of a chemical company and so was also unable to regularly make the after-work training sessions. After this first meeting, I hadn't seen her for weeks. But when I received an unexpected invite to her birthday, I was thrilled. When it was clear we wanted to start seeing each other regularly, neither of us knew where we'd find the time. But that wasn't the point. We were choosing the direction and, while wonderful, it also felt like another scary right turn. On the flipside, the more I was juggling, the more relaxed I became. Or was it the reverse?

I'd signed up for a six-hour race on the 400-metre athletics track in Coburg, and this was being held the weekend after we started going out. All runners ran the track for six hours, and the winner would be whoever covered the most distance in that time.

'Isn't running on a track boring?' I was asked, and the word 'boring' brought to mind a somewhat embarrassing experience of my early childhood. My mother had a few friends over, and I was playing with my toys, when suddenly I felt called to contribute to the boring (to me) conversation. Someone had just pointed out how little time her husband was spending at home and how bored she was. I stood up and went over to her to share the wisdom my mother always imparted whenever I complained of boredom. 'You must be really stupid. My mother says that intelligent people don't get bored.' I probably left the awkward silence for my mother to sort out.

As I ran around the track, I did, however, learn that the challenge we often call boredom isn't typically the issue; the real task is staying focused in an environment with little entertainment on offer. How would I deal with the illusion that those six hours would never end? The repetition of the environment wasn't the problem. The repetitive thoughts in my head, which led to anxiety, were.

The first three hours of the race just flew by. Together with 30 other runners, I was cruising around the track, regularly lapped by faster runners and lapping the slower ones. I was calm and aware of the noises around me — footsteps, heavy breathing, birds having arguments, and the cars rushing past in the distance. Halfway in, everybody changed direction. What excitement. We now ran clockwise, but the change in perspective only marginally enhanced the run. It became more of an inner journey than one fed by new externals. During the last hour the sun was beating down, and the track reflected so much heat that running became a tough grind. How I hated that heat; I was not made for desert conditions. First, I lost my rhythm, and then I lost momentum.

I spent the last hour longing for the sound of the finish gun; it did, eventually, end my misery. Most importantly, it liberated me from the negative self-talk that had had me in its tight grip. I was beyond caring that I'd slowed down or lost focus. Yet, I had gone surprisingly far — clocking 188 laps and conquering new territory. I had pushed my limits just beyond 75 kilometres.

So, what had this tough race taught me? The key insight was that the body followed wherever the mind led. I was sure that without meditation practice I wouldn't have done as well. It was my mind that had taken me to a new level. It was also my mind that had prevented me going any further in the last hour of the race. Training the mind was more important than being obsessed with increasing any other skills. So, I was in no doubt I had more work to do to maintain focus in the later stages of a race. Plus, on the physical level, I had to find a more suitable hydration and nutrition strategy. Only a few hours into the race, I'd been craving salts and couldn't bear to swallow more bananas or dry oat bars.

Luckily, it didn't take long to find the solution for my hydration and nutrition needs. The Saturday after Coburg, a friend took me along to a running symposium at Monash University, where they presented research for ultra endurance athletes. A chance to prepare holistically, I thought. So, on the spot, I signed myself up as a guinea pig for their next nutritional study. This involved a handful of visits for multiple tests, including me eating sugar-loaded jelly while running on a treadmill for three hours. The researchers gathered data, and I learned precisely what my body tolerated. It was a rare opportunity to optimise my race nutrition. The professor in charge even provided me with tailor-made freeze-dried food to take into the desert. I'd be equipped with the perfect mixture for the whole six days.

MIXING IT UP

At another catch-up with Gavin at The Merchants Guild, I recounted my experiences. I was, he agreed, making good progress, but he was most concerned by my lack of focus towards the end of the Coburg track race. I wasn't yet strong enough to keep my mind on what needed attention and was still too easily distracted by my own thoughts. When fatigued or afraid, my own thoughts hijacked me; I became a victim to the storm brewing in my head and was no longer in charge. Even when I didn't have a crisis to attend to, my head could wander off on a tangent. I didn't even notice getting lost in internal dialogues, or jumping from one topic to the next.

Gavin suggested I try zero gravity flotation tanks, which had been in vogue decades ago. But I liked the idea and found a facility in the northern suburbs. I spent an hour in a little pod filled with salt water, where I floated with ease. The tank was just big enough so I didn't touch any side and was free of any external input: no noise, no light. I couldn't feel the weight of my own body, and it didn't take long to start feeling like I was floating through space. Though, I wouldn't have wanted to be claustrophobic.

Deprived of the typical sensory overload, I found deep relaxation. There was nothing other than me and my mind — a perfect starting point to observe what my mind did when it had absolutely nothing to do. I discovered my two favourite topics: the past and the future.

I dwelt on past events that couldn't be changed. I worried about potentially dangerous future scenarios, which hadn't yet arrived. Rationally, I knew the only thing I could influence was the present. Nonetheless, it seemed difficult — a real art, in fact — to not get lost in my own mind creations. Spending time in the pod made this easier, so I incorporated regular floating into my preparation, naming them my 'salt coffin sessions'. Gavin also impressed on me the idea of experiential learning instead of theory. Training based on experiential learning was characterised by just giving things a try and seeing for myself what worked — going for experience as opposed to 'mere' understanding. Gavin did his best to counterbalance my tendency to overthink and stay a prisoner of my head. And I had seen for myself that intellectualising did not help me break free from limiting behaviour. It did not lead to deep wisdom. In our following catch-up, Gavin — unexpectedly for him — mentioned a scientific article worth reading, 'The mundanity of excellence' by Daniel Chambliss.

Usually, anything to do with theory would be right up my alley. But I completely forgot to find the article. I got a promotion at work and, suddenly, was responsible for more than double my original patch. I saw it as the confirmation that my focus on team building, in an otherwise autocratic environment, had not gone unnoticed. The timing of increasing the workload was not ideal, however. With only six weeks to Big Red Run, peak training week was approaching and that captured my remaining attention. I would go through my biggest training load in the following fortnight and get an indication of where my preparation was at.

I had four marathons in the next eight days. I also needed to get used to running on my own. Neither Corey nor Rebecca was joining me in the desert. I ticked off three training marathons within a week: Sunday in rainy Melbourne, Wednesday on the treadmill at the Monash laboratory and Saturday in windy Apollo Bay on the Great Ocean Road. Rebecca and I spent the weekend in Apollo Bay, and on the Sunday they held their annual marathon festival, so I tackled it to complete my peak training week.

The excitement of the race and an end of preparation in sight gave me a surprising boost. The hilly run around Apollo Bay, with constant ups and downs, offered us spectacular views over the vast ocean and tiny enclosed bays. It felt like I was hovering over the hills, effortlessly taking the undulations leading back to Apollo Bay. I got a lot of confidence out of the week. Even more important was that my body felt fine and recovered nicely in the following week.

With the completion of the Great Ocean Road marathon, I significantly reduced my running training until Big Red Run. Finally, the time to freshen up had arrived. It didn't mean my preparation was complete, however — far from it. Before the Berlin marathon, Gavin had reminded me, often, about practising to perform consistently under pressure. Now, we'd take it to another level and think of any possible curve ball I'd encounter. The idea was to minimise uncertainty, so I'd have more capacity to deal with whatever actually happened. This meant I spent two nights sleeping in Corey's garden in a tent, testing my gear and getting used to going for a run after a mediocre night's sleep on the ground. At least in the desert, I wouldn't be licked awake by Corey's excited dog, Emma.

Gavin ensured I never got to the conclusion I was 'good enough'. A challenge this big left no room for complacency. He disrupted the way I was working continually and challenged whether more effective ways to do things could be found. I had put a lot of work into my preparation, and I certainly did not drop my discipline on the last kilometre before it counted. How often had I done exactly that in my job — worked hard on an important presentation and not invested the time to rehearse or check out the meeting room for working technology? This time, I'd prepared for any race condition, until I could rely on rock-solid routines. Most crucial would be the 30 minutes after finishing a stage. I would be exhausted but would need to refuel for the next day and stretch my sore muscles.

DIALLING UP THE HEAT

Just when I thought I'd done everything I could, I remembered the article on the scientific study Gavin had mentioned. I had completely forgotten about it, but downloaded it now — and what an eye-opener it was. It summarised the journey Gavin and I had embarked on perfectly. I saw the irony of what Gavin was doing to me: now, when I was no longer craving theoretical foundations for our approach, he provided them.

The theory of the mundanity of excellence outlined by Chambliss in the article held the key to preparing for any major challenge.

Chambliss had investigated swimmers at different performance levels up to the Olympic standard and identified the factors leading to excellence. The main differentiator for performance was finding step-changing improvement opportunities. Olympians refined their technique, fitness level, sleeping and eating habits, understanding of strategy and ability to master their nerves under stress, and optimised the equipment they were using. They were rarely surprised by heat or wind or rain. Their entire approach to training was worlds apart from a competitor on a local level. They worked on the right things, which made all the difference.

Olympians made it their business to understand where their performance gains came from. It was not about spending more time on training per se but deliberately practising what gave them the edge. They focused on what they needed to learn, rather than what they already knew. It boosted my confidence that Gavin had led me in the right direction.

As I had experienced already, working harder had its limits, due to the law of diminishing returns. Instead, the key to superior performances was a different, more effective approach. That was exactly what turning right was about. For Big Red Run, we had broadened my preparation way beyond the fitness effect of running. No runner changed performance bands unless they also changed the approach. Whether in sports or business, any expert in their field needed to find a few differentiating aspects to lift them to that next level. I could only hope that meditation, the salt-coffin sessions, personalised food and mental training — such as running in circles on the track — would give me an edge.

What had helped me in the previous months was to start quickly with any new idea. The threshold into unknown territory was best crossed rapidly, while procrastination easily led to never getting started at all. Previously, I had gotten stuck in what I had considered to be rational thinking. Now, I saw that it had been cynicism in disguise, protecting me from the unknown and from things I did not understand. The key to my growth was to embrace uncertainty and allow progress. As a consequence, the power balance had shifted from my inner bureaucrat towards the adventurer in me.

According to the article, an athlete's discipline distinguished how good they would become. So-called talent might give someone an advantage on the first few metres, but without hard work nobody got to the top. I could relate to talent not being relevant. It had taken me more than a decade to improve by more than 90 minutes from my first marathon in Cologne. In hindsight, talent was often referred to as a root cause, used to post-rationalise why some people advanced to higher spheres. The real reason was that some were better at what they are doing because they were preparing in better ways than others.

It was crucial to not only learn skills but also embed them sufficiently through deliberate practice into reliable routines. Those routines freed up capacity to deal better with the unexpected. Thinking about basic moves became unnecessary and could be left to the automatic brain. This was where well-measured discipline had its place. Only a diligent approach eventually led to superior outcomes. What was relatively new to me was getting the balance right between being flexible to test out new ideas and being strict at working on consistency. Eventually, both aspects needed to come together. That discipline meant flogging oneself was a misconception.

Inspired by the mundanity required to reach excellence, I put the theory directly into practice before heading to Birdsville where

I'd begin the race. One more new element was to be introduced and diligently practised. I had about a fortnight left, and winter had arrived in the Southern Hemisphere. June in Melbourne is, traditionally, freezing and not suitable for someone to adequately prepare for desert conditions. Training in a heat chamber was the answer; however, location, opening times, combined with the cost to access them prevented me from accessing one. So I found a solution.

I hired a treadmill for a couple of weeks, placed it in my kitchen, closed all the doors and created my own heat chamber. I switched on the heater, placed a second heater in front of the treadmill that blew hot air on me, wore a long-sleeved shirt and ran. My improvised heat chamber was accessible 24/7, required no travelling and was only a short distance to my shower. I completed seven heat sessions, running every other day for up to two hours. I had read that our bodies adapted to whatever they were exposed to, but I still didn't believe it early in the process. The first session was tough. Outright awful. The heat made breathing extremely hard. I was drenched in sweat and, after only 20 minutes, just wanted to stop. But progress was quick. By the end of the first week, I was much more comfortable with the conditions. By the last session, it almost felt normal.

Whatever Big Red Run would bring, I felt ready for it. What had made the difference were the right turns in my preparation. Most importantly, I had the courage to innovate. I hadn't found a single silver bullet leading to performance jumps, but had stitched together many little things I would never have tried previously.

I could see the transformation I had undergone under Gavin's guidance. From working harder to reach the next summit, I had shifted to working smarter to become a better climber. The importance of personal development was overtaking the role of success in my life.

I'd compiled a strong mental toolkit and learned how to tackle unknown challenges, though I was far from certain that Big Red Run would confirm my hopes that I could do this consistently. The time had come to test how all this excellent preparation would manifest under race conditions.

SELF CHECK-IN

- In what areas of your life are you doing 'more of the same'?
- Do you allow cynicism to be disguised as rational thinking? Do you listen to it?
- How could you work smarter?

CHAPTER 5

TURNING RIGHT TOWARDS THE DESERT

> *Having an adventure also shows that someone is incompetent, that something has gone wrong ... At the time it happens it usually constitutes an exceedingly disagreeable experience.*
>
> —Vilhjalmur Stefansson

I was finally heading towards the outback to face my biggest challenge ever. 'Trust yourself; you prepared well', were Rebecca's final words as we said goodbye. Instead of a two-day bus journey from Adelaide, I'd treated myself to the regional plane from Brisbane (via other stops) to Birdsville.

Even before I arrived at the departure gate, I met Dr Adam Brownhill, our race doctor and so a handy man to know. He knew how to treat blisters, could help with gastro issues and help us alleviate any emerging niggles before they turned into injuries. I was about to inundate him with questions when we were suddenly surrounded by athletes. Most of the passengers were runners and, somehow, I felt sorry for any of the other travellers who'd have to put up with the excited atmosphere — mostly pleasant, but also creating a lot of noise and chatter. It felt like a primary school excursion with jumpy kids waiting for the bus. We weren't school kids, of course, and some of us were already past the age of retirement, but the volume we generated would have competed with any school class.

This clutch of excited athletes represented the spectrum of runners: from the insane ultra athlete, who had already run hundreds of kilometres without stopping, to complete novices, who had not even run a full marathon before signing up. I quickly decided I was the only 'normal' person participating in the race, because I was neither of those extremes. But I'd have time for my assessment to be invalidated — an announcement of a flight delay due to fog on the route meant we had more time to bond.

The route, similar to that of a regional bus trip, had us landing at multiple stopovers before Birdsville. Apart from Brisbane, I'd not heard of any of them — Toowoomba, Charleville, Quilpie and Windorah — but the names held some magical feel. Though, of course, I already lived in Australia, somehow flying over 'real' country Australia, and in a plane delivering mail and urgent supplies, made me feel more located here.

We finally got clearance from air traffic control. That was the good news. The bad news was that the cargo, the supplies but also all our bags, was too heavy — despite the strict 14-kilogram limit that had already been enforced at check-in. We'd already had to pare down what we were bringing, which felt to me like a deprivation (I'd already tried to be smart about what I was bringing), but now we heard some of the bags would be left behind entirely and loaded onto the next flight.

TAKING A 'NO WORRIES' APPROACH

We all knew what that meant. This was the last connection to Birdsville before the race start. Any left-behind bags would not make it in time.

Whose bags wouldn't make it? We were united in our hope: let somebody else pick the short straw. How many unlucky ones would there be? And who? I heard my name called and walked to the desk. I (and a few others) had pulled that short straw. We could remove a couple of crucial items from our bags to put in our hand-luggage. Being allowed 'a couple' was like the desert-island question, 'Which three (okay, one extra) things would you take with you onto a deserted island?' Only this time, it was real.

I had already maxed out my carry-on luggage and had my backpack and essential running gear with me. Missing were my sleeping bag, a mattress, my race nutrition, everything on the list of mandatory gear, toiletries and warm clothes for cold desert nights.

What hurt most was that after all the effort to personalise my race food, running three marathons on the Monash lab treadmill and tailoring the results, I'd have to leave my race nutrition behind. I decided to take one day's food and a mattress and, somehow, rely on compassionate runners to share some of their food. Maybe a kind inhabitant of Birdsville would spare a sleeping bag. I was least concerned about the mandatory gear knowing Greg Donovan, the race director, would understand.

As we finally walked across the tarmac to board, I saw how tiny the plane was in front of us; yet I still couldn't see how a few 14-kilogram bags would make such a difference. The bloke who'd instructed me to pick my essentials, looked at me, apologised and, as a farewell, said, 'No worries mate, yer bag'll make the next flight.'

I had lived in Australia long enough to know that most of the time I heard 'no worries mate', it was time to start worrying. I took my seat and could see my bag on the tarmac. What was surprising was I had stayed calm through the luggage 'event' and focused on doing the best I could. My heart was beating at its normal pace, my mind unruffled. It was unpleasant but, from here onwards, I trusted the universe would take care of me. Of course, the race nutrition would have been handy, but not having it would not stop me from seeing the finish line. I stayed optimistic.

In that moment, I knew I was prepared.

None of my usual negative self-talk happened. I didn't fall back into a reactive mode. In the past, I'd have been upset when I did not get what I wanted. This time, even though I wasn't happy with the outcome, I was resilient. I acknowledged I was one of the few unlucky ones whose luggage had stayed behind, but also acknowledged this was a fact outside of my control — and I was learning not to try to control the uncontrollable. Throwing a tantrum at the gate would not have changed the outcome. In fact, it would have been embarrassing and, even worse, reverting to childish habits I had witnessed far too often in my father. So, while none of this series of inconveniences was, in any way, life threatening, it helped me see how far I had come. The difference between my responses now and what they might have been without my preparation was, for me, very significant. Gavin had pointed out that resilience in the smaller things predicted how I would deal with major curve balls. I trusted it would work out.

We finally took off and, when the flight attendant came around, I asked when my luggage was likely to arrive in Birdsville. She smiled and said that they'd found a solution. She explained, unambiguously, that my bag was back on the plane. It seemed that they had used a standard calculation of the average weight of their passengers — until we were all on board, when they realised what they had not factored in was that most passengers were skinny ultramarathon runners. The reduced weight of the passengers left enough room for my bag to come with us after all.

Now, I could fully enjoy the flight. We left Brisbane behind us, and it got rural very quickly. I was sitting next to Natalie who'd already participated in Big Red Run in the previous two years, yet never seen the finish line. One year, she'd pulled out due to an injury; the other year, she wasn't fast enough to make the cut-off on one of the stages. And here she was again, not giving up. She assured me that this time she would make it. I hoped she was right. The race would show whether she was resilient or purely stubborn. Either way, she regarded Big Red Run as unfinished business. I was deeply impressed that she was not giving up.

The chat with Natalie also made it very real that not finishing was a possibility. Injury could strike anyone. But, as soon as I thought that, I also thought that overthinking possible failure wouldn't help. Instead of contemplating failure, I chose to think what success would look like. As was the case in Berlin, I had no specific target. Not restricting myself to an arbitrary goal had served me well. Goals might be motivating; they could, at the same time, be very limiting. The entire intention of my journey was to find new ways to go beyond natural resting points. Overcoming plateaus was more important than reaching a destination. The idea was to stay on my toes and discover what I was capable of. This was a new challenge, and I had no idea what was possible.

In spite of not having a well-defined target, I had a good sense of what success looked and felt like. It included wanting to finish. It meant feeling like I'd given my best. I hoped I'd do well in comparison with other participants. Yet, I couldn't influence who else was in the starter field, so comparing myself to the other roughly 80 runners had limited merit. My placing should not determine my level of satisfaction with the race. It was not about 'beating others' but about my own growth. All up, if I dealt effectively with the unexpected, that would be success. I'd be happy if I acted more in line with my intuition. That way, I was giving miracles a chance to arise — whatever form they would take.

An announcement that we were about to land at Quilpie interrupted my thoughts (thoughts that made me happy; certainly happier than when I'd arrived at the departure gate some hours earlier). The township of Quilpie (home to 595 people) was on the horizon, and it was time for a lunch break and to refuel the plane. I could see only red sand and a dirt track leading to a few houses. The fog had cleared, and it was a brilliant, hot day. This was the climate we'd face in the desert: hot days, followed by freezing nights and fresh mornings, followed by more hot days — and a lot of flies on top of that.

The closer we got to Birdsville, the more I could sense the excitement growing. We were probably masquerading our growing nervousness. What looked unreal from up in the air was starting to take shape. We were in Birdsville and so was my bag. (Until I finally saw it, I'd still had my doubts.)

Everything in Birdsville was in walking distance; you certainly didn't have to be an ultra runner to get around. As I walked past the famous Birdsville Hotel, where the race was going to start and finish, I felt a bit wobbly. The challenge, I realised, was going to be as big as I wanted it to be. And so I was in that realm of contradiction — although I was here for the challenge, another side of me was longing for comfort and security. I had to trust that I'd flourish in moments of unpredictability.

So here I was, helping myself to find inner calmness and otherwise keep busy. I went to the pre-race briefing and then explored the town. The bakery had exotic kangaroo pies on offer and a camel in its backyard. Was that for later consumption? Possibly not. The locals seemed to be very caring. One of them was walking around with a baby kangaroo wrapped in a blanket and told me its mother had been hit by a car. When they'd found the little joey in her pouch, there was no question but to rescue it.

The day before the race — walking around, meeting locals — I felt like I had when I was a little boy and Christmas was approaching. The more I willed the big day to arrive, the more I seemed to hypnotise my watch. It was as if time were standing still while my excitement was skyrocketing. I had done absolutely everything I could do, from sand running, to finding the perfect nutrition to treadmill training in the heat in my kitchen. Most importantly, my mind was in the right spot. Now, it was time to put it into practice.

On race day, I woke at 2 am, with no chance of falling asleep again.

SELF CHECK-IN

- When have you dealt unexpectedly well when life threw you a curve ball? What made the difference to how you handled things?
- What routines help you deal with nerves before big performances?

CHAPTER 6

TURNING RIGHT THROUGH THE DESERT

Whatever the experiences may be, it's how we relate to them that really matters ... Do not develop a craving for even the most celestial content that may come your way.

—Shinzen Young

With five and a half hours to kill until race start, I decided to listen to music and go through my plan. This didn't really take much time because it was so straightforward: focus on the process, run at a comfortable pace (so I could repeat it each following day), drink every 15 minutes and snack once an hour. This all sounded good. Of course, after crossing the finish line, I'd also need to change into dry gear, eat and drink, take care of blisters and roll out the heavy legs. Only after that could I relax for the rest of the day and get the gear ready for the next stage. The plan was so simple that I had the capacity to deal with the unexpected.

DAY ONE: FINDING OUT WHAT'S POSSIBLE

Finally, *the* day. The sun was just coming up when all competitors assembled at the starting line — the famous Birdsville Hotel. We all had to pick up our GPS beacon so we could be tracked should we get off course. And then, there we all stood, a bunch of like-minded nutters, waiting to be sent off into the unknown.

Many new friendships were already forming and, when one of the official photographers approached each of us, he videoed our few last words before the start of the race.

The obvious first question, 'Why are you participating in Big Red Run?' elicited astonishingly similar answers from many of us. I stuttered through my response to camera, without taking any time to think about it: 'I've been running lots of marathons and picked Big Red Run to actually get outside of my comfort zone. This should be a real challenge. I'll see whatever is possible.' Not perhaps as articulate as I'd have liked, but I had nailed the most obvious point for me; my driving force. I'd always found it important to know my 'why', and this strong motivation would get me through what I expected to be some difficult times ahead.

Though everybody had their own reason for running through the desert, I was heartened that so many of us had the desire to challenge themselves. Some wanted to do 'something really hard', some 'to see if I can'. So I wasn't the only one new to this world. I suspected more than a few had the same thought as me: *If I can do this, and others can see this, they can be inspired that they can do anything.*

Some runners had, front of mind, the race's cause to raise research funds for finding a cure for type 1 diabetes — many because either they or one of their family members suffered from the illness. Some spoke of wanting to experience the 'epic vastness' of the Australian outback, running in a 'wonderful place', meeting 'amazing people'. Volunteers from previous years returned as runners to relive the camaraderie, telling many of us that, 'friendships here formed a thousand times quicker than in the normal world'.

The chance for humour wasn't lost on some. 'I've got nothing better to do', said one; 'I'm looking forward to six days of hell', another offered, a big smile on his face. Overall, the wish to 'finish in one piece' was shared. But my favourite answer came from a Hong Kong athlete who declared, 'Life is short, so do something silly, do something crazy before you die.'

It was time to get going. We were excited, we were terrified, we were ready. The inhabitants of Birdsville counted down to the starting siren, 'Three, two, one.'

The siren tooted and off we went, starting with a lap through Birdsville. I was tempted to get carried away by my excitement and rush off. My legs were fresh, and I had waited for months for this moment. A police car led the way out of town and, after about 10 minutes, we left the sealed road and hit a sandy path. I was in the lead, so I did a quick mental check of my pace. No, certainly not too fast. I might have been new to stage races, but I would not make that rookie mistake. My thoughts were interrupted by the thundering noise of a helicopter. As a photographer leaned out and took pictures, I followed his gaze.

Then I saw the first of many sand dunes. More worrying was the puddle in front of them, the size of a small lake. It must have formed from torrential rain that had fallen around Birdsville in the previous fortnight. That meant wet feet with sand and a guarantee of nasty blisters, and we had barely started the race. I was trying to figure out a path through without getting wet when another runner passed me, plop, plop, plop, clearly not concerned about blisters. The puddle was ankle deep and he barely needed five steps to be through it and up the dune. Then, he was gone. I just observed, kept my calm and searched for a better way. Suddenly, I saw pink flags, marking a dry path around the water. I didn't know how I had missed them earlier, but it was time to regain momentum.

Every 20 to 50 metres, small, pink triangular flags had been placed on bushes or stakes in the sand as guides. At the top of the first dune, I came to a second halt. Where was the next flag? Spotting pink in the middle of red sand turned out to be tricky. For a few seconds, I sensed panic rising. Flag-spotting had not been part of my meticulous preparation, and 250 kilometres of me stopping every few metres to find the next flag was going to be awful. This was shit. Why hadn't they chosen a different colour or, better yet, found an easier way to mark the course?

Managing my thinking — or practising 'thought stoppage' — had been part of my training. In similar situations of panic in the Berlin marathon, I'd flicked a rubber band on my wrist to stop me from spiralling further into trouble. I didn't need to wear one now, because I was aware of what was happening inside.

I took a deep breath, didn't buy further into the negative storyline and reassured myself. Everything was alright. Not seeing one pink flag didn't mean I'd be hampered the entire race. The story my brain was suggesting was not grounded in reality. Where was that next flag? I concentrated, searched my surroundings and, in a couple of seconds, spotted it. Then, I got back into a trot. In the following few kilometres, I had to stop a few more times but I got better at spotting the next markers. By the first checkpoint, I'd mastered the pink marker spotting and was back in the lead.

We crossed many more dunes on Day One. Each valley between them presented different challenges, but the worst was the gibber plain. The organisers had specifically mentioned these were horrible to run on but, as I had never seen one before, I was a bit anxious. They were plains of densely packed small and medium rock fragments with small and medium pebbles interspersed. It was a very uneven surface, and I hit my foot on sharp stones several times. I was very concerned to not twist my ankles. So, I had to pay attention, lift my feet and stay patient.

It didn't take long before I felt like I was dancing across those gibber plains. I was having fun. I'd trained countless hours on soft sand, but I was not fluffing. I was running. No, I was racing, and I loved it. Did I get carried away? I didn't think so. I was in the zone, immersed in running, avoiding spiky vegetation, jumping over holes in the dry desert ground, ploughing my way up and across soft sand dunes and belting down the other side, maintaining my rhythm. I felt an effortless sensation of being one with what I was doing, capable of anything, beyond the constraints of my muscles or breathing.

Most importantly, I wasn't worried about the outcome. 'Bring it on, and I'll deal with it,' was my mantra. I didn't have a single thought about the next sand dune, how heavy the next step might become, how exhausted I'd be once the excitement subsided. Nor was I thinking about whether a more conservative approach would be a smarter strategy in the face of a six-day event. I was present in the here and now, body and mind fully synchronised and one with the hostile, yet beautiful desert. I was inhaling the full beauty of the Australian outback and not missing the predictability of a city marathon at all.

The final obstacle on the first stage was running on top of Big Red, the biggest sand dune in the Simpson Desert. If I was prepared for one thing, it was running on soft sand. With each step, I sank deep into the dune and had to work hard to keep going, while my heart was thumping against my chest. I could taste the win of this first stage. All I had to do was plough through two kilometres of sand, and then run back down and through the finish line. Ahead, though, another surprise was waiting.

At the top of the dune, I noticed footsteps in the sand. Then I saw him — another runner, a few hundred metres ahead. How could that be? I was surely in the lead. I hadn't seen anyone for more than 35 kilometres, other than the cheerful volunteers at the checkpoints and a photographer taking pictures of this crazy bunch in action. How could I be behind anyone? What I could do, though, was increase my pace and catch him before the finish line. This guy was not very fast, but the finish line was getting close. I'd better get him quickly. All the sand training had taught me how to run fast without getting bogged down, before fatigue would eventually get me. I got closer and caught up with him, just as the pink flags were guiding us off the dune and towards the first campsite.

I hadn't expected anyone in front of me, but it seemed this guy equally hadn't expected anyone to catch up with him. He almost jumped out of his skin when I approached silently. When he turned around, it all made sense — he was the course marker. The course had been set up the day before, and his job was to ensure enough pink flags had been set to guide us the full 42 kilometres to the finish.

I passed him and a minute later crossed the finish line. Actually, I crossed what was going to be the finish line — it hadn't been set up yet. I had taken both the course marker and the race director by surprise; nobody had expected me to turn up this early. I had just completed the first stage in a new race record of 3:44 hours, an improvement of more than half an hour.

I was bombarded with questions. When people heard I was a rookie in the world of ultramarathons and multi-day racing, however, no more explanations were required. Allegedly, I had over-paced. It was no surprise that the feedback I got was mixed: congratulations for a great run on the one hand, and pity for not knowing how to pace myself on the other hand. My run was proof of me being new to this world, committing rookie mistake number one on a multi-stage race — exhausting myself on the first day.

Only, I didn't feel exhausted. I felt good. Good about finally racing after months of preparation, good about how I managed the heat, and good about how I dealt with the unexpected — whether it was puddles, pink flags, gibber plains or course markers. My right turn had been to let go of the illusion to control the uncontrollable and simply focus on the process. When worries emerged, I caught myself, stayed calm and trusted I could deal with the situation. It was like the luggage incident at Brisbane airport. I hadn't expected that dealing with curve balls could be so rewarding. My preparation had been spot-on. Training to run faster would not have helped me with any of those unexpected challenges, while training my mind had made me a much better athlete. My inner adventurer had become my best friend. Now, how many more surprises were out there?

In less than four hours my confidence in being capable of running 250 kilometres had sky-rocketed. I was no longer terrified of this ridiculous distance. According to the comments and tone of other runners, volunteers and spectators throughout the day, the following day would be entertaining for everyone. Apparently not for me, though. Day Two would teach me the lesson many beginners, myself included, needed to learn.

DAY TWO: ALLOWING MIRACLES TO HAPPEN

For the second night in a row, I hadn't slept well. Sleeping in a tent after a marathon didn't make for the best recovery. Eventually, the first signs of life in the camp indicated it was time to get up, even though it was still dark. The desert night had been freezing and many runners huddled around the camp fire, their breakfast in hand; mine was porridge and a treat of hot chocolate with milk powder. While the prospect of yet another marathon was daunting, I preferred to be here instead of going to work. So I stood close to the fire and looked up to the night sky, in a prime location to look out for satellites and shooting stars.

With 10 minutes to go until the start gun, I changed into running shoes and shouldered my backpack. Suddenly, every step produced a sharp pain on my heel. I'd missed a sizeable blister and, though it was late notice, I rushed to the 'blister clinic', for Dr Adam and his crew to perform their miracles. He had just enough time to fix me up, and I got back to the start line in time to head off with the whole cohort. Another day, another marathon.

I quickly forgot about the blister. Certainly, none of us felt as fresh as on Day One. On the flipside, all of us now had a better sense of what we were in for. So, we relaxed. We ran a different course, which early on led us over a dusty station track.

It was a welcome change to completely let go of any concerns about twisting an ankle and just run. I flew through the vast valley. I was back in a state of flow, beyond thinking and worrying. I noticed that, again, I was leading the pack and running on my own, reaching a decent pace — just over four minutes per kilometre. Regulate my speed? No, not yet. I was having too much fun.

It got much hotter than on the previous day, and by mid-morning the sun was already burning down with a brutal intensity. The halfway checkpoint gave me an extra boost of energy, as I was cheered on by the support crew. For the rest of the run, I was completely on my own, apart from a bunch of loyal flies. The energy from the cheer squad got the flies and me around the next bend and then, out of nowhere, my legs felt heavy. They were getting tired.

Strangely though, it didn't strike me as bad news. I didn't judge it; it was a fact that made sense. I'd run one and a half marathons and my legs were tired. This was simply cause and effect, the laws of nature. My mind stayed empty. No alarm bells were going off. I kept running with tired legs, maybe a bit slower than before, but I was not concerned. I knew, from deep within me, that my legs were transforming into desert legs.

'Desert legs' wasn't a real term, and I hadn't picked it up from anyone else. Perhaps the sun had gotten me, and I was losing my sanity. One part of me was well aware desert legs didn't, technically, exist. But, as I pictured with clarity what was happening, the term was reassuring. My legs were going to hurt until they'd fully adjusted to the desert. Then they'd be fine again. I had no need to panic or resist what I concluded to be a natural process. There was no doubt about it.

Letting go of the usual limitations of my mind made running much easier. I stayed strong and ticked off the remaining kilometres, one by one. I didn't chase down the course marker, because he'd started his shift early after the prior day's experience. This time, I crossed the finish line in 3:27 hours, more than 40 minutes faster than the previous record for Day Two.

I'd allowed a miracle to happen, similar to outrunning Corey on the hill in Lysterfield. The key to unlocking the magic was the absence of both fear and rational thinking. While fear would have triggered a fight-or-flight response, rational thoughts would have been rooted in my beliefs and experiences from the past. They would also have limited me. Instead, I bypassed fear and thinking by tapping into my intuition. That allowed me to surpass my expectations and witness a surprising performance.

I hadn't even had to try hard. On the contrary, all I did was to let what would happen to happen. I wasn't actively thinking or problem-solving or drawing on previous experience. While I was in a state of flow, my intuition just presented me with the answer, offering me a constructive alternative to the default route towards catastrophe. This was very different from wishing the pain away. I was not rejecting it; I just stayed present. My conclusion was that when I suspended the typical drama in my head, I was no longer bound by my usual limits. Those were the perfect conditions to see what was truly possible, and I wasn't relying on the thinking mind, which I had been brought up with, to respond to them. This was a much more powerful mode. As astonishing and unconventional as it sounded, I had no doubt. Following my intuition led to the magic. This was a big discovery and stood in stark conflict with any rational model I had of the world.

DAY THREE: MANAGING THE PRESSURE

After two new race records in a row, a lot of talk in the camp was about how fast I could run the third marathon. I started to feel the pressure. Even the race director publicly called out that he was confident I could maintain this pace. I didn't like having external expectations piled on, but I had to acknowledge to myself that pressure was an integral part of any performance — whether in sports or at work, what made the difference was how one dealt with pressure.

Up till now, I hadn't been running to prove a point to those who had doubted me. Now, I was not going to run to prove a point to those who believed in me. I was in the desert to find out how far turning right could get me. In the overall classification, I already had a lead of 90 minutes. But I still had more than 160 kilometres to run. Just after breakfast, I recorded a short video to capture what was on my mind:

The big question of today is how to attack the remainder of this run. Take it a bit easier or keep going as I've been going? I've given it some thought, and the key to answering it is why I am here. The primary objective definitely is not to win this run. I am here to try something new, get out of my comfort zone and see what is possible. I've done the necessary work. I've done anything which is possible and, over the last two days, I have seen that if I don't have a game plan, if I don't do all the things I normally do, actually, I can still achieve the impossible. It's more risky, but I will go with the flow today, see how I feel, and why not repeat that? Let's see how the day goes. As you can see from my eyes, I am slightly tired. It has been a shocking night with lots of wind. Several tents have broken, and it is a multi-day event.

> *Everybody starts feeling it, with blisters, sleep deprivation and only eating dehydrated food. But it's a great atmosphere.*

So, I didn't take it easy on Day Three. That was not what I had come for, and I was not going to overthink my approach.

This day started with something special — a send-off from the traditional owners of the land who came to the camp and wished us all the best and fired the start gun. After this special send off, we knew the day would be tough, with dozens of dunes to conquer, more gibber plains and unrelenting heat.

From the start, we got straight back into the challenges, ascending, yet again, Big Red. I remembered overtaking the course marker on this dune on Day One, and I felt surprisingly good. My headspace turned out to be compensating for my fatigued body — those aches and pains were forgotten. I was not focused on protecting my lead, or trying to merely survive the day. I went straight into attack, was the first to arrive on top of Big Red and ran another solitary race from there on. Neither winning nor posting records was on my mind. On the contrary, I didn't think about it at all. I was here to do my best, immerse myself into the new challenges as they popped up, and just run.

I was curious, patient and, at the same time, aware that nothing was a given. I was comfortable with that, knowing that one of the key ingredients allowing me to fly up and down those dunes was simply focusing on the process. I ran, drank my sugar solution, ate the occasional snack bar and concentrated on spotting the next pink flag. Nothing else. No wondering how far in front of the next runner I was. No calculation of how much of a lead I might have by the end of the day. I didn't try to predict how my legs would feel by the end of the run, or how I would pull up on the following day.

Before working with Gavin, I had a favourite game — time travelling. In my version, I'd indulged in imagining wishful scenarios or unproductive storylines, giving me the illusion that I could predict the future. The danger with time travelling in that desert was that I wouldn't pay attention to the very activity that contributed in that very moment to a favourable result: running. How easy would it be to miss a pink flag, because I was day-dreaming? So many athletes choked when they focused on the outcome rather than the process. I'd practised for countless hours to stay present to seemingly mundane or routine activities. That skill, now, prevented me from zoning out, overthinking and, eventually, choking.

As I went into a zone of deep concentration, I recalled a random memory from my childhood. I must have been 11 and in the physical education class. We were running for one kilometre around a canal and, at that age, it felt like an ultramarathon. I'd never run any further and was proud to be the fastest kid. To get me through, I applied a technique from one of my favourite books at the time. The protagonists, a Native American called Winnetou and his white friend Old Shatterhand, had to run extremely long distances through the 'Wild West'. They were pursued by evil villains and had to avoid their horses leaving any traces. Their trick to not getting tired from running was to focus on the right leg at every step, until it got tired. Then they switched their attention onto the left leg. That way, they could almost run forever without needing to rest.

I'd been curious about these heroes' trick and mentioned using it to the teacher. When I shared my little secret, I got laughed at by everybody in the class. Even the teacher brushed away the idea, patronisingly saying she was happy it had worked for me.

How did something that far in the past reappear on my radar during Big Red Run? But, though the question was decades old and had remained unanswered, now it just clicked. It hadn't been a magic trick from two fictional characters; it made complete sense. A focused mind could keep going forever.

As this thought formed, I could see I was approaching the finish line. Evidently, my legs had transformed into desert legs; they'd carried me to another record run on the toughest terrain so far. Overall, I was relieved and pleased to have managed the pressure I had felt in the morning. It gave me confidence beyond running in the desert — managing pressure would come in handy in other areas of life. My seeking of better experiences was not about avoiding difficult situations but about relating to discomfort in new ways. As I could see, the outcomes were taking care of themselves.

DAY FOUR: GLIDING ALONG

Everybody called the fourth day the 'sprint day', because we had 'only' 32 kilometres ahead of us. The previous afternoon I'd enjoyed a helicopter flight over the Simpson Desert. The views were breathtaking, and I got a preview of the terrain that was expecting us. All I could see up to the horizon was one dune parallel to the next — a sea of red sand and stone, with limited scrub and vegetation, and barely any trace of human existence. What would be new was to run through a dried-up salt lake. Only, due to a recent intense thunderstorm, it might not be that dry.

I'd come to terms with not sleeping well the entire week and had not noticed any negative impact on my performance. It seemed that the more exhausted my body got, the more my mind relaxed. So far, it had been my mind that had effectively cut through any mental blockages. And again, once the stage started, I continued where I'd left off the previous days. As soon as I'd crossed the first dune, I was back in flow, and running was effortless. I was fast and didn't feel the need to save energy. To my mind, now, selecting the safe approach was the first step towards a motivation to avoid failure; the opposite of what I needed. From selecting safety it was a slippery slope to being run by fears and, as a consequence, cutting myself off from the intuition that allowed me to thrive.

When I got to the salt lake, I motored through it, even as I sank more than ankle-deep into the humid salt mud. I had a comfortable rhythm and was calm, free from anxiety and stress. My focus was on the pink markers, and everything else had vanished from my consciousness — even my sense of self. This was my new mode: racing, not pacing. I'd read Mihaly Csikszentmihalyi's work on 'flow' (discussed in his book of the same name), but reading it, even analysing it, was nothing compared to the richness of experiencing it.

Ten years had passed since I'd experienced a similarly intense flow-state as I was now. Back then, I was unsuccessfully training to break the three-hour mark for the marathon. I joined a bunch of fast runners for a long run and regretted it very quickly. It was a miserable day with pouring rain, the guys were significantly fitter and faster than me, and we were training on hilly terrain, which I was not used to.

In the second half of the run, things changed. I was not locked up with my own thoughts anymore but was embracing the forest, the mud and the rain. I sensed the birds complaining about the weather. I was no longer hanging in but running, confidently, in the middle of the pack, and it felt almost effortless, as if I were gliding through the woods. I wasn't worrying about how far I had to go, I was one with the activity and the surroundings. Yet, it was a fragile state. Once I started thinking, I was kicked out of paradise. That was my direct route to banishment and why I'd rarely accessed the state of flow. I was a thinker, constantly judging and evaluating the situation, others and myself.

It wasn't a surprise that since my first right turn, I got into flow more often. Both turning right and entering flow required letting go of control and being fully present. Now, racing through the desert, my body and mind were in full harmony, synchronised, and I was at peace with myself. No conflict existed between what my body wanted to do and what my mind allowed to happen. My mind had, apparently, let go of the typical constraints it burdened my body with.

This was a feeling of connectedness, not only within myself but also with my surroundings. I was running beyond my usual limit. The storm happened around me, time slowed down, and I was in the eye of the hurricane. There, everything was calm and measured. Both risk-taking and creativity went up a notch. I was in an uncomplicated state where anything was possible.

Given that Day Four was the sprint day, I sprinted for the final metres of the stage. What amazed me was that the result had really become secondary. What I was craving were the growth experiences that had happened every day so far. A common insight across all four stages was how often I'd limited myself by my beliefs of what I thought I was capable of. My creation of 'desert legs' was an example of what happened when I let go of those limiting beliefs. A force was set free, and miracles became possible. From that place, I could deal with the unexpected and come up with surprising and innovative solutions. If I had learned one thing, it was to trust my intuition and allow whatever was happening to happen.

Because it was a shorter run than previous days, all runners were back in camp early. I still diligently went through my post-run routine. Blister management had become a task in itself, and the medical team did a phenomenal job with my feet. By now, they were au fait with every foot of each of the 80 runners and how best to help them — a medal-worthy achievement in my books.

Afterwards, we had time to freshen up, exchange stories and enjoy a lazy afternoon. Another welcome surprise was the barbecue lunch that the local land owners put on for all of us to celebrate cracking the $200,000 mark in our fundraising efforts. It felt like an eternity since we'd eaten proper food. Steaks, sausages, bread and especially fresh fruit were a massive treat after our freeze-dried meals.

But the relaxing afternoon didn't lull any of us into a false sense of security; the race was not over yet. The following day was going to be brutal. Since the very first day, everybody had been talking about the 84 kilometres of the daunting Day Five.

DAY FIVE: DEALING WITH ADVERSITY

Few runners needed a wake-up call the next morning. The crisp desert morning was saturated with runners' nerves. The mood was more serious. For the first time, we put on our reflective vests and head torches. It was still pitch-black when we stumbled over the first kilometres of gibber plain. My legs were still asleep and, several times, I almost twisted an ankle on the uneven, rocky ground. It was not a great start. What also played on my mind was that I wasn't in the lead. Two other runners had gone out fast, and I could see their torches in the distance, teasing me. I'd been warned. In previous years, not a single runner who had led the classification on the morning of the fifth day could defend that lead to win the overall race.

Shortly after we had conquered the first gibber plain, I got even more impatient. I was stopped by a volunteer, who let me know that race control had radioed to check my GPS beacon because it wasn't working. Similar to my legs, it must still have been asleep. What the volunteer couldn't fix was my negative mindset. The darkness outside reflected how I was feeling inside — I was in a gloomy spot. Where were my calm and my focus? How could I go back to that state of bliss and cruising along?

My inner voices were talking over each other to complain, but their message remained unclear. The problem-solver in me just wanted to know what I had to fix. My legs didn't feel any worse than the previous days. It couldn't be the early morning start in darkness, given that most of my training happened at an ungodly hour — the only way to squeeze it in before work. I also doubted I was panicking about the two runners ahead. I enjoyed the role of chaser and thrived on the satisfaction of catching people.

While I climbed up another dune, I suddenly knew what was wrong. I almost felt embarrassed. Simply put, I was afraid. I was running my longest run ever, and I knew, very well, how painful those runs turned out towards the end. I was anticipating agony I didn't want to deal with. I was afraid to endure pain.

At least, I now knew what it was. But what could I do about it? The kilometres ticked by, and the drama in my head didn't let up. On the contrary, it added extra detail around how bad my legs would feel later. It would get tough. Very tough. Right now, the sun was just rising, and I threw a long shadow ahead. I would have to run all day, probably until after sunset. It reminded me of my days as a consultant, when I'd entered the client's office at the crack of dawn and often didn't leave until after midnight. I didn't miss those long work days and had vowed to not get back into that unhealthy habit. Something inside me couldn't stand the idea of still running tonight when it got dark again. My thoughts, spinning and hysterical, were not helping me to get back on track. I had to stop them.

An hour into the stage, I'd caught the runners in front and was back in the lead. But the chaos in my head remained. The dirt track made a sharp right turn, and the race director's son was standing at the bend, indicating where to go. 'Kay,' he shouted, 'you're awesome!' 'Far from awesome', I wanted to yell back. He was kind, but just a spectator; he had no way of spotting the difference in my performance from the previous days.

The difficult times struck out of nowhere. Wasn't this what I'd trained for? At that moment, I knew how to get back into a rhythm. I had an entire arsenal of techniques in my mental toolkit to get me back on track. Focus on the breath. One, two, three — in. One, two, three — out. Unfortunately, the voice of my inner bureaucrat was louder than the counting, and he was spoiling my good intentions. 'Listen to the birds,' a different voice suggested, eager to get me back on track. Moving the focus to something external tended to help. Bummer, no birds were around. The only animal I'd seen, other than flies, was a cow or, better said, the skull of a long-deceased cow.

I might not have been able to hear birds, but an hour later I did hear a helicopter. When it got closer, I saw two photographers and the race director leaning out of it. They were having fun and so was the pilot as he veered in, whipping a cloud of sand and dust around me. This gave me a boost.

They were having fun and, though I was only accompanied by my misery, it did make me remember why I'd entered the race in the first place. I was here to be out of my comfort zone, find out what was possible. It was time to change my attitude. It was time for a serious conversation between S (my solution-oriented self) and W (my whingeing self):

S: So, you are afraid.

W: Yes, I don't want to go through the pain.

S: But the legs are feeling fine.

W: They won't be later. Just wait and see.

S: Kay, you can do it.

W: No, I can't.

S: But, yes, you can.

W: No, I can't.

S: But you did it the other days?!

W: Yes, that was easy.

S: But why isn't this easy?

W: Well, that was 'only' a marathon, and this is much more.

The conversation went back and forth for a while, obviously leading nowhere.

S: Kay, just have the same self-confidence as on the other days. And just run. Don't think about it. Just run!

A few moments of silence.

W: What is in it for me?

S: You will be at the finish line quicker. Even if we don't make it entirely there before the pain starts, it will be more bearable.

This resonated. S was getting somewhere.

S: You know what, we keep running at this pace, and we will arrive in camp by 2 or 3 o'clock. Just in time for a late lunch.

W: Food?! I'm in. Let's go.

I knew that solution-oriented Kay had won this argument and was not letting it go. I'd found something worth focusing on — getting to eat.

When I passed two volunteers at the side of the road with a little bonfire in front of them offering me a roasted marshmallow for breakfast, I just ran past and shouted, 'Sorry, no time, I have to get to camp for lunch.' The fun was coming back, and I dropped the seriousness that had been holding me back. It took another hour before I fully reconnected with what running had felt like on the previous days. A tailwind helped me to glide effortlessly across the desert. I was cheerful and rushed through the next checkpoint, full of energy. I was on a mission; I was on my way to lunch.

My legs did start to get very tired, shortly after I got to the halfway mark — with still a marathon to go. On top of the fatigue, I now had to run straight into a strong headwind. It couldn't be much longer battling against the wind, I naively concluded after a few kilometres. Almost two hours later, I was still fighting the relentless wind. I stopped expecting anything. I was tired, but the idea of getting this done propelled me forward. For a short moment I lost my motivation when my whingeing self resurfaced:

S: This is better than the experience we went through for 30 kilometres this morning.

W: Dehydrated food for lunch? Yuk.

Even so, I battled against the headwind until I hit the border fence between Queensland and South Australia, where the course changed direction. The finish line was within reach. The final stretch led over a wide-open plain of dried-up soil, with the occasional scrub growing out of the cracked ground. On the horizon our campsite appeared like a Fata Morgana. It hushed away any tiredness and pulled me silently towards it. I had done it.

I crossed the finish line in another record time of under eight hours and improved the overall race record by over five hours.

Before I could sit down or celebrate — with a final dehydrated meal for lunch — I got handed a microphone as the race director asked me to share my impressions. In the brightness of the mid-afternoon sun, I talked and talked, and talked. He shouldn't have given me the microphone. Rarely had I felt that alive and that clear.

I talked about what I'd learned, the struggle I had overcome that day, and my other realisations over the course of the race. The glory didn't lie in how fast I could run or in how I compared to anybody else. I was proud of who I'd become in the process.

The most intriguing incident of that day was that I'd run into trouble and had to slay the metaphorical dragon. For the first time that week, I had faced my inner demons — head-on, and in a battle that had lasted several hours. The issue wasn't the distance, and it wasn't my body or fitness. The issue had been my head. For hours, I'd lacked that sense of connection from which performances came effortlessly. While body and mind were separated, it was impossible to get into a rhythm. In hindsight, I understood; it took the same effort to be miserable as it did to do something about it.

It reminded me how difficult it was to be consistent under pressure. Just the day before, I'd concluded that all I needed was to not overthink and to trust my intuition. However, there were worlds between knowing something and being capable of applying that wisdom. I might have shrugged off some inner demons this time, but they were far from defeated. Even the euphoria of winning the race could not dim the certainty that the war was far from over. More battles were to be fought.

All afternoon and late into the night, runners arrived at the finish line. We cheered, jointly, for every single one. Everybody was exhausted, often very emotional, and certainly keen to tell their stories. The real heroes were still out there, not having lunch in the camp, still battling their personal fights. Those 84 kilometres offered plenty of opportunities to give up, yet nobody did. The most emotional finish was the final one of the night. Natalie, who had sat next to me on the plane, made it just before the official cut-off time. She made it, after her two previous attempts when she hadn't managed to. But she didn't let that break her and stayed committed, when many others would have given up. She had the key to keep believing in herself during dark times and dealing with the setbacks.

DAY SIX: SEEING CLEARLY

On the final day of Big Red Run we ran only eight untimed kilometres back into Birdsville to round out the 250 kilometres. Before we left, a little girl wearing a fairy dress in the camp asked me to wear a pink tutu for this final stage, and her appeal was so convincing I had no choice but to say yes. Without knowing, she created a new race tradition. From then onwards, the winner of Big Red Run would run in a pink tutu into town. This last part of the run was all about the camaraderie. In less than a week, friendships had formed and deepened, and joys and challenges were shared. Then, we all enjoyed the lap of honour. I was glad I didn't have to run on my own anymore and used the opportunity to connect with other runners. The cold beer waiting for us was refreshing, but the highlight of the day was something else.

This highlight was also wet, but somewhat larger than a bottle of beer. After almost a week of using baby wipes for personal hygiene, nothing was going to be better than a long, hot shower. I checked in to the Birdsville Hotel and stood under the shower for (almost) an eternity.

I was so pleased and so satisfied with my experience in the desert, and not because I had achieved something I would not even have dared to dream about. Over and over again, I'd experienced how short-lived success was. The illusion of personal greatness always faded away quickly.

This time was different. I knew I'd grown as a person. The most vital and life-changing realisation was that the really significant stuff we could do with our lives was not to achieve great things. It was to dare to pursue who we were capable of being.

I'd come to find growth, and what I encountered was a sense of meaning and purpose. Participating in Big Red Run had enriched my life, and it was up to me to ensure I stayed on the path of personal transformation. What that could look like, I didn't know. But what I did know was that I'd become more comfortable with letting go of control. I could tap into reserves I didn't even know existed. I'd been curious to find out what was possible and had encountered three surprising insights.

First, I had always regarded challenges as the problem. The sheer size of Big Red Run had scared me. Now, I could see that the issue was not the mountain to climb but becoming a better climber. The answer lay within me. Focusing on technical expertise was never going to cut it. Getting paralysed by the perceived problem would not have bridged the gap between what was required and what I was capable of. What made the difference was working on me. I was asked to transform my view of the world in order to handle much more complexity, with far greater ease. It was as if I had been upgraded with a more mature operating system. My desperate urge to succeed shifted towards the pure joy of exploring. Creativity took the place of reactivity, and peak performance was no longer an end in itself; it was just a welcome side effect. If consistency led to greatness, turning right led to magic.

Second, I'd discovered that the intellect had its limitations. I had been brought up in the belief that the intellect could master anything. Yet, I'd experienced that intuition was much more powerful in solving complex problems. It was striking how well my intuition knew what best to do. One of the biggest shifts in my perspective had been to let go of preconceived expectations of how I should feel and perform. Judgements, such as right versus wrong or good versus bad, were more and more replaced by the acknowledgement that life, my life and the lives of others, was more nuanced than black and white. I was undergoing a complete shift in awareness; things that had been 'logical' previously were no longer valid. How much more could I discover, if only my intellect didn't stop me, based on its convoluted view how the world was operating?

Third, I found a new appreciation for how essential it was to step out of my comfort zone. The magic happened when conditions were far from perfect. Growing 'desert legs' had been a prime example. For growth to occur, I could not cling to predictability. The hard training wasn't primarily what got me to where I was. What gave me the edge, and easily got lost, was the fact I'd dared to walk unchartered territory and try out new things. The trick was to find smarter ways of preparing, rather than working harder. The logical conclusion was that anybody could be great at whatever they were passionate about. To my surprise, that was the part few people wanted to hear. Maybe because it was too scary to face the obvious question: 'Who would I be, if I wasn't this anymore?'

The internal struggles on the double-marathon day clearly indicated that my most powerful opponent was within me. He had far from surrendered, and I would be a fool not to expect more vicious fights in the future. I still had to learn how to relate better to my inner critic. How great would it be to get past the constant worries and inner battles? There was certainly more to life, and it sparked my curiosity to explore what else it had on offer.

The best week of my life was coming to an end. The next morning, I boarded the flight back to Brisbane. I would have loved to prolong my stay in the desert yet, at the same time, I was also excited to see Rebecca again. She was staying with her parents in Brisbane and was about to race herself. She'd entered the Gold Coast marathon and I relished the idea of being there to support her, and just being a spectator without having to run myself. I was also due to meet her parents for the first time. Luckily, I was too exhausted to be nervous.

The weekend with Rebecca and her parents was wonderful and passed far too quickly. For the first time in months I relaxed. The icing on the cake was when Rebecca ran a new personal best in her marathon. We were both desperate for a time with less running training and more time for seeing friends, for entertaining, for others and ourselves — and for long afternoons of wine and cheese. Now, as her race was done and dusted as well, it was time to get back to reality.

SELF CHECK-IN

- What do your inner demons sound like? Are they the voice of reason? Or are they critical and complainers?
- Think of peak experiences in your life, when you were in deep flow. What did you do differently from the times you weren't in flow? How did you feel?
- What new possibilities opened up when you were in flow?
- How can you provide the grounds for more miracles to occur?
- Who could you be if you weren't what you are now?

CHAPTER 7

TURNING RIGHT ONTO SHAKY GROUND

> *We are at war within ourselves ... the brain giving directions which the body will not follow, and the body giving impulses which the brain cannot understand.*
>
> —Alan Watts

After our major runs and enjoying the warmth of Queensland (the north-eastern state of Australia), Rebecca and I arrived back in full Melbourne winter with its short and cold days. The struggle didn't end there. The daily grind, which I'd been away from for only a week, had become soul-crushing, and work had become more sinister than ever; employees now called the office the 'Death Star'.

The decline in the culture at work had been gradual at first. But at some point, it had become swift and unshakeable. Where we used to have cooperative discussions and meetings, now most interactions seemed to be characterised by power struggles or intrigues. I felt collaboration had given way to people tearing each other down, publicly as well as in whispered tones. Everybody craved inspiration and, more fundamentally, a sense of achievement; however, they were too busy chasing the flavour of the week. The direction from the top changed all the time, and we could barely keep up with which battle we were fighting. I wished I had the skills to fix what was essentially broken.

Coming in daily contact with such hostility and tension was even more frustrating after a week full of magic in the desert. The management's 'Inspiring the Magic' program, aimed at unlocking everybody's full potential, seemed to have long been buried. As things stood now, employees considered meetings successful when we survived them without getting humiliated. We all wasted a shocking amount of emotional energy.

During my preparation for Big Red Run, I had had bigger fish to fry and turned a blind eye to what had been happening at work. Now I could no longer ignore the darkness spreading its cloak over my place of work. The prevailing rhetoric was the language of war — 'defeating the competition' — rather than focusing on our customers. Time and time again, just when I thought we had hit rock bottom, it got worse.

INHALING TOXICITY

One particular morning, as we sat in the boardroom and the person in charge hit the button to turn the big, clear glass walls opaque to conceal us from our colleagues outside the room, I had unambiguous confirmation that I had to leave. Apparently, we were all being managed far too loosely, and that wasn't the kind of weakness that would be tolerated — a much more dictatorial organisational style was the preference.

The meeting was afterwards downplayed, swept under the carpet, but it was a massive turning point for me. I could no longer ignore the clash with my values.

I was all too familiar with autocratic posturing and aggression, and also had a wealth of experience about which coping strategies were doomed for failure and which ones could work. For years I had made myself small in my relationship with my father. It never stopped him. For years I had tried to figure out what his underlying expectations of me were so I might satisfy them, only to find out that I could never satisfy his hunger for more power and control. After complying, I tried the next strategy — avoiding confrontation and trying for a peaceful coexistence.

When an opportunity presented itself for that option, I grabbed it. I moved from my bedroom on the first floor into a cellar room. The location was more remote and would have reminded most people of an old-fashioned prison. Little natural light came in through the windows, which were burglar-proofed with solid iron bars. The damp walls and cold floor tiles meant it was not the cosiest spot in the house. Yet, because it was tucked away and designed to not allow entrance to harmful people, it allowed me a measure of freedom. I had a chance for time away from harmful influences and, even, time to develop my own personality. Having fewer interactions where I had to fight to be myself allowed me to nurture my authenticity and find out, more deeply, who I wanted to be. While marginalised physically, I kept my pride and my head high. However, I couldn't constantly hide and, therefore, it was a temporary rather than perfect solution. I learned that the autocrat of our household would not let a week pass without some reminder, large or small, that he had absolute control.

As a teenager, I may not have had a lot of experience of politics, but I did conclude a revolution was needed to overturn this governing body. Sadly, the coup I envisaged failed. One day, I had had enough of getting beaten up by my father. It was a grey, miserable day, and I ventured out to the police station, reported him and asked for their support. They were not remotely interested in leaving the cosy police station for something as meaningless as a few slaps in the face.

I felt hopeless, but at least the episode taught me to not count on external help in dire situations. In the following months, I realised that the only way to put an end to my misery was to step up and remedy it myself. I may have grown up, but I'd not yet learned how to stand tall. The days of sobbing into my teddy, however, were numbered.

Just as my childhood realisation had been sobering, so too did I know that the toxic environment at work was not going to get better without a change in leadership style. Had I come all the way from Europe to Australia to encounter the same story? What seemed true, though, was that wherever I went, whatever I did, I found confirmation that the world was hostile and I was on my own. I had sworn to myself so many years earlier that I would never, ever again be a victim. So, I had to do something about the work situation, urgently. The options of sacrificing my values or initiating another unsuccessful coup were equally bad moves.

Also, I could no longer hide behind the strategy I'd used so far — which was to set up a high-performance team that could withstand the prevailing culture. It just was not strong enough. I was too senior to limit my vision to the team reporting into me. If it was true that I was on my own, then it was up to me to make a difference. So, I volunteered to drive a project that had been sold to me as the solution to reset the culture.

It didn't take long for that to also fail and for me to not only become disillusioned but also recognise the extent of my naivety.

The 'solution' I'd been sold was a mere restructure of the organisational setup. I'd bought the dream that moving boxes around on the org chart could fix the problem. But it never could have. For me, the fundamental problem was rooted in the leadership approach and behaviour. To lift the outer game, we would have needed to step-change the maturity of the inner game. I felt the only option was to resign. But I would do it on my own terms.

I wasn't going to act on the same kind of emotional impulse as I had, much to my regret, in primary school. On that memorable occasion, I'd experienced the pain that comes when the main intention of an action was to harm somebody else. When I was seven years old, my sister was born and we moved from an apartment in inner Cologne to a house in the outer suburbs, with a garden. I had to make new friendships and ended up spending most my time with Laura, a girl from the neighbourhood. One summer in the school holidays Laura and I had an argument. I quickly forgot what it was about, but I can still remember how it made me feel. First, I was hurt. Then, I was furious. I acted on that and kicked Laura out of my life. I wanted her to learn her lesson. I never set foot in her house again. I never again inhaled the smell of the adventures we had in the attic or the tree house in the garden. With a heart as cold as stone I cut our strong bond. I've regretted it ever since.

So now, instead of reacting mindlessly and angrily, I'd resign in the way that suited me. The question was no longer whether to resign but when, and what to do next. I was also hooked on a share incentive scheme, which would come in handy while sorting out my next career move. Therefore, I was going to withhold my resignation letter for another four months. That plus the company six-month notice period would give me plenty of time to sort out my next career move. Ideally, I wanted a way into coaching executives and building high-performance cultures, as well as being able to leverage my experience as an athlete more holistically.

TESTING THE LIMITS

In the short term, I needed to find inspiration outside of work. I longed to return to the amazing world Big Red Run had opened up for me. That was where I belonged. There I was excited, felt on top of the world and able to conquer my own mental limitations and insecurities. I had not forgotten the struggles — the early morning starts on rainy winter days and the challenges of juggling sport, work and a social life. But those struggles were worth it. The journey was its own reward and brought brightness into my life. Not only did unsolvable dilemmas dissolve in the new reality but also, as a welcome side effect, each transformational shift went hand in hand with step-changes in capability. I knew I wanted to turn right again. I had probably only seen a glimpse of what was possible if I put my mind to it. What else would I discover?

Turning right had taught me that I didn't do all the hard work in order to get to the end and sit back at home. My future was about the process of putting myself out there — leaving my comfort zone, taking on any curve balls, fighting adversity and, eventually, learning my lessons. True and long-lasting satisfaction did not come from the glory of achieving anything great. It came from winning the battle against my own demons. Satisfaction came from a sense of being at the edge of defeat, close to giving up, but then striking back unexpectedly and claiming victory. I needed another challenge, big enough to unlock more of that magic. If I now settled for my new comfort zone, I would get stuck again. The open question was, what adventure was big enough to thrive on?

Only a few weeks had passed since the race, and I had stayed sensible, giving my body the required recovery. I used the time to select my next quest. If I was honest, the next expedition had already chosen me, rather than the reverse. At work, I regularly found myself daydreaming about how I would conquer Mount Kosciuszko — specifically, during Coast to Kosci. This was the pinnacle of Australian ultra running and it had become the race I was passionate about. Runners started on a beach at Twofold Bay on the south coast of New South Wales and ran for 240 kilometres, to the summit of Australia's highest mountain — 2,228 metres, accumulating 5,500 metres of climbing overall. The clock didn't stop, and everybody had a maximum of 46 hours to complete the distance.

It was the perfect race — an adaptive challenge that was far beyond my capabilities and thus would force me onto another steep growth curve. I had reached a stage where the challenge would be my best teacher and, while Gavin offered his mentoring support, he pointed out that his role would diminish. The race was held every December, but I first needed to satisfy the qualification criteria of running a 24-hour event and completing at least 180 kilometres, and running a secondary 100-kilometre event. While not a formal requirement, I was also expected to crew for another Coast to Kosci runner to get a better sense of the event. That in itself would take me about a year. Overall, this adventure had an 18-month horizon and was a true test of my ability to embrace delayed gratification. But I was determined to give it a go. The words from the Hong Kong runner at Big Red Run came to mind. 'Life is short, so do something silly, do something crazy before you die.'

An unexpected phone call put an end to my daydreaming. Rob Boyce introduced himself as the president of AURA, the Australian Ultra Runners Association, and congratulated me on my stellar run in the desert. He encouraged me to get onto the Australian 100-kilometre world championships team and run 'at the worlds'. I would have almost a year to run the necessary qualifying time and, a pure formality, become an Australian citizen. His suggestion left me speechless. Becoming a national representative on the world stage had never crossed my mind. That was for serious athletes, not for me.

While I was tempted, my loyalties lay with Coast to Kosci. I was hesitant to sacrifice my dream race, just to pursue an unrealistic chance to become an elite runner. But Rob had a few aces up his sleeve. First, he assured me that I had what it took to get selected. Second, the world champs would be in Spain, where I had lived for almost three years when I studied for my master's degree and doctorate. And third, the race was scheduled on my birthday. What could possibly go wrong?

Before I had the chance to second-guess whether I was good enough and politely refuse, I was too deep into this new adventure. An hour later, I received a call from another stranger, Gary Mullins. He was on the national team himself and a running coach by profession. Gary offered to be my first-ever personal running coach and teach me what it would take to compete with the big boys.

Needless to say, it didn't take long for me to decide that Coast to Kosci would have to wait for another year. The prospect of wearing the national colours was too appealing to give up. Gary was Sydney-based and so would coach me with regular phone calls and spreadsheets, which we would send back and forth. He knew exactly what it took to be selected, and the statistics were scary. To have a realistic chance, I had to run faster than four-and-a-half minutes per kilometre (or almost 14 kilometres an hour), for 100 consecutive kilometres. The ideal qualifying race would be the New Zealand 100-kilometre championships in Christchurch, which gave us more or less nine months — enough time to prepare. The course promised fast times, a flat running surface and, typically, favourable autumn weather conditions. Back in my mind, I just hoped to not experience a shake-up; after all, Christchurch, a hotspot for earthquakes, trembled frequently and violently.

I instantly clicked with Gary. What made things feel even better was that Gary was open to cooperating closely with Gavin and, jointly, they'd get me world-champs ready. The three of us agreed to jointly turn right. Gary would take care of the physical preparation and, therefore, was in charge of my training program. In parallel, Gavin would keep an eye on my mental preparation. I had to let go of control and trust them. My resilience would be tested in an environment where the pressure of having to perform was real. While 'seeing what would happen' and 'racing without a goal' approaches had unlocked new levels, we all had to face the reality that this was a very different challenge. I had to be one of the fastest Australian runners, or I would stay at home. Many amazing athletes were competing for the same spot on the team.

Gary's program had three phases. In the first three months, we'd lift my basic speed. I only hoped that the first training session wasn't an omen for what was to come. It was a hard interval session, covering four times four kilometres. From the beginning, I worried what would happen if I didn't hit Gary's target times, which appeared too ambitious. I feared he would be disappointed in me and even regret having assumed the assignment of getting me to the world's stage. I wanted to show him I was a worthy student; however, in the first interval, I only just managed to get to target pace. From there, I deteriorated. In the second repetition, my left hip joint felt locked up. Next, my left knee was sore. I hobbled home, defeated.

Next morning the pain was no better, so I saw a sports doctor and was diagnosed with bursitis in the knee. Big Red Run must have done more damage than I had been aware of. After only one training session, I was prescribed a week of rest. It was far from an optimal start into a fresh adventure with a new coach, but time was on my side. After a week of rest, I hit my stride again. With minimal training, I ran a new half-marathon personal best. Not such a bad start after all, and certainly a reminder not to judge too early.

The following weeks went to plan. I kept worrying about not hitting Gary's speed targets but always managed to, in the end. The first training phase concluded with the Melbourne marathon, and I was in good shape to smash my personal best. The race started well, and I remained patient. At the 18-kilometre mark, though, I had a feeling of déjà vu. Similar to Berlin, my heart was burning and I could hardly breathe. My air supply was restricted. 'It's all in the head,' I kept saying, yet my body disagreed. No mental technique I could think of got me back on track. Instead of speeding up, I slowed down for good. Shocked, frustrated and full of self-pity, I crawled towards the finish for the remaining 24 kilometres. What a failure.

Gary and I were equally devastated, and both of us struggled to find the root cause. Was it that I had resumed training too early after

Big Red Run without bouncing back fully? Or was it the situation at work as I held off my resignation? We did not know. Doubts crept into my head. Would I ever be good enough to make the team?

Four weeks of easier running to fully recover helped me get back into a positive headspace. Gary moved to the second phase of our preparation, which was all about strength. As we got back into nature and onto trails, I was surprised how much it lifted my spirit.

This was also the time I was able to hand in my resignation at work — and the moment I did, I felt a weight lifting from my shoulders. From one day to the next, my already low resting heart rate dropped by five beats. Physiologically, I could measure the emotional burden. I still had to work through a six-month notice period, but merely the certainty of the end date made everything much more bearable. I'd also negotiated with my boss to start later on Wednesday mornings, so I could fit in a long, midweek run. This bit of creativity led to significant improvements in training. After many sessions I could demonstrate I was on the right trajectory. From there onwards, things turned. Unfortunately, they turned badly.

The second phase ended with the Six Foot Track Marathon, a scenic 45-kilometre race on the beautiful trails in the Blue Mountains outside of Sydney. Everything was going my way when, an hour into the race, I didn't lift my feet high enough. I was winding down a narrow path and stumbled over a rock. Boom! Face first, onto the trail. My right knee took a knock and was bleeding heavily. So were my hands and even my chest. I was lucky that my jaw just missed another rock. First, I was in shock, and then in pain. I got up and hobbled myself back into the race. My rhythm stayed behind, however, and with it my confidence. I was afraid to fall again. Concerned volunteers offered their help at every checkpoint. I looked like a zombie from a bad horror movie. Somehow, I made it to the finish line but stayed far below my capabilities. The last time I hurt my knee had been when I fell off my bicycle as a kid. I found that, in my late thirties, wounds healed much slower. The same was true for my demolished confidence.

The first training phase had concluded with a disastrous marathon in Melbourne and the second phase with a shocking Six Foot Track Marathon. Dwelling on what had happened was pointless, however. We had to move on to the final phase of training — race-specific fitness. But instead of building confidence, I was swallowed by a black hole. Rebecca pointed out that my mindset was very different from what it had been before Big Red Run. My motivation having shifted to avoiding failure was visible. I was no longer master of my inner world. During my peak training week, my training diary included the comments, 'Afraid of downhills', 'Not a good day, at all', 'Bad mental space', 'Really concerned that I lost mental calmness' and 'Pacing mind and restless'.

I felt the pressure of 'having to qualify' and knew that the stress I was experiencing was counterproductive. All I wanted was for that horrible feeling of being stuck to go away. I was caught in a painful situation with no control, and decided to have an honest chat with Gary and confess where I was at. I called him and shared my doubts, telling him I did not have what it took to make the team. Gary took a deep breath. I sensed he was no foreigner to these types of conversations. Dealing with low self-confidence was his bread and butter, and he did an amazing job in listening to everything I had to get off my chest. When I ran out of words, he just said, 'Now listen to me, Kay. You are ready, and we will both travel to the world champs.'

That was all I needed to hear. What a relief to have somebody trusting in my abilities. My spirits and hopes lifted. I wanted to prove Gary right. Even more desperately, I wanted to run for Australia. I wanted it so badly that I concluded, 'I better make the 100-kilometre team. If I don't, I will have to make the 24-hour team. That sounds like even more work.' Running as far as one could within 24 hours was the only longer race format that offered world championships. Gary laughed and encouraged me to stick to Plan A. The calibre of Australian representatives for 24 hours was exceptional. I should not be under any illusions; it would be much harder to get into that team.

With a few weeks before the main race, I had one remaining important task to complete. I had to train my support crew. Both Rebecca and Gavin were accompanying me to Christchurch, and their role was to be on top of my nutrition and hydration. Also, I did not underestimate how important cheering me on would be. Having Gavin present for any mental emergencies would be invaluable. The race consisted of 50 two-kilometre laps through Hagley Park in the centre of Christchurch. We conducted a short race simulation session, where I ran at race pace and my crew handed me drinks. Everything came together that morning and lifted my spirits. I reminded myself that for miracles to happen, not everything had to be perfect. We had all done everything we could. Hopefully, it would be sufficient.

RUNNING INTO TROUBLE

Roughly 30 runners huddled at the start line in Hagley Park. Gavin and Rebecca were standing with the other supporters, cheering us on. I was freezing, wearing my shorts and a singlet on a six-degree morning as we waited for the gun to go off, but I could not complain about the perfect racing conditions Christchurch had put on for us. I was in a much better mental spot than I had been for months. Training had been a roller-coaster ride, but all that counted was consistency under pressure. I was good at that. Before I could contemplate what might happen in the next few hours, we were sent off.

The dark night sky still had Christchurch under its grip when a bunch of still enthusiastic runners stormed off onto their first lap. Every few metres I checked my GPS watch to ensure I kept to my intended pace and wasn't going too fast too early. Gary had reminded me often enough that the race did not start until kilometre 70. It was a patience game. My pace was fine, yet my thoughts did not settle. I could not switch off the voice of an internal commentator who judged every move I made. My inner critic was wide awake, which was not the news I wanted to hear.

After a few laps Rebecca was on her first drink duties. I had compiled a sheet, outlining which drink bottle to hand me at what time. My only instructions had been to be decisive. I wanted to focus on just running and not having to make any unnecessary decisions on what and when to drink. When I approached my crew, Rebecca looked flustered and asked me, 'Do you want the yellow or the blue drink?'

I lost it. I was disappointed. Was asking for decisiveness too much? The anger took hold of me and I heard myself shouting, 'I don't know! That's your job to know.' Bang! The instance I said it, I realised how inappropriate my behaviour was. Instantly, I regretted my outburst, which was a mere reflection of my frustration with myself. The colour of the bottle didn't even matter. I was running the most important race of my life, and I didn't know how to relax. Too much was at stake. Yet, we were a team, and I promised myself that, regardless of my frustration going forward, I would show my support crew the respect they deserved.

Apart from my early tantrum, the first few hours were uneventful. I ticked off one lap after the other and took on sugary fluids as intended. My pace felt slow, but that was the plan. Invisible to my crew, a storm was brewing inside of me. I did not manage to get on top of my fears. My inner voice constantly recommended I watch my pace, stay patient, focus on the breathing. It was unnecessary advice and not helpful. I knew what to do and just wanted to be left alone so I could do what was required. Yet, the advice kept coming. Through meditation I had practised how to gently refocus my attention on an object of my choice. But now I could neither focus on my breath nor on the rhythmic pattern of my feet hitting the tarmac.

It barely surprised me when, at kilometre 32, all alarm bells went off. My legs were as heavy as lead, my glute muscles were burning and the clear message was, 'I cannot run at this pace anymore.' Out of nowhere, trouble struck, reminding me of my blow-up in the Melbourne marathon. The message was the same. Slow down! But I was not even fast, and it was early in the race. Again, I could find no apparent reason for feeling the way I did. Only this time my goal of qualifying for the world championships was under threat. When I ran past Gavin, I shouted 'orange' — the code we had agreed on, should I get into trouble.

It was time to rely on my mental toolkit. I tried everything I could think of: thought stoppage, tuning into the pain, distracting from the pain, breathing deeply. Nothing worked. Absolutely nothing. This was not mental. This was physical. My legs were getting heavier, and I was forced to reduce my speed. 'Red' was the next shout-out to my support crew. The message was unambiguous. I was in serious trouble.

I was flooded with utter fear, and almost in a state of panic. Every step got me deeper and deeper into trouble. I hadn't even completed a marathon distance, and my legs were cactus. My body was slowing down, while my thoughts were accelerating. All I could think was, *This is not working. I can't do this.* I felt awful and had to battle hard to not give in to the urge to walk. Next, my tummy announced that I urgently needed a toilet stop. My body was complaining on all channels.

I stopped at the toilet in the start–finish area. So far, my support crew had not been helpful at all. This was my life's story — I was fighting on my own. With no backing from anyone, I was losing ground. Gavin looked as shocked as I was and didn't know what to do either. While I was on the loo, Rebecca talked to me from outside, reminding me of a story Gary had shared. He had been in major trouble at the previous world championships. He was dizzy and crashed into a support table. Yet, he found the strength to push through to the end. Sharing that story was a well-intentioned attempt to cheer me up. It had the opposite effect. All I did was to brush it aside with a snappy response. 'F*#% Gary! Good on him! I'm not as stupid as Gary!'

I had lost belief. It was obvious I wasn't capable of running the required qualifying time. Even worse than that, I could see no way I'd even finish this race. The pain was unbearable, and I was not even halfway. The race was over for me before it had properly started. In a last desperate attempt, Gavin told me to switch off my watch and just run. I hoped that he was right and even went a step further: I took off my watch and, full of frustration, threw it at his feet. From here, I would navigate my way without a GPS device. I was far from the role model for dealing with adversity. Again, I was taking my frustrations and fears out on the very people who were trying to help me.

I'd dug myself a hole, and now I felt trapped. Why could I not access that quiet place within me, where body and mind acted in perfect harmony? I was no longer the amazing runner I'd been in the desert. Instead, I was in pain, without even the prospect of finishing the race. It was just too far to go. I could not beat my body into submission.

The chaos in my head expanded with every step I took, until I was convinced that the situation was unbearable. I would not feel any better unless I gave up. I was desperate to just stop and make that pain go away. I had no choice, other than to declare defeat. The next time I passed my support crew, I announced, 'I will stop, and we go home. Three more laps.'

SELF CHECK-IN

- Think of a major instance in your life when you felt that you completely failed. What happened? What were your thoughts at the time?
- Can you think of a time when your mental fears and frustrations manifested in physical pain? How did you deal with this?
- Typically, when we don't succeed with a stated goal, our identity feels threatened. When this happened to you, why do you think the 'failure' hurt so much? Who did you think you had given up being?

At the start of Big Red Run, worrying about puddles ahead—wet feet mean blisters!
© EYE SEE IMAGES—Patrick O'Kane.

BIG RED RUN

Clockwise from top left: Day 3 or 4—still smiling; welcomed after 84 km on day 5; starting day 3 (© Brad Baker Photography); signing the camera at the finish line; final day celebrations. All photos © EYE SEE IMAGES—Patrick O'Kane, unless otherwise specified.

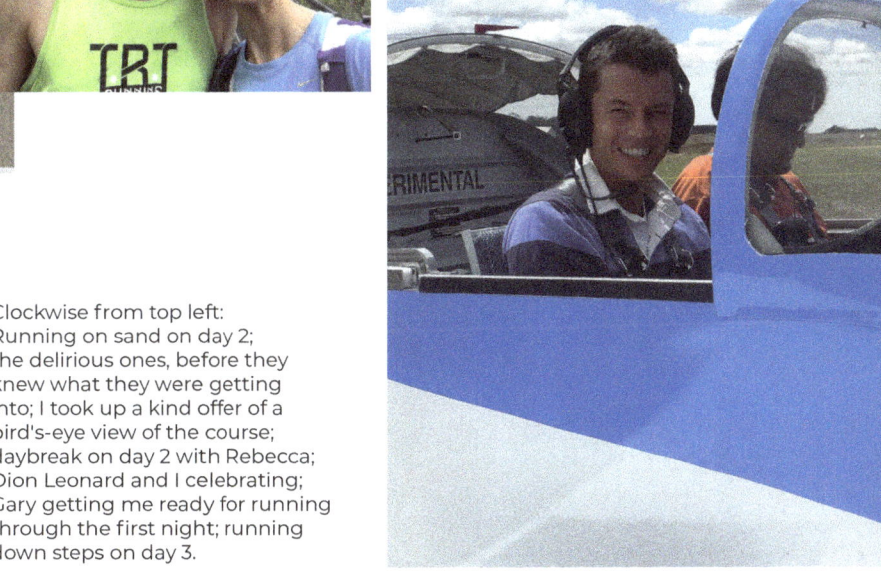

Clockwise from top left: Running on sand on day 2; the delirious ones, before they knew what they were getting into; I took up a kind offer of a bird's-eye view of the course; daybreak on day 2 with Rebecca; Dion Leonard and I celebrating; Gary getting me ready for running through the first night; running down steps on day 3.

DELIRIOUS W.E.S.T.

24-HOUR WORLD CHAMPIONSHIPS

Clockwise from top left: Passing a drinks stop during the race; celebrating a successful debut with the Emus; all smiles (© Martin Fryer); the Australian team, the Emus; winners are grinners; opening ceremony through Albi.

BERLIN MARATHON

Main: Brandenburg Gate. © MarathonFoto.
Inset: Time to fly. © MarathonFoto.

COAST TO KOSCIUSZKO

Clockwise from top: The road ahead at daybreak; my crazy Kosci crew, from left to right: Rebecca, Mario, me and Gary; crewing for David at the summit.

CHAPTER 8

TURNING RIGHT AT THE END OF THE WORLD

> *The basic difference between an ordinary man and a warrior is that a warrior takes everything as a challenge, while an ordinary man takes everything as a blessing or as a curse.*
>
> —Carlos Castaneda

I had made the call to give up in Christchurch, desperate to just stop and make the pain go away. Possibly the most difficult part of it was that I could not beat my body into submission. My body and my brain were both saying the only way to feel any better was to give up and declare defeat.

So, in the most important race of my life, for the very first time in my life, I would earn the label DNF, Did Not Finish. I couldn't really explain why I had even committed to another three laps, but it was probably because I wanted to be on my own. The prospect of dealing with my embarrassment and disappointment in front of other people was even worse than the physical pain.

Just before I started my final lap of walking, Gavin tried to haggle. 'Two more,' he demanded. But I was firm, as black and white as I'd been before meeting Gavin. My response left no room for misunderstanding.

I started walking, and Rebecca joined me for the first few hundred metres. She didn't know how to help, what to say, or what to do. I was beyond finding a solution, and it was not the time to seek anybody's understanding. But it was some comfort for her to just be there for me. I wanted to spend the remainder of the lap on my own. I decided to test my legs one last time and tried to get into a slow jog. But the pain instantly forced me back into a walk. This meant that I was within about a marathon's distance from the end, and in second position overall with a lead of six kilometres from the third runner, and I had to give up. That, to me, was a disaster.

With less than a kilometre's walk to the finishing area, I knew that if I didn't complete this, I would miss out. Because this whole event had a deeper meaning. What I would miss out on was less about not completing the race or even claiming a podium position, and more about my conviction that I was here to learn something. The thought rolling now around was, *If I stop now, what then? If I'm going to get the insight I'm meant to, I have to finish the race*. I couldn't just pull out; I had to get to the end and find out.

BECOMING AN EXPLORER

My inner, calm voice had somehow come into my mental space to remind me, 'I'm an explorer. I run to find clarity.' And along with this voice came a dramatic change. Suddenly, within 100 metres, everything had changed. As if somebody had pressed a reset button, I could run again. It was miraculous. I was filled with a deep level of purpose and had no doubt at all. I would finish the race. I'd re-encountered the reason I loved running in the first place, so there was no quitting. Moreover, I'd grow through this experience.

What had just happened? My head had tricked me. This wasn't a physical issue; it was primarily a mental crisis, and the result had been a horrible race. It was painful that I would not achieve my goal to qualify for the Australian team. Yet, from one step to the next, my motivation shifted. Unexpectedly, my passion for running took over from my desire to succeed. I was here to know myself better and grow as a person, not for that podium finish or spot on the team. From here onwards, I could still do my best. It looked like I'd kept on running because a grain of hope had been still alive in me. Needless to say, when I rushed past Gavin and Rebecca and, full of enthusiasm, shouted, 'We're back on again!', their reactions were equally dramatic. Surprise and delight, in equal measure.

I was as surprised as my support crew. I'd never experienced such a big swing in energy in such a short time. How had the pain in my legs, which had forced me into walking, vanished instantly? I thought about it for a few laps and, going over it, realised it had all started with a slight twinge in the body. From that, the catastrophising began, and soon I was convinced it would last forever. From there, the tragedy took its course.

I'd resisted the pain and wanted to make it go away, which had the opposite effect. I got caught up in my own reactivity. The pain hadn't been unbearable — in fact, it was only unpleasant — but the narrative I had spun around it made it so. I added in repetitive negative thoughts and became terrified about how bad the pain would get.

I was no longer dealing with the here and now, but with an imaginary future. My fears created a platform for the discomfort to get out of control. It got worse and worse until the suffering was too much.

The downward spiral stopped the very moment I pressed the pause button and became curious about it, asking a deeper question. Yet why was the answer so significant? With those words — explorer, find clarity — came the magical moment when my mind had gone quiet. The storm calmed down, and the mind chatter disappeared. Peace emerged. The battle between hope and desire on one side, and pain and despair on the other side, no longer needed to be fought. I had the choice of how to respond and so, with that perspective, following my purpose became an option.

When I completed the next lap, I saw Gavin cheering me on, and I suddenly understood why the term 'explorer' was so powerful for me. Gavin had had a strong role to play. After the Berlin marathon, he'd challenged me to change the language in order to embed the new perspective I'd gained through turning right. My choice of words mattered more than I was aware of. He'd questioned what my new terminology would be, substituting my old perspective of being in control, but I hadn't found an answer. He had warned me that I risked reverting to old patterns without this new language. I could see now that my transformation had never been complete. The emerging butterfly was clinging to the language of the caterpillar; instead of flying, I fell over my feet.

This was exciting. I'd encountered the answer — the old self was highly bureaucratic, desperate for efficient results. The new self was more of an explorer, free to pursue an inexplicable calling.

While I was thinking about it, I passed the 70-kilometre mark and, according to Gary, this was when the race really started. Interestingly,

I was running better than anybody else in the field. Even the runner in the lead was in serious trouble. As I passed the start–finish area, I saw him sitting on a chair in a world of pain with his support crew massaging his legs. I, on the other hand, was not running as fast I had wanted to, but I was consistent in my progress. I could see, from the scoreboard, that he still had a very comfortable lead because he had lapped me multiple times. So, being realistic, I could only win the race if he gave up. Time would tell.

In any case, however, this race was no longer about running a qualifier or even about winning. It was about a lesson. Up till then, I'd never had so many consecutive failures: I had blown up in the Melbourne marathon, cut my knee open in the Six Foot Track Marathon and, in this race, lost all faith very early on.

Big Red Run had been a high in my running career. My bureaucrat seemed to have claimed credit for it and then crept in through the backdoor and begun running my life again. I might have told myself that I was after personal development but, deep down, all I'd really cared about was success. The bureaucrat had tricked me by imitating the voice of the explorer. I was back trying to control the uncontrollable and resurrected the drive for perfection. On top of that, I'd suffocated my intuition. My sole focus was on great achievement, qualifying for the world championships and finding those moments of glory. As soon as that goal became unachievable, I'd had no reason to keep on running.

Now, though, for the first time in the entire race, my drive to find the insights pushed me forward. But I was too exhausted to think straight and couldn't put my finger on what the latest insight was. At least my mind allowed my body to do what it was capable of. They acted in harmony and found a good rhythm.

I never did catch the first guy but was happy to claim second place in a time of 8:19:59 hours. Both Gavin and Rebecca hugged me, and I did not let go. If I had, I'd probably have fallen to the ground with exhaustion. I was disappointed with myself and had hoped to run almost an hour faster. At the same time, I could just feel that this race was one of the most important experiences I had gone through in running. The old saying was very apt — it was not what I wanted, but it probably was what I needed.

I couldn't kid myself, though — facing failure was painful. The emotional pain after the race was much worse than the physical pain while running. My body bounced back quickly, but the disappointment sat deep. I wanted to hide away — or, better yet, run away from my misery. I had worked very hard, and the result was not even close to what I'd been capable of. I had short-changed myself. After repetitive fiascos since Big Red Run, I stood with empty hands. No world championships for me. In hindsight, it was a sign of poor judgement to sacrifice Coast to Kosci. I'd traded in something I had been passionate about for the attempt to shine in glory.

Friends and family did their best to cheer me up. A raft of sayings arose: 'You are not your results', 'Everybody looks good when they win, but the true test is how you deal with a bad day' and 'Failure is the stepping stone to success'. None of them softened how broken I felt. I was still missing the key learning of the catastrophic experience and, without learning my lesson, I knew it'd keep haunting me. It terrified me that the streak of disasters might never end. I was desperate to shrug off the misery, but I was equally compelled to understand further.

Had I encountered the limit of turning right? Were there situations where right turns just didn't work? Was I too ambitious? Several friends commented that I was very driven and, maybe, even overly ambitious. Toning down my ambitions would save me from further painful experiences. I did have very high expectations for myself, and those ambitions would have played their part in choking me during the race. Perfectionism, excessive drive and control were the opposites of what had led me to an amazing experience in the desert. But I fundamentally disagreed with my friends' conclusion that lessening my ambition was the solution. Self-protection was the wrong path. I was not going to dial down my aspirations. Avoiding tough situations would just be another reactive play, reinforcing my motivation to avoid failure. The solution to overcoming reactivity was not to become more reactive.

I'd approached the race as a mere running challenge, and my inner bureaucrat had taken over. He'd completely ignored the lessons from Big Red Run and had come back in through the backdoor to claim the unexpected achievement as his success. My egoic mind wanted to protect who I had become — a successful ultra runner. For Christchurch, I fully disregarded that I didn't deal with a technical but with an adaptive challenge. Therefore, it was a question of mindset, not of skill alone. A change in technical capabilities was never sufficient when new ways of thinking were required. I had pretended that pure running training would bridge the gap between my capabilities and the demands of the challenge. Instead, I lacked the adequate mindset. I had crossed a very fine line: in the desert I did my best; in Christchurch I wanted to be perfect. The paradox in the desert was that incredible achievements occurred once I dropped the need to be successful.

Although my intention had been to turn right again, I'd done the opposite. From the moment I ditched Coast to Kosci, I was back on autopilot. Obsessed by the need to be perfect, I had become a slave to a training plan. Worse than ever before, everything was highly regulated. My program prescribed which session to do on which day and had clear success criteria for every single run. I worried about not being quick enough and falling behind. Each day I asked myself whether I had made progress. It did not speed up my improvement. I was not marching to the beat of my own drum but trying to please Gary. Filling in spreadsheets with my training was suffocating my creativity and left no space for the unexpected. The honest verdict was that I had completely missed the right turn in this adventure. It was nobody's fault, other than my own.

I was still missing what exactly I had to do to prevent taking the wrong turn in the future. The inner bureaucrat had convincingly imitated the voice of my inner explorer and had been exquisite at masking that I was not even close to turning right again. I hoped Gavin would give me a hint to prevent a repeat in the future. His counter-question was to ask what my conclusions were. Otherwise, he remained silent. He surely had a view, having watched the race play out in person. But it was another one of those instances where, apparently, it was essential that I came to the answer myself. Only, I did not seem able to find it.

DISCOVERING A NEW PERSPECTIVE

I was ripe for a proper break from running to freshen up both physically and mentally. The timing coincided almost perfectly with me wrapping up my job in Melbourne. It might have taken a year from making the decision to resign to actually leaving, but I'd stayed true to my work ethic and the commitments I had given. Finally, I was trading in a stale, toxic environment for the excitement of a four-month trip around the world. First, I would see my family and friends in Europe, followed by a stint through Peru, Galapagos, Brazil and Argentina with Rebecca.

While Rebecca would then have to go back to work, my journey was going to be topped off by a three-week ship expedition to the end of the world. In what would be the highlight of my trip, I was going to follow the journey of Sir Ernest Shackleton, a legendary explorer from the early twentieth century. We would set sail to Antarctica via the Falklands and South Georgia. I did not even have to worry about what would await me after that expedition. While I wanted to drastically change career paths, the timing wasn't yet right — and the competing supermarket (with its headquarters in Sydney) had chased me down with an offer I could not resist.

Rebecca and I snorkelled with turtles on the Galapagos, hiked to Machu Picchu and enjoyed cocktails at the beaches of Brazil. I just enjoyed the travels. No striving for anything. The break did wonders and, by the time I reached Patagonia in Argentina, I was desperate to put on my running shoes again. I reencountered the joy of experiencing the landscape by running through it. The following three weeks took me on a ship bound towards Antarctica. On the ship, I kept running. Even the heaviest swell through the rough seas did not stop my daily runs on the treadmill. Again, I was not striving for any event but running because I loved it. Spotting penguins, seals and icebergs through the porthole as I ran was priceless.

Following Shackleton's journey made me feel almost like a polar explorer myself. A few years after Roald Amundsen had won the race to the South Pole against Robert Falcon Scott in 1911, Shackleton and his men tried to be the first to cross Antarctica from sea to sea via the pole. Unlike our trip on a comfortable ship through the icy waters of Antarctica, Shackleton's ship got stuck in the pack ice. What followed was a long battle for mere survival. He and his men saw their ship, the *Endurance*, get crushed by the ice during the black polar winter.

Lost in the endless ice, they faced almost certain death; however, they never gave up and made an unlikely escape in a tiny life boat. Like a little boy, I could have listened to his adventure stories forever. Seeing some of the hostile places they got stranded on, such as Elephant Island near the Antarctic Peninsula, brought the stories even more to life. What a resilient leader, who failed in his endeavour to cross the white continent but succeeded in not losing a single one of his men when disaster struck.

Now, as I had stopped dwelling on my Christchurch disaster, a complete shift in my awareness occurred. Shackleton had role-modelled the mindset I was lacking. My travel to the end of the world helped everything to make sense, and it was as if a blindfold had been stripped from my eyes. I wanted to be an explorer, but without all the pain that came with it. I wanted the glory without the disappointments. The sun without the shadow. I was chasing the shiny side of adventures, yet was not willing to relate to its ugly counterpart. As if the two could be separated, I pushed away any afflictive emotions in my incapability to bear them. I was too fearful of that dark side within me — afraid of pain, of not being good enough, of failure.

Those fears had deep roots. I remembered how afraid I had been as a kid — afraid of the dark, afraid of being alone, afraid of not being safe, afraid of not being loved, afraid of being helpless, afraid of getting laughed at.

Then there was the fear of getting hurt. How I hated pain. The day I decided not to feel the pain anymore, it got much more tolerable. My dad had just smacked me, and I was alone in my room, crying. I must have been an adolescent already. That was when I decided not to cry anymore. Cutting myself off from those unbearable emotions was such a relief. With that decision, I regained control. I was no longer an emotional wreck but could disassociate from my feelings and keep a clear head. I left the adventurous, imaginary world of Winnetou behind. It had not delivered on its promises that I could hide away in it. Instead, thinking, planning and the success that came with it kept me safe.

My ability to keep a cool head in the middle of emotional eruptions came in handy when trapped in boardrooms. Staying rational had become one of my core strengths, allowing me to function when others became overwhelmed.

It looked like I had gone too far, however, in expelling my emotions from my life. Avoiding pain in all parts of my life was comfortable. But what were the costs? I was not relating to a significant chunk of the human experience. Similar to outside my garden gate, territory still needed exploring, if only I dared to turn right. No doubt, this territory had a lot of untapped potential on offer. For example, I had seen snippets of the power of intuition. Intuition was strongest for me when I let go of the models in my head and trusted my feelings. Did I ever believe that I could rely on my intuition if I rejected my emotions?

How would I have led Shackleton's men? While I always avoided unpleasant experiences, Shackleton embraced what actually happened and made the best out of extremely poor conditions. He too started off with enthusiasm. Different from me, he maintained composure in spite of the hardships he faced. He could see through the veil of desperation that accompanied seemingly hopeless situations. Pursuing one's ambitions with stamina and perseverance in spite of painful setbacks along the way was far from easy. It required true resilience — resilience, way beyond that which comes from flicking a rubber band. I could not keep going through life hoping that every painful situation could be avoided or, if necessary, managed away. Thinking that way meant I lacked the ability to deal with any situation effectively, regardless of its nature.

My relationship with the unwanted was very frosty. My urge to always be on top of things and control constantly changing circumstances was not serving me. I always had something to worry about. I struggled when what I desired was not aligned with what the world had on offer. Once again, I had become dependent on external circumstances and lost sight of my dreams. While I got stuck in my ambitions, Shackleton adjusted his perspective and demonstrated extraordinary agility. When everything was stripped away from him, he drew on the resources he had within himself. He didn't waste his time on what couldn't be changed. Instead, he took ownership of the controllable. He created his future pursuing his vision. I got caught up reacting to my fears.

A clear vision formed before we left the waters of Antarctica. I was going to turn right again. It was time to let go of the pain from Christchurch and move on. This time, I would learn my lesson and get comfortable with discomfort. Success on my next endeavour would not be measured by blissful achievements but my ability to not be a pawn when adversity struck. I would no longer avoid the battle with my own demons. Resisting discomfort was the main reason

I repeatedly got stuck in my life. I had not only thoughts but also feelings. To keep growing, I had to readjust my relationship with my emotions. If I wanted to be a true explorer, I also had to descend into the depth of my less shiny side and face my doubts and fears head-on.

Shackleton was proof that an entire expedition could be a disaster and yet, on a different level, be an amazing achievement. For the magic to emerge, I did not even need success at all. The magic happened when I provided the grounds for it to happen, regardless of the outcome. Its biggest enemy was the longing to be amazing and great. Going forward, I had the choice to perform to grow my ego, or to reduce my ego and perform beyond measure. It was a no-brainer what my next adventure would be. Finally, I would run Coast to Kosci, tackling 240 kilometres in one go and running from the beaches of New South Wales to the heights of Mount Kosciuszko, the top of Australia. It had been my dream for a long time, and I had gotten side-tracked by the seductive sounds of the world championships.

SELF CHECK-IN

- How far do you go to avoid pain or your emotions?
- How have the most challenging times in your life shaped who you are today?
- What realisations about yourself emerged?
- What language did you (or can you) adopt due to this transformation?

CHAPTER 9

TURNING RIGHT TO NEW HEIGHTS

> *So, it is not always the pain per se, but the way we see it and react to it that determines the degree of suffering we will experience. And it is the suffering that we fear most, not the pain.*
>
> —Jon Kabat-Zinn

Shortly after returning from Antarctica, I moved to Sydney to start my new job. I had left an increasingly toxic environment just before my round-the-world trip and, now, I was fully recharged to bring my full self into work. My intention was to not only build a high-performing team but also help the organisation transform and leave behind the challenging times it was going through. My new boss told me he'd hired me for my expertise and to help him transform culture. I was stepping up in responsibility and felt, finally, I could make a real difference in where the buying team was heading. For the first time in years, I reconnected with my sense of purpose in the business world.

I was part of a leadership team whose role extended far beyond running our respective departments. The environment was invigorating and rewarding — we were responsible for how we collectively lived our values. My most challenging mission was to embed a new way of working internally and with our suppliers, focusing on customer needs and collaboration. No longer was I primarily working just to get my pay cheque.

But the price I had to pay was travelling often between Sydney and Melbourne to see Rebecca; we'd not yet found a more sustainable solution.

SEEKING GROWTH AND MEANING

While I learned how to navigate the new ecosystem, at least the direction of my personal development was clear. If I wanted to thrive — both in a more senior position at work, and in a race such as Coast to Kosci — I needed to upgrade my inner game. I had treated Christchurch as a technical challenge where I'd merely focused on developing my skills. This was important but was also nothing more than horizontal development and, therefore, led to a disappointing race result. Coast to Kosci demanded a fundamentally different approach, because it was another adaptive challenge, meaning I had to grow vertically and stretch beyond the boundaries of the world as I knew it. The next chapter in my life would be another inner journey; it would need a major personal rethink.

I had a sense, luckily, of what part of me needed strengthening. It was the explorer in me, and I needed this explorer to be able to stand up tall against my very reactive, and restrictive, inner bureaucrat. The bureaucrat reacted to fears; the explorer was driven by purpose and had a vision of where that purpose could lead. I could see very clearly now. One motivated me to avoid failure; the other encouraged me to succeed.

When I started my new job in Sydney, Gavin asked me what part of my personality I'd have to let go of in order to step up and fill the big shoes waiting for me. I answered that it was my identification with success. In Christchurch, I'd sought external validation to boost my self-worth. The pain of failure accompanied me down to Antarctica. Who was I if not my success? Failure was an attack on the very core of my recently created identity — the successful ultra runner. But if I wanted to make the transition from caterpillar to butterfly, I could no longer define myself through my achievements.

The adventure stories of Shackleton and his men had shown me that life was not about achieving something extraordinary. Rather, it was about responding to the challenges life threw at us. In that regard, my sense of identity had two flaws. One, validating myself externally did not give me the freedom to pursue any real growth. As long as success was paramount, growth and meaning would always come second. Two, my high level of reactivity, driven by fear, left me ill-equipped in the extreme challenges that excited me. If motivation to succeed was the mindset that kept me going, I needed to be less dependent on my external circumstances and build on the strength within myself. Coast to Kosci would be the quest to realign what I did with what fulfilled me.

What fulfilled me, my values, were growth, curiosity and clarity. If I was going to find that fulfilment, I needed to strengthen my inner explorer. As a child, I'd dreamed of becoming an explorer or an inventor — at the time, they were synonymous. I listened as we were told the thrilling adventure stories of Amerigo Vespucci or Christopher Columbus. They served as a great escape from the grim reality of the relentless and regular aggression in my household. Those heroes showed a constructive use of their energy, instead of releasing it in the face of their own children.

I was disheartened as a child when I realised I'd been born too late in human history. All the continents were already known and mapped. The major invention I thought of already existed. At each turn I was stymied, and it did not take long for me to bury my elusive dream.

My grandfather suggested that, anyway, simply becoming successful and wealthy was a more promising alternative. For the next few years, the plan was that I would become a rich dentist. And so, the fear of failure, disguised as the voice of reasoning, held me back from becoming an explorer. My dream had already lost colour; next, it faded altogether. But when it came to choosing a degree at university, I realised that becoming a dentist was too restrictive; also, exploring other people's mouths was not for me. I wanted to broaden my horizon. I opted to study a master's degree in International Business and completed a Doctorate in European Law.

It was surprising how much clarity I had as a young kid. I knew what I wanted and, more importantly, who I was. While the clarity faded away as I grew up, it never disappeared completely. However, multiple personalities within me seemed to be all fighting for their place. On one side was my reasonable self. It wanted to keep me safe and, therefore, loved control and bureaucracy. Christchurch was a reminder of how dark and vocal this side could get when the bureaucrat was under threat. On the other side was a more nuanced and quieter character. I hadn't yet figured out this other self. That version of me was adventurous and intuitive; a higher version of myself, who fearlessly pursued meaning and fulfilment rather than getting intimidated by the prospect of not succeeding. As I had experienced during Big Red Run, his power was unprecedented.

How many wake-up calls did I require? I was about to finish my doctorate and had just secured my first 'proper' job as a consultant when I got diagnosed with a melanoma on my left forearm. From one instant to the next, the reality of not living forever kicked home. I was lucky enough to have found the cancerous cells in my body before any metastasis spread through my body. When several life-insurance companies refused to offer me cover, due to my medical history, I realised that I'd been given a second chance to stop and ask myself what I really wanted to do with my life. I was still thirsty for success but not if I had to sacrifice finding fulfilment. Life was too short, I concluded. Yet, I had gotten back into a lull, and a decade had slipped past until I had turned right. Whether I would let the next decade drift past or inject my life with more meaning was up to me.

I was determined to be more responsible with the time I was granted. My next mission was to find a better balance between the demands of my inner voices. My inner explorer, particularly, was craving more space to flourish. If I managed to make friends with my emotions, I might even relate to the shadow within me. I'd experienced my feelings being better signposts than my rational mind would ever be capable of. These feelings were essential to tapping into my intuition. Coast to Kosci would be like resitting a failed exam. The true measure of success was whether I would be capable of accepting any outcome. Mastery and insights did not rely on the result.

To have a realistic chance of being selected as one of approximately 50 competitors in Coast to Kosci, I needed to tick off three criteria: cover 180 kilometres within 24 hours, run a 100-kilometre race and crew for a competitor to experience, firsthand, what it took to be successful at Coast to Kosci.

I urgently needed to create the right conditions to thrive again. First, I needed to have a courageous man-to-man conversation with Gary. I knew he had so much experience on offer, but we hadn't found the right rhythm — at least not yet. The answer, which worked for both of us, was shifting from a coaching to a mentoring relationship. I did not require a coach who set rigid training plans for me. Going forward, Gary was going to be my invaluable thought-partner, who challenged and inspired me.

On the running side, I had to boost my general fitness level back up, working on hill strength in particular. All my life, I'd lived in pancake-flat cities such as Cologne, Seville or Melbourne. What Sydneysiders called 'undulations' looked like mountains to me. After a few months, I felt sufficiently prepared to participate in another 45-kilometre trail race in the Blue Mountains, the Mount Solitary Ultra.

My ability to run on hills had improved significantly. For most of the race, I found myself well within the top 10 runners. With about 10 kilometres to go, I ran into trouble from one step to the other. For kilometres, I had raced down a sharp descent, when my left quadricep muscle just above the knee went into spasm. Pain shot through my body. Luckily, the trail levelled out for a few metres, or I might have stumbled. The cramp didn't ease off, however.

The situation was not promising. How would I climb back the seemingly vertical ascent out of the valley to get to the finish line? To make it worse, the muscle on the other leg started cramping as well.

My response was surprising. I stayed calm. All I did was tune into the pain and try to determine its exact location. I didn't judge or condemn it but stayed curious. Instead of going down the well-trodden route of panicking about the prospect of pulling out of the race after coming this far, I tested what I was still capable of doing. My muscles twitched a few more times and then relaxed. They did not cause any more trouble.

The fact that I lacked the conditioning to defend my top 10 position was secondary. Several runners overtook me on the long ascent to the finish line. And I was content. I'd just taken another right turn. In a pressure situation, I had not pushed away intense pain; I'd switched off my autopilot and taken the route less travelled. I had the recipe and was dealing effectively with the situation: from upset to awareness to choice. The cramp had been an external trigger, upsetting me. As if at a stop sign, I paused and became aware of what was happening while it was happening. And instead of reacting mindlessly, I stayed present. That interrupted my autopilot and, with that, created the possibility of turning right. It was now my choice about how to respond to the situation. My choice.

My experience reminded me of the message Viktor Frankl had crystallised in his book *Man's search for meaning*. Frankl had been a Jewish psychiatrist, and he witnessed unbearable cruelty during his incarceration in four concentration camps during World War II. In Auschwitz, he promised himself he would not only survive and help others but also study the psychology of survival.

Frankl realised it wasn't necessarily the healthiest who made it through those extreme conditions — it was the ones who were able to give meaning to their suffering. And those who oriented themselves towards a goal to complete in the future had the best chances of survival. Frankl concluded that, even when we were triggered by what appeared unbearable, we still had a choice:

Between stimulus and response there is a space. In that space is our power to choose our response. In our response lies our growth and our freedom.

The power each one of us holds is the choice, the individual response when triggered. Regardless of the circumstances, we never have to be a victim. Frankl even went further and summed up yet another realisation: 'When we are no longer able to change a situation, we are challenged to change ourselves.' That shone a new light on the simple formula of moving from upset to awareness to choice. This formula was nothing less than the path to personal transformation. Whenever I left my comfort zone, I was triggered by upsets. Instead of externalising and reacting mindlessly on autopilot, I was invited to alter my perspective. Upsets created the fertile ground for transformation. By becoming aware and staying present, turning right became an option.

I had come a long way since Christchurch, where pain had captured my consciousness and led to an automated response pattern. This time, I was not immune to the pain of a cramping muscle, but I chose to not take on board additional suffering. My curiosity about the nature of the pain had made the difference. I had let go of my limiting belief that pain was endless once it surfaced and, therefore, had to be avoided. By believing it, it was self-fulfilling, if not even self-reinforcing. I was not only starting to familiarise myself with my feelings, but also starting to challenge the assumptions driving my behaviours. 'I have to avoid pain' was an illusion, stopping me from pursuing the vision of exploring the unknown. My takeaway from the race was that I was on a great trajectory for further personal transformation. I was proud of my early progress towards Coast to Kosci.

SLOWING DOWN

The very next morning my enthusiasm took a significant hit. My right heel had flared up, and I could hardly walk. Each step was excruciatingly painful. Although I tried to get on top of the injury early, all attempts to get a diagnosis failed. Hundreds of dollars later, I was advised to keep running. But the pain kept growing — and with it my frustration.

I recognised the upset and was aware what was happening — I was being tested in the very lesson I was trying to learn. That powerful lesson of dealing with whatever was happening, including the unpleasant.

But I hated dealing with situations I did not want in the first place. Time was running away like sand between my fingers, and I could barely run. What was the choice in this situation?

I had to learn the hard way that at times things would be beyond my control, and I had to accept that. My choice lay in how I related to the situation. It sucked. But was I going to soak in my misery for weeks? Potentially months?

I chose to focus on what was in my control. While I could barely run, I found two meaningful actions I could take. First, this upset was the perfect opportunity to familiarise myself further with my own emotions. Christchurch had taught me the lesson that cutting myself off from afflictive feelings was preventing me from going to the next level. Second, I further intensified my meditation. It helped with being present and, therefore, widening my awareness and spending more time observing myself objectively.

I had read about scientific studies that indicated meditation could help with dealing with pain. In *Full catastrophe living*, Kabat-Zinn outlines how participants of the studies were exposed to slightly painful impulses. In investigating the differences between meditators and non-meditators, the researchers found that non-meditators experienced the pain for much longer than meditators. They even felt the pain before they were exposed to the impulse, just because they were anticipating it. It also took them longer to recover from the sensation, and longer to not feel it anymore. Meditators experienced the pain only when they were actually exposed to it. They did not attempt to resist the pain and so had the ability to stay present and experience what was actually happening.

What intrigued me was that the study confirmed my own experience during the Mount Solitary Ultra. The degree of pain I'd experienced during the muscle cramp was intense but not unbearable, because it did not morph into suffering. The key difference was not letting myself be dominated by the unpleasant experience. When I'd acknowledged the pain without resisting it, it disappeared as soon as the pain impulse stopped. By not having the anxious desire to suppress the pain, I avoided a considerable percentage of pain sensation that, previously, would have had me feeling overwhelmed. It was a great reminder to continue my meditation practice — not necessarily to feel less pain but to become more comfortable tuning into discomfort and thus avoid unnecessary suffering. I wanted to master the inner game.

Physiologically, our brain patterns are responsible for what happens during any upset. Whenever the amygdala — near the base of the brain and part of our limbic system — senses a threat, it triggers a fight, flight or freeze response, and that includes releasing stress hormones. Those emotional patterns (the 3 Fs) are primarily shaped in our early childhood, before our rational and creative brains are fully developed. Evolution set these responses up as being highly effective for self-protection, along the lines of the motto 'better safe than sorry'. This explains why our emotional reactions are so often out of proportion to the actual incident. The good news is that our brains are 'neuroplastic' — that is, they are capable of rewiring themselves — meaning we have the capacity to strengthen new neural pathways and replace old habits with new ones. For me, meditation was helping that process.

What I did during meditation practice was to focus on an object of attention, moment by moment, without judgement. At least that was my intention. But my brain was conditioned to problem-solve, to come up with future plans or to reflect on past experiences. I was a thinker. Whether I tried to focus on my breath, sounds, thoughts or sensations in the body, it never took long for my mind to get hijacked and go off the next best tangent.

Meditating did lead to surprising insights about myself. Since working with Gavin, I knew how detrimental my urge to control was and worked on overcoming that reactive tendency. Through meditation, I realised that thinking was just another method of giving myself the illusion that I was in control. I'd been blind to how my self-protection mechanism governed my life. By escaping emotions, I had armoured and protected myself, spending a huge amount of my energy to keep safe.

A few months after asking the police for protection against my father, and them taking no notice of it, I took control of my dire situation for myself. Yet again, my father was chasing me down the staircase into the cellar and was about to hit me. Instead of turning my face away and making myself small, I did the unimaginable. I witnessed myself going towards my father, both arms held up in protection, standing tall and announcing with unmistakable determination that he was never going to hit me again. It was as if time stood still. I saw a broken man in front of me, and he looked much smaller than I remembered him. Dad's hands were shaking uncontrollably, as they always were when he was stressed. (Since he was a little kid, he'd had a neurological malfunctioning that meant he could never keep still.)

It felt like an eternity, yet was only the time it took for both my father and I to realise that our relationship would never be the same. In another few weeks I clarified the situation further, letting him know that he was mistaken if he thought he only had to stop hitting me. Nobody in our entire household was going to get hurt again. We were on the top floor of the house when I intervened and stopped him hitting my mother for the last time. I did not need any aggression or force; pure determination was sufficient. Yet, inevitably, we drifted apart, a side effect of the developments between him and me.

CUTTING THROUGH THE DRAMA

So far, I had been working on reducing my need to control. Now, I recognised that I had been blind to another reactive tendency: self-protection. I achieved that by distancing myself emotionally. When under threat, I escaped into the thinking mind. Most of my life, I'd lived in a mind-created world, where being rational was paramount. All my protection mechanisms of staying rational, being in control, and loving order and discipline were highly rewarded in the academic and business world. They led to regular achievements.

But what was the price I paid? It was no longer a surprise that the magic in the past had happened when I not only let go of control but also stopped excessive thinking.

My intensified meditation practice loosened several of my unhelpful patterns, and I could see tangible benefits. At first, I noticed I felt more relaxed and less stressed, and the change was not even while I was meditating but in everyday life.

Next, I became more aware of moments where I had a choice. The moments that mattered most in my meditation practice were those when I noticed that I'd let go of the object of attention. I could choose what to do next: beat myself up for being a bad meditator, or gently but firmly bring back my attention to the object. It was as if the space between external triggers and my response increased, giving me more of a chance to choose my response, rather than react mindlessly. This space opened up new, expansive possibilities.

What did not improve was my heel pain, and it actually got significantly worse over time. A colleague suggested I see his sports physio, Michael Brierley, who'd worked with many elite athletes. I followed the advice and found myself in very capable hands. Michael reassured me he'd get on top of the issue. He diagnosed that my Achilles tendon insertion had flared up, and it was a textbook case. I had to dial back running for a few months to regain strength.

Due to the injury, I also had to decline a fully paid invite to an elite race in China. Gary had managed to get me onto the invite list of this 50-kilometre race around the Fuxian Lake, and it was devastating that it came at the wrong time. My priorities were clear, however, and I chose to be sensible and fully recover first. Hopefully, the opportunity of being an elite athlete for a few days would come up again the following year.

The sensible approach to recovery paid off, and I was back to full strength a few months later and ready to start preparing for a 100-kilometre race through the Australian alpine region. One Thursday night, to test my physical endurance and mental stamina, I decided to run a particularly tough training session of 50 laps on a 1.2-kilometre loop in North Sydney. Already exhausted from a long day at work, I parked my car next to the path, packed with drinks and food to test my nutrition strategy.

I was curious about how I'd deal with my emotions during the predictable roller-coaster ride of such a session. Surprisingly, the run itself was not too challenging. The distress I encountered wasn't mine but that of a couple sitting on a park bench under a tree close to the loop I was running. They grabbed my attention around sunset — and theirs was a scene full of tension. Every few minutes, when I completed another lap, I got to see another snippet of their story unfolding. Unambiguously, conflict was in the air. When I first saw them, they were not talking at all. That had changed by the next lap, when the guy was moving his arms a lot to explain his point of view. Her body language suggested that she was not agreeing with him. But she stayed mute. On one of the following laps, she had exchanged her silence for vicious gesticulation. Even I clearly understood that she was not happy. Now it was him who was silent as he sat in his misery. Only one lap later, they were hugging and passionately kissing each other. On the next lap, they had gone.

I felt like an episode of a soap opera had just ended, and I'd watched a lesson on anger, frustration and emotional pain. Regardless how real any of those emotions felt at the time, none of them was eternal. The couple dealt with their feelings and moved on.

My takeaway from the episode was to do the same the next time my emotions overwhelmed me.

I kept running until 1 am. Luckily, the entertainment continued, ranging from a drunk adolescent falling asleep on a bench, to the local wildlife taking over the park. Bats flew over me and fed off the trees. Possums ran around or froze to look at me. Even rats came out of the gutters in search of a midnight snack. When I finished the run, I was proud of my concentration. Lap after lap, I hadn't let repetitive negative thoughts seduce me into giving up. What did concern me, though, was my realisation when I completed the session. I had 'only' run for six hours and was exhausted. How would I ever manage to run for 24 hours in order to qualify for Coast to Kosci?

Deep doubt had me in its tight grip. Never being capable of running Coast to Kosci felt real and had huge seductive power. I took a deep breath. Back on autopilot, I was following the negative storyline. In spite of my exhaustion from running 60 kilometres and it being past midnight, I caught myself. I became aware what was happening. I had been overpowered by my emotions. In a loud voice, I called it out, 'Here we are again. Same old story.' The ghosts haunting me disappeared the moment I faced them. Luckily, I remembered that regardless how weak, helpless and full of doubts I felt, I still had a choice.

Months of setbacks had taught me many valuable lessons, and I would not have learned them if everything had gone perfectly well. I was in good shape to tackle the qualifying criteria for my dream race. First, I would run 100 kilometres through the Australian alpine region, and then I was going to serve as the support crew for an elite international runner from Poland at Coast to Kosci. Finally, I would run a 24-hour race myself. I was most excited about supporting the

Polish runner, whose credentials could hardly be more breathtaking. I was going to look after somebody who had claimed the silver medal at the previous 24-hour world championships, covering 267.187 kilometres. How exciting to work with and learn from a potential race winner. Another upside was that we would be done much earlier than the last runners, who battled against the 46-hour race cut-off. He did not even need me to pace him in the later stages of the race.

I should have known not to tempt fate. The Polish guy got injured, and it looked as if I would not be able to crew at all. I did not know anybody else in the starter field.

Then, out of nowhere, the race director contacted me and took care of me. He paired me up with David Billet, a domestic runner in need of more crewing support. David had successfully run Coast to Kosci five times with his mum always crewing for him. The first few times, he'd been close to missing time cut-offs at checkpoints, but the previous year had improved his personal best by almost nine hours and finished in the middle of the field. I would learn a lot from him and couldn't believe my luck. His mum would take care of his nutrition and hydration, and I would run about 120 kilometres with David, once he was allowed a pacer. My main duty was to ensure that he didn't stop to sleep. David's instructions were unambiguous, and I would remember them in the tough times.

The sacrifice I had to make to crew for him was to downgrade my own 100-kilometre race to the 36-kilometre option. With only a fortnight in between races, I otherwise didn't have enough time to recover. I could not recall ever before being tested that often on my adaptability. It helped that my priorities were clear.

SELF CHECK-IN

- Our dreams and highest purpose are outside of our comfort zone. What are you dreaming of?
- What idea of your own success are you holding on to?
- How could you slow down to speed up?
- Who do you want to become in this life?

CHAPTER 10

TURNING RIGHT TO EXTREME HEIGHTS

> [A] whole range of reality we hadn't noticed before is coming into focus. With this openness, flexibility, and curiosity, we begin to see certain truths about the way things are.
>
> —Sakyong Mipham

I had finally made it to the start line of Coast to Kosci — I just had to ignore the fact that this was, really, David's race. He and a bunch of exceptional ultramarathon runners were heading off towards the mountains. I quickly realised how important crewing was. Attempting the race without getting a glimpse of its challenges might have been possible but was certainly not advisable. I got much more out of the experience of being a support team member than anything the 100-kilometre race could have given me. It was amazing to see what level many other runners had reached, through dedication and continually challenging the limits of what they deemed possible. One of them, for example, had run more than 1,100 kilometres, travelling from Broken Hill to Sydney. And the most inspiring part was that no limits were placed on anyone. I heard, often, people being reassured they could do anything, as long as they worked on themselves.

REACHING THE SUMMIT

I learned a lot from David. He was patient and very comfortable at the back of the field during the first day, and he interrupted his run with plenty of walking breaks. That way, he conserved precious energy and never lost momentum. From sunset, I was allowed to run with David and saw how his strategy paid off. While other runners slowed down at night, we had a lot of fun catching one runner after the other. The mental advantage was obvious, and I had to do very little during the night to encourage him to keep going.

David was on track for another personal record. We had survived the darkness of the first night, without the sleep monsters catching up with us. By now, the poor guy had been running non-stop for 24 hours, and we would probably be on the road for another 10 hours. But sunlight made the whole race much easier, and I thought we had it in the bag.

Then, out of nowhere, David could no longer run or even walk in a straight line. He was exhausted and desperately needed sleep. My orders, which I took seriously, were to not let him sleep, so I promised him a caffeine drink the next time we caught up with his mum's car — she always drove a few kilometres ahead and was never far away. When we reached her about 40 minutes later, she took one look at David and overrode my instructions, announcing that David would have a nap.

I was tired myself but suddenly on high alert. I couldn't believe what I was hearing. David's instructions had been unambiguous, and

I reminded her what he expected from us: 'Never, ever let me sleep. Regardless of what happens.' My sole purpose of being here was to get David as quickly as I could to the finish line. Yet, his mum had decided. She stared at me, unwavering, and then coldly stated that she was his mum and knew best what her son needed. She played the mum card.

I was stuck between a rock and a hard place. Accepting her decision meant letting David down. Starting an argument between any members of this sleep-deprived team could make things even worse for him. I recalled a friend of mine, Buzz, who had failed to finish this very race because his support crew had fallen out with each other. As a result of the conflict, Buzz avoided his crew and didn't eat or drink enough. Only one kilometre from the summit of Kosciuszko, he gave up, too weak to continue.

It was one of those moments with no clear-cut answer. Stick to the plan or adapt? I had no more time to think it through, so I followed my intuition. I figured adapting was less risky. What I did manage to negotiate was to limit David's nap to 10 minutes. He woke even sooner, fully refreshed and eager to get going again. An eight-minute nap had worked miracles. We had taken the right path.

I was glad I had not reacted automatically to the trigger. It was yet another instance where suspending judgement and letting go of the original plan was better than forcing what seemed the intellectually correct answer. From there on, David struggled with fatigue; it seemed these intermittent attacks were trying to wrestle him down. Regardless, we made it to the top of Kosciuszko and back to the finish line at Charlotte Pass with no more major stops.

I understood that this was all about rhythm. I could sense when he was struggling, without him having to say anything. First, his running gait lost its rhythm and, soon after, his negative self-talk got hold of him. All I did was to help him find his rhythm again. Rhythm left no room for distress. Only once did I make the mistake of asking him to speed up; his response was fury. I had stirred the anger of an exhausted man, who had run more than 200 kilometres in the previous 30 hours. On the flipside, when I reminded him to get back into a rhythm, there was no negative emotional charge, and he started speeding up.

After almost 34 hours of running, David finished in the top 10. He'd also shaved off another hour from his stellar performance the previous year. When I sat at the finish line, my own feelings surprised me — having helped David excel felt much more satisfying than any of my own athletic achievements ever had.

At the same time, running for somebody else was so much easier than running my own race. My sole focus had been on getting David to the finish line. I did whatever was required, whether that was showing compassion for his fatigue or cracking the whip on the homestretch. The entire race was not about me. A new quality of magic came from being connected to something bigger than myself.

I had not even needed a single drop of caffeine to stay alert myself. Nor did it occur to me at any time that my own muscles were sore. No 'I am tired', 'My legs hurt', or 'I wish this was over' voices came into my head. Two and a half years after Big Red Run, I was finally back exploring what was possible. For the first time, I was grateful for my Christchurch experience.

In hindsight, the failure of Christchurch was much more of a blessing than the success of Big Red Run. Had I not experienced the pain, I would not have learned my lesson. It was clear that chasing the magic without it relating to painful experiences wasn't possible; magic and pain were inextricably linked.

Apart from new ideas of how to approach Coast to Kosci myself, I was now confident I could be a finisher in the following year. What helped was a lengthy chat with Paul Every and Diane Weaver, the race directors, testing my understanding of how to qualify. They were very encouraging — I was on the right track, as long as I incorporated significant hill training. It felt like I'd been knighted when Paul concluded that he would love to see me at the start line. Then he presented me with a gift. He said that it might take more than one attempt to make it to the finish line, even for experienced runners. With that, I was freed and allowed to have a different mindset. I would definitely aspire to finish, but I'd not let it become something I expected; I wouldn't be tied to the idea of having to finish.

My credo was to maintain a beginner's mind and test out new ideas. I gave David's run–walk strategy a go and was impressed by how much energy it saved. My biggest challenge was still dealing with my emotions. With David, I had seen firsthand how short-fused one could become when sleep-deprived in the final hours of an overnight race. No doubt, I needed more practice running with an impatient mind, and therefore shifted more training sessions into the night. The best advice I'd picked up during my crewing duties was to make the night my friend, rather than to dread it. This would help me during my next part of the qualifier — running at least 180 kilometres in 24 hours.

GETTING READY FOR ANOTHER PEAK

In April 2018 I went back to the athletics track in Coburg to tackle their 24-hour event. I had to complete at least 450 laps; the main challenge, then, was going to be not getting dizzy. From the get-go at noon, I regularly walked for a minute every few laps, to be able to finish strongly during the last race hours leading to lunchtime the next day. I got lapped and lapped and lapped by other — much more bullish — competitors. It was a very hot afternoon, and I struggled with the conditions. My heart rate was significantly higher than I was comfortable with, while lots of runners seemed to be less affected by the heat. Without question, I had to pull back my speed even further. I must have dropped to eighth position and could sense one of my well-developed emotional patterns taking over — impatience.

This time, however, I kept my cool. The impatience, coupled with my competitiveness, made for a strong emotional impulse, tempting me to run faster and go with my desire to chase the other competitors. Instead, I kept my attention on an unpleasant sensation. I didn't wish it away. I didn't fight it. Figuratively speaking, I looked my impatience straight in the eye and observed how it made me feel. In being able to distance myself enough to truly observe, I resisted its seductive message and didn't drown in its darkness. It felt real and powerful. It also had a limited half-life — so what seemed true one moment was revealed as less reliable soon after. The emotion just faded away.

As soon as night fell and the temperature settled, the results on the leader board turned. Now I was the one persistently creeping up it. I didn't even have to increase my speed. Many of the runners in front of me were paying the price for the fast pace they had set early on. Most slowed down, some even withdrew. Shortly after midnight, I was in second position. I was having fun and thoroughly enjoying running at night. It was cool, and I had momentum. The floodlight and rising fog made for an eerie, rather surreal scene. And all I did was execute my strategy and, most importantly, keep my mind still.

At sun up, the heat struck again and the race changed for me. For the last two hours, I battled with heat and exhaustion. I never got close enough to challenge the winner, but I was absolutely thrilled with my result. I had covered 531 laps, totalling over 212 kilometres, significantly above the required 180 kilometres for Coast to Kosci. Surely, that would be enough to get an entry to my dream race.

One of the most important aspects of the run, however, was that I felt the past several years of racing, with one setback after another, had finally come to an end. Big Red Run had been the apex for me, and I couldn't immediately reach a higher peak — the only way upward was after crossing another valley. That success came as I recognised my diminishing dependence on the emotions automatically triggered by negative repetitive thoughts. These fundamental changes had taken almost three years, but the patience and resilience had been worth it. Racing at Coburg was a demonstration that I was better than I'd ever been at dealing with what the world had to offer, rather than clinging to the world as I pictured it in my head.

As the Coburg track had no elevation, I still had to prove in my final qualifying race that I was hill-fit. Three months later, I raced the inaugural Elephant Trail Race near Port Macquarie. Over a distance of 108 kilometres, we climbed 4,600 metres. My smartest decision during the short training cycle for this event was having the diligence to drive up to Port Macquarie and train on the course for a weekend. It meant a four-hour drive after work on a Friday so I could familiarise myself with the course, before coming back home on Sunday. I was glad to get an idea of what to expect, because the steepness of some of the climbs and descents would have freaked me out if I'd faced them for the first time on race day. A few weeks later, I took part in the actual race and nailed it. It took me just over 13 hours to claim the win.

By the time registrations opened in September to apply for Coast to Kosci, I had done everything I could to prepare. All I could hope for was that Paul and Diane would give me a crack at their event. Regardless of what would come, I felt I'd matured as a runner. I was surrendering my urge to control more and more. And the more I backed off from striving for results, the more balanced and faster I became.

Of course, being greedy for even more glory or trying to claim great results or the demanding voice at the back of my head hadn't disappeared. But so far, I had not forgotten the lessons from Christchurch. I now couldn't do anything else but wait until the race directors announced the starter field.

After submitting my application, I went to the North Sydney pool to swim and then use the sauna. I met another friend from my running group, who introduced me to a guy who had run Coast to Kosci twice. I jumped at the opportunity to learn more. I asked for advice and, interestingly, the first thing he could think of was to be wise about choosing my support crew.

I was very comfortable with my crew because they knew each other well, were all amazing runners and all had crewing experience. My partner Rebecca had done a phenomenal job during my 24-hour race in Coburg. Both Gary and my running mate, Joe, knew me sufficiently well to not be surprised by a sleep-deprived version of me. We would keep the plan simple and flexible. The key for all of us was to stay present. It was the secret to having surprising solutions fall into place.

I took a lot out of that conversation in the sauna. What inspired me most was his report of what to expect at the event: 'It's just a great bunch of people. With them you don't have to explain anything. Anybody else tends to ask, "You're running how far?!" Most people do not really understand. Not them, though. They don't ask why we run; they just get it.' He had summarised exactly how I had felt crewing for David. It was that feeling of arriving, of feeling at home, surrounded by like-minded people.

STAYING GROUNDED

On the Sunday a fortnight later, we were supposed to hear who had been selected for the race. That weekend I demonstrated that patience wasn't one of my strengths. The entire day I stayed glued to my iPhone, refreshing the inbox every few minutes. I received neither an email nor a phone call to say whether I was selected. Eventually, I went to bed, still in limbo.

The next morning, I got the exciting news that I was in. Paul had sent a confirmation email congratulating me after midnight, and it meant I had 10 weeks to get race-ready. Everything was suddenly falling into place.

Another piece of exciting news arrived via Gary, who said I was also invited to race 50 kilometres in China — the same event I'd had to miss out on the previous year due to my Achilles injury. This time it was near Wuhan (a city I'd never heard of at the time, but would hear much more about in the years to come). The race fitted well into my preparation for Coast to Kosci. I would approach it as a solid tempo run, with the intention of backing it up with a final big training week. The best news was that my entire support crew for Coast to Kosci would race the 100-kilometre event in China — Gary, Joe and Rebecca would be the high-calibre people supporting me.

Rebecca, Joe and I had never been to China before, and we had a really good experience. For the first time ever, we were classified as 'elite', treated like celebrities and even had locals and event staff queuing up for autographs. Joe's autograph in particular was much sought after, especially when news spread that he was single. Around 100 athletes from all over the world raced — for decent price money — over the 50-kilometre and 100-kilometre events. Most runners had recently competed in the 100-kilometre world championships. None of us was a serious contender for the podium, yet Rebecca surprised with a strong ninth position and world-class time — 9:02 hours — in her debut 100-kilometre race. Such a result would have given her a ticket to the next world championships, if she'd been an Aussie. (Rebecca is a Kiwi, and the New Zealand qualifying standard was to run in less than 8:30 hours.)

The race was tougher than any of us had anticipated, yet what surprised me most was the high percentage of runners who pulled out early. It was, admittedly, much hotter on race day than on the days leading into the event, and many of us had underestimated the constant undulation of the course. Nonetheless, I had expected more adaptability from such a world-class field. In particular, many male contestants struggled with what was thrown at us and not being able to let go of their original expectations.

The female completion rate was high. Did that mean they were more capable of shifting their perspective to fit the circumstances? The male completion rate was low. Was this a sign of bigger egos, of fewer males running smart races? They seemed to stick to their original expectations, which prevented them dealing with what was thrown at us. When I raised the matter at dinner, a Hungarian female team member, with plenty of world and European records over both 100 kilometres and 24 hours, responded, 'Kay, if you want to do well, run like a wise woman.'

Soon after returning from China, I reduced my training load to freshen up for Coast to Kosci. I was ready, both physically and mentally. Within two more weeks, we'd be standing at the start line on the beach at Twofold Bay near Eden, on the Australian east coast. It would be sunrise, the waves would be rolling out on the beach and we'd leave from there to tackle the heights of Kosciuszko.

The next morning brought an unexpected and devastating twist. I was greeted by an email from Paul, the race director, with the subject line, 'Probable cancellation of Coast to Kosciuszko 2018'. A nail-biting 24 hours later, it was confirmed. The race had been cancelled and, very likely, would never happen again. After more than a decade of a smoothly run annual event, the council and road police hadn't given clearance for the event to go ahead.

The email was like an arrow through my chest, and my heart felt like it had been pierced. I had put everything into running Coast to Kosci for almost 18 months. Three days before my 40th birthday, it was cancelled. I had missed my chance. I would never run Coast to Kosci; not now and not in the future. I'd wasted a year on Christchurch, but I couldn't do anything about it.

I still hated being out of control, but I now had the ability to be self-reflective; what feelings were coming up? I definitely felt disappointed, deflated and sad. The unexpected had been thrown at me; a race cancellation had not been on anybody's radar.

If only I had a problem to fix, but there wasn't one; only new circumstances to accept. The 'unpleasant' was the teacher I'd asked for, and it was my turn to embrace the situation as it was. I'd prepared myself to deal with any race outcome. But was I ready to accept there wasn't even going to be a race? Had I really built up enough strength to deal with setbacks more skilfully?

Through this misfortune, I could experience how far I had come. When everything was going my way, I could easily claim I had evolved. Thoughts could float in my head, *focus on the controllable, be resilient and bounce back from adversity*, or *choose how to react to difficult situations*. But now I was facing disaster, I had nowhere to hide. My true colours would shine through.

To my surprise, I experienced a deep stillness. That was a fundamental change. A mere few months ago, I would have been beside myself. My previous tendency had been to speed up my thoughts, which only led to tackling the picture in my head but not dealing with the real issue I was facing. This time, I slowed down and sat with what I was feeling. I was astonished that I wasn't angry, or distressed or wanting to blame someone. My thinking had changed and so had my emotions.

That did not mean I liked the cancellation. Far from it. I was staring at the pieces of a shattered dream. But here I was, filled with pain but not getting carried away and tilting into suffering. The important shift was that I did not have to look away from the pain. Years of meditation and resilience training must have shifted my brain patterns.

The realisation that, at any point in time, we always had a choice was sinking in. This was Viktor Frankl's message in action. The upset of the race cancellation was triggering me. But I noticed and acknowledged it, neither clinging to my desires nor pushing away my aversion. When I stayed present, I felt time slow down. With my still mind, I could deal with what was happening in the moment. Despite not having control, I felt much more in charge. Instead of an automatic reaction, I chose to respond purposefully.

STRETCHING HIGHER

My measure of success for this quest had been to accept any outcome. I had succeeded — without the trouble of running 240 kilometres, I concluded cheekily. The journey had never been about summiting Mount Kosciuszko but about freeing myself from an old identity structure not up for the demands. I was not somebody because of what I did, what I was good at or what others accepted me for. I was not my success, just as I was not my failure. The test had been to what extent I followed my calling. I was a human being on a quest to inspire the magic. And it seemed that not running Coast to Kosci catapulted me to a new level, perhaps much higher than summiting would have achieved.

In a way, the Coast to Kosci cancellation brought to mind a feeling I'd embraced during Big Red Run. It was the feeling of exhilaration, which came from being aligned with my purpose and vision. In both cases, my challenges were empowering me to navigate my path through the unknown. I felt completely alive and encouraged to embrace my passion for exploration. After Big Red Run, I was attracted by the bright light of the magic, which was more fantastic than any of my wildest dreams had suggested.

This time I was on a downward current into the darkness of my dream race evaporating into thin air. The darkness, wrapping me in its tight grip, was even more mesmerising than being on top of the world. I wasn't afraid of failure, because I could see through the illusion. With my inner guiding light ignited, I was equipped to explore the darkness I found myself in. I was called to go with the flow of the current to the bottom of the abyss, without taking the seemingly horrible story too seriously.

Each of the 50 runners, their crew, the support teams and, first and foremost, the race directors, Diane and Paul, were devastated. It seemed the entire Australian ultra running community was in mourning. Our pinnacle of ultra running had been destroyed. When clearance to use the roads hadn't been provided, even the president of the Australian Ultra Runners Association had been involved in the negotiations with the authorities. From his report, it sounded like a new appointee was in charge who had more conservative views on safety measures. The new requirements surpassed anything that could be met, especially with the little remaining time before the scheduled start. Regardless of how sound the reasons might or might not have been, the reality was that the race was cancelled. All I could do was to look ahead and take in the implications of this cancellation for me.

I had a deep trust that another worthwhile event would pop up to replace it. But time was not on my side if I wanted to leverage the peak fitness I was in. The longer I waited, the higher the risk of injury or chronic fatigue. A look at the Australian and New Zealand ultramarathon racing calendars did not justify my faith. The summer months were bad timing for the type of extremely long event I was desperate for. Instead, I started to hope that one of the other disappointed Coast to Kosci runners would come up with an alternative. We were all facing the same dilemma. Surely, somebody would channel their energy towards a worthy replacement. A few ideas were floated, but I quickly recognised that I needed to take fate into my own hands.

I skimmed through the same list of races again and this time noticed I prematurely had discounted a race that could be what I was looking for. In February, Western Australia would host an inaugural 200-miler, covering 350 kilometres of the Bibbulmun Track between

Northcliffe and Albany. This race had not drawn my attention at first because it was too crazy. Within a split second I'd come to the conclusion, 'Too big. Not achievable.' Reflecting on it, this was exactly what I was looking for. Coast to Kosci had been a challenge too big to imagine years ago. Instead of running 240 kilometres on the road, why not run 350 kilometres on a trail, including lots of sand dunes?

Turning right again was the main selling point for the 200-miler. Over such a long distance, I would surely encounter plenty of obstacles. I would not be able to avoid crises; instead, I would have to conquer them. Only by turning right, could I get a chance to overcome my own demons. That was a 180-degree turn from how I'd led most of my life. My game had been to chase the next high and become a master in avoiding the lows. The cost was not only immense energy spent in doing so but also missing the point. I could learn more in the low moments than from what was on offer with highs. Every low indicated where I got stuck. If I only accepted blissful success, I missed those lessons and stayed a mere pawn when adversity made its move. Through my experience with Coast to Kosci, I gained a different understanding of the game. It was not about reaching delightful moments. It was about the ability to just be present in any given instant.

Before I could reach out to race director Shaun Kaesler, he sent a message to all Coast to Kosci casualties, encouraging us to enter his event. He was feeling for all of us, especially because Coast to Kosci had influenced his own running journey — he had both crewed for another runner and participated himself, finishing in the top 10.

He even offered a generous $240 discount — a dollar for every kilometre cancelled — to us disappointed Coast to Kosci runners.

At this stage, signing up was only a formality. I refrained from letting my rational mind argue this challenge away by convincing me that it was impossible. My intuition that something would emerge from a disappointing situation had been spot on. The name of the race summed up what I was committing to: 'The Delirious W.E.S.T. (Western Endurance Scenic Trail) 200-miler'.

SELF CHECK-IN

- How do you deal with the 'darkness' of pain or disappointment?
- What is the biggest challenge you're trying to overcome at the moment?
- What steps are you taking to do that?
- What can you do to ensure you build or find the right support for the shift you're seeking?

CHAPTER 11

TURNING RIGHT TO BECOME DELIRIOUS

A high-performance mind is one that can enter at will the state of consciousness that is most beneficial and most desirable for any given circumstance.

—Anna Wise

Speaking to race director Shaun a few days later confirmed that the Delirious W.E.S.T. 200-miler was exactly what I wanted. It was going to be tough, and the race just got bigger and bigger with every piece of information he revealed: lots of elevation, seemingly endless sand dunes, plenty of snakes, burning summer heat and not a lot of sleep for days. He expected a winning time of around 80 hours, with a cut-off at 104 hours. A typical work week had fewer hours.

This was a different beast from Coast to Kosci, where I'd have expected to finish in around 30 hours. We would start on Wednesday at 7 am and have until Sunday 3 pm to finish. Shaun casually added that, unless authorities reopened the original trail in time, we would have to run a 'short' diversion. So what were supposed to be

350 kilometres might become 380. He reassured me, though, that he wouldn't charge extra.

To my surprise, the growing running challenge didn't keep me awake at night, although the demands of the race were beyond anything I had ever attempted. I was comfortable not knowing how to solve the escalating complexity. Surely this was what several years of turning right had taught me? I couldn't stay comfortable and follow my passion for development. To thrive in the chaos of the aftermath of Coast to Kosci not going ahead, I had to unlock hitherto unknown mental reserves. For that to happen, I had to trust that along the journey to the finish line, I would figure out who I needed to become to keep going in this race. In past races, many insights I'd gained went beyond running. Hopefully, this time as well, I would learn valuable life lessons by putting myself out there.

EXPANDING THE CHALLENGE

For once, running wasn't making me restless, but work was. I'd been living in Sydney for two years. And they'd been great years. We had shifted the ways the organisation worked and improved the culture. Now, though, my growth curve was flattening again. The job felt repetitive and stale, and a familiar inner voice was getting louder. I could hear it daring me to pursue this passion beyond running. Apart from a few timid attempts at bringing the idea of turning right to my professional life, I had played it safe in my work environment.

Yet the voice was getting too loud to ignore for much longer, and the time was coming for fundamental changes. Since the days of working with Gavin and immersing myself in mystery runs, I sensed that what I had been practising and learning from — the act of turning right — had potential application way beyond running. It held the seeds for inspiring the magic of individuals, teams and organisations.

With that sense of a new energy for work, I wondered how much longer I'd still feel fulfilled pursuing an increasingly difficult race such as the Delirious W.E.S.T. While this was a challenge, this type of challenge had become my new comfort zone and couldn't conceal the fact that I was avoiding the really scary prospect — bringing turning right into the work context.

I had been confining myself to what felt relatively safe. In terms of my running, I'd come a long way in my quest for meaning; for my work, I was still at the beginning. Throughout my career, whether as a consultant or a retailer, I'd always been passionate about building high-performing teams and developing the next generation of leaders. Upgrading culture was especially close to my heart. I'd worked in more than a dozen countries and immersed myself in a handful of them by living there. Each place's cultural dynamics fascinated me. I'd say, half-joking, that home was where my laptop was. Now, a new meaning of this sad joke was emerging. If the field of work culture became my new home, why not make a profession out of my passion and integrate it with what I was learning about the inner, mental game through running?

My vision became clearer: I wanted to find a way to support individuals, teams and organisations to reach what they dreamed about, and to do that using turning right in the professional arena. I was passionate about unlocking step-changes, when incremental improvements didn't move the needle sufficiently. Transformation was the key, and this required us to courageously explore new territory beyond the limitations of our restrictive mindsets. I had the dream of setting up my own business, one that facilitated those transformational journeys. My role would be to inspire the magic, providing cultural transformation programs, executive coaching and keynote speaking. I was excited. It was also obvious I had a lot of work to do. For starters, I had to learn the fundamentals of coaching and gain some credentials. But I had no idea where to start.

For the first time in years, my professional development became as important to me as running. While I was preparing for the daunting Delirious race, an unexpected dinner with my first boss from my consultancy days triggered some momentum. Harald Fanderl was on a family holiday in Australia when we caught up in Sydney. We hadn't seen each other for almost 10 years, though the dinner was comfortable enough for me to feel like we'd been in touch yesterday.

We did, however, have a lot of updating to do. Harald told me about life as Senior Partner at McKinsey, and I shared some of my turning right experiences and my passion for growth adventures. Harald had always been very supportive, and this time was no exception. He put me in contact with a few outstanding executive coaches from around the world. Talking to them would give me a better understanding of what I needed to get started and have an impact in that field.

Apart from valuable contacts, Harald also passed on an intriguing comment he had learned in a leadership course himself: 'We all have our childhood wounds. To become amazing at what you are doing, you have to overcome whatever yours are.'

In an instant, my thoughts went to my father hitting me on my face with his flat hand — again and again and again. I saw myself crawling under my blanket in my bed, crying and railing against the unfair world. I certainly didn't lack childhood wounds. Growing up, I learned what it took to be safe from erratic, harmful behaviour. It had been a tough journey, but I was now successful at whatever I put my mind to. The reward was intellectual and financial independence.

Most importantly, though, I had never modelled my father's aggression. For generations, all males in the family had displayed some use of domestic violence. I'd committed to never following their footsteps. Thanks to my mother, I'd learned alternative methods of conflict management. Contemplating Harald's remark, I concluded that I'd overcome my trauma. Hadn't I, though? Or did I have a blind spot? Were some memories still too raw to look at?

With the privilege of being linked to a global network of extraordinary people, I was guided and encouraged to learn the fundamentals for inspiring the magic. My ex-boss from Germany connected me with an Italian executive coach living in Switzerland, who got me in touch with Lisa Doig from America, who now lived on the west coast of Australia in Perth. Lisa and her husband, Malcolm, were the founders of Corporate Evolution, a company offering highly acclaimed accreditation programs for facilitators and coaches to drive sustainable corporate culture transformation. I would learn how to help leaders transform their personal and professional worlds by focusing on values and purpose. I sensed that accessing transformation by stepping into one's values was the approach I'd been missing when trying to share with other people the magic I experienced through running. Transformation needed to be experienced, not thought about. This understanding was exactly what I needed. How marvellous that I could meet her in person a few weeks later, given that I'd be flying to Perth for the Delirious race.

WIDENING CONSCIOUSNESS

The race was approaching and, together with my support crew, I made my way to Western Australia. Rebecca and Gary had kindly offered to take care of me at aid stations and pace me in the later stages of the race. Before we left Perth, I met Lisa for breakfast at a beach café with views of the Indian Ocean. I was curious and glad for any opportunity to take my mind off the crazy adventure ahead. The instant we met, I knew that I was in good hands.

Lisa seemed to understand that I no longer wanted to lead two separate lives, one as a manager and one as an athlete. Integrating both lives had more on offer than the sum of the parts. Lisa challenged my quest for magical moments through running, which she called my 'little, safe experiment'. Had I transformed beyond the world of running? Her conclusion was similar to Gavin's a few years back — I was still clinging too tightly to control; I was still protecting myself.

I was under no illusion that I had a lot of work ahead to become a credible executive coach and facilitator of transformational journeys. At least my having worked with top management, both in the capacity of a consultant and as a senior leader, proved to be valuable. The content I had to learn was the straightforward part. The real effort was working on my reactive patterns. Habits such as my urge to control, being judgemental, or distancing myself during conflict would hold me back from being of service to others in unlocking their full potential. The 'inner work' was the differentiating factor, and what would allow me to effectively facilitate transformations. As a true leader, I had to be at the forefront of any fundamental change. Was I prepared to embark on yet another confronting journey and transform my engrained reactive habits?

Lisa hinted at traumas we all carried, which reminded me of what Harald had called 'childhood wounds'. We would have to surface the limiting beliefs keeping me from fully living my purpose. Those beliefs and assumptions typically had their origins in early childhood. I instantly felt the urge to shout out that, in my case, there was nothing to see. I had gotten over the flying kitchen objects aimed at me, those shattered coffee cups dripping liquid and misshaped heavy frying pans. But I was wise enough to recognise that an open, curious mind was a more appropriate response to Lisa's challenge than withdrawing into my shell. She was talking about a world I still understood very little about. If she was right, something else would still be lurking, a story I turned a blind eye to and didn't want to see. What resonated with me was the idea of expanding turning right beyond running, and finding ways to make the magic accessible to anybody — without them having to run hundreds of kilometres.

A lot of respected research underpinned Lisa's approach to transformation, and I sensed this research would support and explain most of my turning right experiences. Lisa encouraged me to start with Richard Barrett's seven levels of consciousness, with Barrett's article 'From Maslow to Barrett' providing a good first taste. Before we parted, I verbally committed to joining her accreditation program soon after Delirious. We agreed that, for now, staying in my job and leveraging any spare time to set myself up for the pending career change would be best. Maybe even an in-house opportunity at my current employer would come up, Lisa speculated.

Rebecca, Gary and I had a few hours' drive ahead of us to get to the start line and meet the other participants. I used the time on the backseat to familiarise myself with the first concept Lisa had mentioned. Barrett had evolved Maslow's pyramid of human needs to seven levels of consciousness, which shed light on the motivations for each of our actions. The first three levels were almost identical to Maslow's model reflecting our ego's concerns to keep us safe, and focusing on viability, relationship and performance. These were homes for all our fears, resulting in nothing ever being good enough on these levels. This explained our unquenchable thirst for success, recognition, or money and material goods.

Barrett had then expanded Maslow's highest level — self-actualisation — into four separate parts, levels four to seven. The fundamental difference from levels one to three was that, with an evolved mindset, we wouldn't be all-consumed by upsets. Instead, we could choose how to act purposefully, with awareness. We could respond to our ego's needs from the more mature perspective of our Higher Self. I recognised that these responses had created the difference in my experience between the disaster at Christchurch, and when Coast to Kosci was cancelled. In the former, I regressed to an ego consciousness, obsessed by success; in the latter, I stayed present, focusing on personal development.

Barrett's level four was all about transformation and evolution, which introduced a completely new perspective beyond the needs of our ego. I concluded that turning right unlocked this level. The key realisation of this fourth level was that, to evolve, we had to let go of what got us here and focus on the requirements of the journey ahead. The signpost for this level was a new set of values becoming important to us, such as courage, growth and adaptability.

I was fascinated by the model, because it not only explained what had happened in the past but also outlined a path forward.

My intentions for the upcoming 200-miler were in tune with a level five consciousness, which was concerned with meaning and personal alignment. I wanted to trust myself and stay true to my purpose. Levels six and seven, which focused on collaboration and contributing to the greater good, were particularly relevant for my professional journey. The model even described my leadership journey ahead — by becoming more conscious, I developed as a leader. Lisa had referred to this journey from the ego to the Higher Self as the inner work. Each level widened consciousness and broadened our perspective, resulting in completely new possibilities. I now understood why turning right led to the ability to naturally access higher levels of capabilities. The Barrett model was, it seemed, gifting me a compass to find my way.

Interestingly, the journey was not about leaving behind levels one, two and three, or even denying them. Instead, it was an integration process, increasing our ability to toggle between different views. Research showed that the most effective leaders were capable of operating at all levels and switching their attention to whatever was required, without becoming stuck in any perspective. This allowed them to master their challenges purposefully.

All of this meant that the magic I was pursuing was the same as accessing a different level of consciousness. Therefore, the vision for my own business, to inspire the magic, was to help individuals and organisations widen their consciousness. The path that organisations would take was no different from that of an individual's journey. No organisation could operate at a higher level of consciousness than the personal consciousness of its leaders. Barrett's most prominent call-out was that any transformation started by working on oneself first. As he argued in *Building a values-driven organization*, 'Cultural transformation begins with the personal transformation of the leaders. Organizations don't transform. People do.' And as Lisa had pointed out, unlocking the magic in other leaders started by working on myself.

SURROUNDED BY LEGENDS AND BOGANS

As interested as I was in finding out how to develop professionally, I had to switch focus. Rebecca had stopped at a supermarket to stock up on things we needed for the upcoming race, and we filled our rental SUV to the ceiling. However many days the race was going to take me, I was now sure none of us would starve. We continued to Northcliffe, where the race would start the following morning. The weather was stinking hot already. We would definitely be tested over the next few days.

It was late afternoon when we arrived and met the other participants. While all runners could relax, the support crew participated in a fun run before dinner. The 'Bogan Run' lifted the tension and was entertaining to watch — demonstrating that the best strategy for keeping our nerves under control was having some fun. Most crew members had changed into dress-up outfits, mostly from the '80s, with wigs and mullets being very popular. Shaun explained the rules, and it couldn't have been any more bogan: participants had to scull a can of beer, and then load up with an empty beer keg and run with it to the halfway mark — 1.5 kilometres down the road. There, they'd sit down on the keg, scull their second beer and sprint back without the keg. When everybody inhaled their first beer and searched for the optimal way to run fast with a keg on their shoulders, we sensed the competitiveness of the field.

Gary was the first to cross the finish line. Initially, it looked like he and lots of other runners were going to be disqualified, because they'd come from the wrong direction. They had lost their orientation and not followed the course marking. Eventually though, Gary was declared the winner and received his prize — a 30-pack of Emu Export beer. Beer was the last thing we needed for the upcoming days, but more valuable was the reminder to pay attention (unlike our crew) to the course markings. The distance of 350 kilometres was far enough without any added mileage due to getting lost. Luckily, at least the potential diversion of an extra 30 kilometres had been removed by authorities.

At the race briefing in the evening, Shaun dedicated this new race to Paul and Diane, who had organised Coast to Kosci during its existence. The Delirious W.E.S.T. would be its own beast but lived in the spirit of the race I had originally wanted to run in. We were thousands of kilometres away from Mount Kosciuszko and still all part of the same running family, sharing the same passion and values. This dedication confirmed that I was meant to be here, and could hardly have found a better substitute.

The highlight of the evening was the introduction of each of the 36 runners, and I soon learnt I was surrounded by an impressive field of serious athletes, who had earned their stripes to be here. Among them was Dion Leonard — a celebrity since a race through the Gobi Desert in China when a little dog followed him. Dion eventually went back to find and adopt the dog and wrote the wonderful (and best-selling) *Finding Gobi*. Recently, Dion had mastered the 'Triple Crown' in the United States, running three 200-mile events within a nine-week time frame.

The standout female athlete was Candice Burt, 'the queen of 200-milers' and organiser of the Triple Crown series. Then, there was Gene Dykes, who was the oldest finisher of the Triple Crown and had recently run an unofficial world record over the marathon distance for his age group — 2:54 hours at the age of 70. Others held national records or had summited Mount Everest. A few years earlier, I'd have felt inadequate. Now, I was just in awe.

I was lucky enough to get some advice from Dion, a veteran in 200-milers. He cautioned me against over-pacing early in the race. Secondly, he warned me to not stay awake for too long. The longer I pushed out sleep, the more I would struggle falling asleep. Doing well in these races highly depended on one's sleep strategy, and his advice reminded me that this was completely new territory for me. I had neither a strategy for sleep nor any experience of how to transition from running to sleeping and back to running again. The only way to learn was the hard way, exploring what worked for me.

When it was Shaun's turn to introduce me, he had nothing to say, as if I were a nobody. Everybody examined me when I was put on the spot to stutter a few words on who I was. My body sent me mixed emotions. I loved the opportunity of flying under the radar with nobody expecting serious competition from me. But a part of me was deeply hurt, and I was thrown back to how much I'd hated my parents referring to me as the 'gypsy from Romania', as if they were rejecting me. Our ancestors were Germans who had lived for centuries in Transylvanian Saxony, a region that was part of many different countries as borders where redrawn over the course of time. At school, at work or with my friends, saying I was German was so much simpler than explaining that I was born as a German within Romania and had migrated to Germany as a one year old. Whenever the topic came up at school of why my parents spoke a weird German dialect at home, my friends teased me that I was a foreigner.

I was so grateful when I recognised Janine's welcoming and familiar face. She was sitting behind me and had run Big Red Run with me. She predicted that I would blitz the course, as I had in the desert. While I hoped she was right, nothing was a given. Janine would be following my progress and, given that she was the race medic, hopefully not have to intervene. She was so excited to see me she offered a flight in her propeller plane *when* I finished early — not *if*. She told me her husband could show me the course from a bird's perspective. That was an extra incentive to hurry up and finish early.

I told myself that I had to be careful. Getting carried away by my ego and focusing on my finishing time would be too easy. My reasons for participating in the race had not changed from Coast to Kosci. I wanted to immerse myself in uncertainty and deal with whatever was thrown at me. It was time to thoroughly embed the learnings from Christchurch, and remember my goal wasn't to demonstrate that I was a fast runner. Chasing glory was the path to another disastrous race. Instead of focusing on the finish line, I had to stay present.

My intention was to switch off my rational mind and trust my intuition. Thinking about what lay ahead was terrifying. If I listened to my analytical brain, the conclusion would have been straightforward: it was impossible to run almost eight consecutive marathons. However, if I let go of my rational limitations and trusted myself, I would find a way.

Success in this race was to embrace whatever emerged during the long adventure. With that in mind, it was impossible to fail. I was guaranteed to learn something valuable. I had never been fitter and, most importantly, my state of mind gave me confidence. I felt composed, yet realistic enough to expect the unexpected. It was time for bed, and I needed to get as much sleep as I could.

SELF CHECK-IN

- What are your top three values? Why are they so important to you?[1]
- How well are you living your top values in all areas of your life?

CHAPTER 12

TURNING RIGHT UNTIL DELIRIOUS

It was very unpleasant to turn back, even for this short distance, but on this job one must expect reverses.

—Ernest Shackleton

Full of anticipation, I opened my eyes at 3 am and was instantly wide awake. I meditated, had an early breakfast and spent a long time taping up every single toe. After testing my patience trying to prevent blisters, I closed my eyes and listened to calming music. I just lay on my bed, breathing in and breathing out. Eventually, I rocked up at the bustling start line. Several photos and a few big hugs later, we were sent into the unknown.

DAY ONE: AWAKENING EGO

The race director poured a can of beer into his shoe and drank it to signal us that the Delirious W.E.S.T. had officially started. A cohort of 36 runners left behind Northcliffe and dashed off into the bush.

After a few metres we were guided left onto a windy, singletrack forest path. When I could see that I was in second position, I recalled Dion's advice to not get carried away by my excitement. After the realisation that I was going too fast, I deliberately dropped back into mid-field. It was a decision that would soon save me a lot of grief.

We got to the first clearing and a woman from the back shouted that we were on the wrong track. At first, I was as confused as everybody else, and then, 15 minutes into the race, I found myself, together with the whole pack I'd been running with, back where we started.

We'd all taken a wrong turn and needed to backtrack. We were no closer to the finish line, and so still had 350 kilometres to go. The front runners didn't realise their mistake for another 20 minutes. Shaun had warned us, yet none of us had learned from the mistakes during the Bogan Run that had come from not paying attention to course markings. Apparently, we had to make our own mistakes. Somebody had guided us to the left, while we needed to turn right. I should have known. Such a big endeavour just had to start by turning right.

When I began the course again, my task was to settle into the race and apply everything I'd already learned. The more I switched off my thinking mind and tapped into my intuition, the higher would be my chances of seeing the finish line. At the race briefing, we'd been warned of upcoming obstacles — ranging from overheating to snake bites. There was no room for error and discipline was crucial. I drank and ate regularly, stuck to frequent walking breaks, changed socks once in a while to avoid blisters, reapplied sunscreen and watched out for any chafing (which was invariably painful). I paid extra attention to not stepping on snakes (especially necessary in sections with thick plant coverage). I was obsessed with following the correct path, too.

Most of the time I ran on my own, and only sporadically was I in the company of other runners. Around two and a half hours into the run, a pack of four runners rushed past, unsettling me. Those were the front runners, led by Candice and Dion, who had taken longer to notice their wrong turn at the start of the race. Now, they were gunning past and soon out of sight.

I realised what was happening and why I felt unsettled. They had woken up the competitor in me, who wanted to prove himself superior. I could feel the conflicting emotions stirring in me as the group vanished. I understood, though, that I did not have to keep up with them. As much as I felt the urge, I knew that looking good now would lead to feeling bad later. A troubled body would escalate the disturbed emotions and lead to a troubled mind. Satisfying my ego's desires now meant I could, literally, run out of energy too early.

Soon after, the midday heat burned down from a cloudless sky. Even in the shade the temperature exceeded 30 degrees Celsius. There wasn't much of cover, and I was cooking. My heart rate climbed into territories that indicated trouble and gave me déjà vu of the Coburg race: I had to let go of the leading athletes because of the heat. I chose to stick to what had worked in the past — patience and discipline. The smartest thing to do was walk more and run less. Additionally, I had to be even more diligent with my hydration. The mantra shared with me in China kept me focused: 'Run like a wise woman'.

At the next aid station, I told my crew about my concerns of blowing up. Gary instantly took action and demanded a 10-minute rest in the stationary air-conditioned car with an icepack on my neck. I had to cool down. The break also allowed me to empty my shoes from the accumulated sand and have a solid lunch of instant mashed potatoes with an extra portion of salt. Those few minutes proved to be gold — as my core temperature dropped, so too did my heart rate, and never got as high again. With less effort, I was moving faster than before, now regularly passing other runners.

The burning afternoon sun sent me into a lull, where my focus diminished. That changed from one second to the next. I was running on a path covered in white sand when, about three steps in front of me, a big, fat black snake noticed me before I spotted it. It was about two metres long and must have been enjoying a sunbath. Luckily, it was as terrified as I was, and jumped into the air and then disappeared into the scrub. This was my first snake on the Bibbulmun Track, reminding me to stay alert. I wasn't keen on using the three snake bandages I was carrying in my mandatory gear.

We'd been told that we were unlikely to encounter snakes once it cooled down, but I learned that even during the night I had to be careful of snakes. At about midnight, I spotted something and came to an abrupt stop. Only a few centimetres from my feet was a baby snake crossing my path. Surely, its mum wasn't happy with it being out so late. It looked like a dugite — a highly venomous member of the Australian brown snakes family. I could see its little tongue coming out of its mouth. It wasn't bothered by being in the spotlight of my head torch and moved slowly. As fascinated as I was by this beautiful creature, I didn't want the situation to turn, and nor was I on a mission to study the deadly Australian wildlife. I stepped around it and, from then, didn't see any of its brothers and sisters for a while.

I preferred running during the cool night. Once the full moon was out, I almost didn't need my head torch. Within a short space of time the forest opened up, and I was encountering more sand dunes — a sign I was approaching the coastline. I hadn't seen any other runners since sunset, and I was in a comfortable second position, chased by Candice. As expected, the pace of the fast runners in the heat of the day was claiming its toll. Only Dion was ahead of me — and I gathered he must have been well ahead, based on the number of spider webs I had to navigate. Surely, he'd had to navigate them too, but the spiders must have had enough time to rebuild their traps since Dion had passed. I had made it through the first day of the race, but my mind was still unsettled. I was still too concerned about how I was going, instead of focusing on what I was doing. I had not yet managed to tap into my intuition. That bossy inner bureaucrat was still wide awake, and even doing extra shifts.

DAY TWO: LOSING SLEEP

I reached the first 'sleep station' — one of four aid stations with beds to sleep on — before sunrise. The Walpole Motel offered us runners a proper room for recovery, and the advantage of my fast progress was that I didn't have to share it with anybody else. Dion had already continued on without sleep. I wasn't particularly tired but decided to stick to my strategy of running like a wise woman. And this kind of wisdom would agree that one should sleep at night. Regardless of how many other runners might pass me at this stage, I knew that sleep would help me later. We had 200 kilometres to go, and a 30-minute nap would be worth the investment. After a bowl of salted Japanese ramen noodles, I tried to switch off my mind and fall asleep. Yet, going from exercise mode straight into sleep mode seemed impossible, and within 15 minutes I was back running. Even though I was up and moving, I suspected sleep would play a major role in how this run would develop. It would turn out that I was right.

I was surprised how well my body was holding up, as a strong sense of progress kept my spirits high. Also, from Walpole onwards pacers were allowed, and I no longer had to run on my own. Gary and Rebecca alternated in keeping me company, and jointly we celebrated every milestone we could think of. Plenty were available, and we celebrated every aid station, every full hour, the first 100 miles, the halfway mark and the 200-kilometre mark. Particularly meaningful were the moments when I passed 24 hours and, a few hours later, 212 kilometres. I entered foreign territory in both cases, because I had never run any longer or any further previously.

Around lunchtime of the second day, my sense of progress took a dent, and my positivity started slipping away. The battles with my ego on the first day had been exhausting, and the physical struggles on this second day indicated much more trouble on the horizon. I had run for 30 hours without sleep, and a heavy fatigue was trying to crush me. My eyes weighed more than lead, and I would've given a lot for the ability to fall asleep. Rebecca reminded me of the importance of rhythm when I seemed to be drifting into the land of trouble, applying the same winning recipe I had used when pacing David at Coast to Kosci. While helpful, I was not sure for how much longer I could keep it together.

I desperately tried to bundle my remaining willpower and plough on. I knew these were dark patches and I had the mental toughness to get through them. I was trying hard and yet, with the hours passing, so was my level of determination. I'd reached the limits of my willpower. With my exhaustion levels rising, my attempt to stay tough was only fuelling my motivation to avoid failure. The strict commands from my inner bureaucrat were counterproductive. Stress and adrenaline weren't getting me to the finish line.

I was about to lose the solid ground under my feet. I swam against the tide countless times, wasting precious mental energy. I was getting less and less tolerant of things turning out differently from what I wanted them to be. For example, I protested when the trail was overgrown or too steep. I even lost my temper when an aid station didn't appear when I'd expected to reach it. 'It should be here, but it isn't!' was my complaint, as if Rebecca, pacing me at the time, could help me gain control over what I perceived to be a hostile world.

Despite being aware of what was happening, I couldn't change my attitude. I lacked focus. From there, my mood got worse. We hit one of the most troublesome sections of the course — hours and hours of climbing over sand dunes, without any sense of progress. I recognised that inner voice seducing me, spinning a disaster story, but was too exhausted to fight it and stay positive.

Rebecca had an amazing idea, which we immediately put to the test. I lay down on the trail for five minutes, used my backpack as a pillow and closed my eyes. Even though I couldn't sleep, the rest reinvigorated some positivity in me, and Rebecca's gentleness tapped into a completely different energy. This was a smart and successful recipe to keep me in the race, allowing me to recharge. Lying down for a few minutes every so often also seemed to allow me to reconnect to my surroundings, instead of putting myself in opposition to them. For a while, I was one with nature again.

But the sun was about to go down, and the sleep monsters would soon creep out of their caves, waiting for their opportunity to wrestle me down. Was the recipe going to hold?

I had hot chips for dinner and hoped to cling to my good spirits, moving along well in Gary's company. My mood changed when we hit the next section of sand dunes. The sand got into my shoes and into my head. Its grainy fragments penetrated my mind's machinery, causing friction and frustration. That second night was also pitch-black, and the darkness consumed me. Gary and I got slower and slower. It reflected the difficulty of the terrain more than my performance. We were, unexpectedly, closing in on Dion and, in one instance, even saw his head torch in the distance. It lifted my spirits, and I started singing 'There's a light … Over at the Frankenstein place … There's a light' from *The Rocky Horror Picture Show*.

My enthusiasm burned off quickly. Before we could catch him, I needed another lie down on the trail. After five minutes, I started shivering as if a severe fever had come over me. I was freezing and my body seemed to be shutting down. The challenge was no longer to catch Dion, but to not collapse and, somehow, finish the race. I had 120 kilometres to go.

Gary helped me onto my feet, and we continued our journey, with me desperate to warm up again. Next, my vision got blurry and I couldn't focus on Gary in front of me. All I saw was the green of his calf guards but no distinct shapes. How could I stay in the race, if my entire body was letting me down? I kept talking to Gary describing the detail of what was happening. His mission was to get me to the car at the next aid station. He decided that I needed an hour of rest on the passenger seat, regardless of whether I was able to fall asleep or not. Continuing like this was pointless, and the remaining eight kilometres to the aid station seemed endless. They took us around three hours.

By the time we arrived at the Parry Beach aid station, all life had leaked out of me. Rebecca was shocked by what bad shape I was in and offered some solid food to warm me up from the inside. I got into the passenger seat of our car, and I was rugged up. When Rebecca closed the door, it felt as if a coffin lid was falling shut.

I no longer cared about getting caught by other runners. The game had changed — it didn't matter how the others performed. This was now a battle against myself to keep my dreams of seeing the finish line alive. My legs ached. Random pain shot through my knees and kept me awake.

My thoughts wandered to David at Coast to Kosci. He had been a similar situation and was miraculously resurrected by an eight-minute nap. Also, my race in Christchurch had demonstrated that new life might wait for us the very next moment. What was holding me back? What did I have to let go of?

Within what seemed barely a few minutes, the car door opened. Brightness filled the car, and I could barely open my eyes. Rebecca's head torch was shining straight into my face. The agreed hour had passed, and this was my wake-up call. Rebecca cautiously investigated how I was feeling. After 46 sleepless hours, I had finally slept.

This was terrific. I instantly knew that I had awoken in a different world. I felt rejuvenated. There was no, 'Another five minutes, please', and nor did my legs complain about having already run for two consecutive days and nights. My exhilaration must have been infectious; Rebecca mirrored my joy and declared the lazy times were over. She grabbed our backpacks to tackle the next section jointly, giving Gary a well-deserved break. The race was back on, and we had work to do.

The next seven kilometres led us along the beach to William Bay. The high tide was just withdrawing, allowing us to power-hike through the wet sand, which was firm in places and pretty loose in others. There was no need to waste valuable energy and attempt to run this section. While we were marching over the dark beach, I reflected on what had just happened. It was much greater than the fact that I had fallen asleep. I had woken up a different person.

It felt miraculous, and I saw clearly what had happened: I had let go of my ego. The bureaucrat had gone to sleep in the car and the explorer had woken up. The fear of failure was replaced by the excitement to extend my limits. I no longer identified with success. Richard Barrett couldn't have outlined the journey any better with his seven levels of consciousness. My ego had been in charge for two days, making the whole race one almighty battle. Consequently, I was utterly exhausted and felt defeated. Instead of dealing with the circumstances as they were, I'd created a disconnect between my expectations and reality — the perfect recipe for trouble.

The path out of my misery was to become aware of the choice I'd had all along. That choice was to widen my consciousness and let go of the urge to stay in control.

I could now have knowing without any thinking involved — I had surrendered. Surrendered any need to control and surrendered to circumstances as they played out. I had conquered my mind by letting go. I was relying not on a future promise but on an instantly available reality. I felt in harmony with the world and myself; tranquil. I had no more battles to fight. I hadn't surrendered because of the sleep; I had slept because of the surrender. I had been convinced that my circumstances were the issue. That had kept me stuck, until I realised that it was my perspective that trapped me. Everything needed to be stripped away for me to discover the resources I had within.

The inner magic emerged again because I was playful and connected. The difference was that I allowed everything to arise as it did.

For the first time in this race, I fully embraced uncertainty. I was going to deal with whatever would come. The saving ground was within me, not somewhere external, where I had been searching. How much energy had I wasted by not letting go of control from the beginning? And if that was the perfect way to run an ultramarathon, what would happen if I led my life with that attitude? What if I brought this mindset to everyday life? It would be even more powerful if I could help others access this state.

We barely stopped at the next aid station in order to keep our good momentum. The couple in charge of the checkpoint had been asleep, and we were sorry for waking them. It was even their wedding anniversary, and they were celebrating by supporting crazy runners trying to make it to Albany. I became aware that it wasn't only my crew who'd barely slept much more than me. By now, anybody supporting this event was sleep deprived, equally testing their limits.

We stayed for a couple of minutes at the aid station; just long enough for Rebecca to adjust her gear and for me to take one of the fortune cookies. I wanted words of wisdom from the oracle, and perhaps an answer for how to approach the remaining 105 kilometres. I couldn't have been further off the mark: 'You don't marry someone you can live with; you marry the person whom you cannot live without.' After Rebecca read it, she looked at me full of expectation, until she laughed out loud. It wasn't the moment to pursue this topic.

DAY THREE: CONNECTING WITH NATURE

We continued and maintained a good rhythm for the rest of the night. I was still in second position, but Candice was closing in, and Dion had pulled away. I wouldn't catch him, unless his sleep deprivation caught up with him. Anything could happen in a 200-miler, especially in the final hours of the race. My mind was calm, and my focus felt sharp as a knife. I was in full flow, observing everything that happened within and around me simultaneously — like watching a movie in slow motion. I ducked every spider web, took in the sounds in the woods and felt my body gliding over the sandy trail.

Shortly after daybreak, we climbed Monkey Rock — one of the highest hills left to climb. We'd been told the downhill that followed into the township of Denmark was runnable. Instead, the trail was full of boulders and felt never-ending. I complained to Rebecca, 'We should be running, but we're rock-climbing.' Scrambling our way through the worst-marked section of the race, we suddenly realised we were lost. Rebecca showed the first symptoms of having been infected by my contagious negativity. We were in dangerous territory, losing track of what we were here for. 'We just have to regain focus and rhythm,' I called out. Instead of continuing with our bush-bashing, we backtracked until we found the trail again. In all, our detour probably lasted only 10 minutes. As we learned later, other runners were less lucky and lost for up to four hours in this section.

The third day was unexpectedly hot, much worse than the first day. Gary decided it'd be best for us to not run at all during the hot part of the day. We hiked instead, and I took a few 10-minute naps every few aid stations. I was at ease with myself and enjoyed the journey through the stunning landscape along the ocean, full of dunes and cliffs. Also, sleeping was no longer an issue. The moment I sat down, I fell asleep, so I regularly used short breaks for strategic recovery. I wanted to be in good shape during the night to finish off the race before sunrise.

Later that afternoon — during snake rush hour — we had to be extremely alert. We couldn't afford an incident. We hadn't come this far to step on one and get bitten. I suddenly stopped when we were running along a narrow, windy path through low scrub. So did Rebecca behind me. A 20-centimetre 'stick' on the ground had grabbed my attention. It differed slightly from the other sticks, and I wondered whether it was a snake. Rebecca found a long branch, poked it and confirmed that it was a snake. But, lucky for us, it was dead. Rebecca tried to push it off the path so none of the later runners would step on it — and that was when the apparently dead snake resurrected, made itself tall and, in full flight, hissed at us in fury.

Both of us instantly tumbled several steps backwards. We did not want to be bitten as Gary's wife had been a few weeks back when she had accidently stepped on a snake during a training run. Luckily, it had been a 'dry' bite, or a bite without poison. In contrast, we could be sure that if this creature bit us, we wouldn't be that fortunate. It was angry at having been disrupted in its late-afternoon nap. Or it was afraid what delirious runners were capable of doing to it. Resolutely, it let us know that it was going to fight for its life. Until the snake moved out of our way, we could not pass and carry on. It kept hissing, standing its ground. Our intention was not to escalate the situation any further, and so we backed off even further. The snake mirrored our behaviour and finally disappeared into the scrub.

We were deeply relieved and kept going with our journey, surprised that after less than a total of two hours of sleep over the last three days, we were still alert enough to distinguish a stick-like snake from all the other sticks. From then, every stick looked like another snake but, luckily, we didn't have any more snake encounters.

For the rest of the race, I did not need any more sleep and barely stopped at aid stations. We'd already entered the third night when we were told that Dion had won the race in just over 61 hours. What a champion and what an incredible achievement! He had pulled off the race of his life with no sleep at all. Inspired by Dion, we increased our speed. Finishing in less than a total of 70 hours felt realistic. For the first time, I could smell the finish line.

I was in tune with nature and spotted an owl sitting on a branch. It seemed to be curiously observing what we were doing. I'd never seen an owl in the wild and, probably, the owl hadn't seen any runners at this time of the night either. I almost expected it to speak to us and share its wisdom. Instead, it spread its wings and vanished in the dark. Gary and I kept on running silently through the serene night.

Out of nowhere, an idea occurred to me. A deeper knowing emerged, and I heard myself ask Gary whether he could introduce me to Martin Fryer when we got back home. I had never met Martin, but had heard that he was an amazing long-distance running coach. My intuition told me that Martin could lift my ultra running to the next level. I felt he was the man to speak to if I wanted to pursue these long-distance runs more seriously. Once again, Gary proved what an amazing, selfless mentor he had become for me. He didn't take my question to be in any way undermining his own worth. He loved the idea and reassured me I'd click with Martin instantly.

Soon after, I announced that if we ramped up our speed even more, we'd finish in less than 69 hours. I felt strong and knew that I had more in me for the remaining three hours. I was in a deep state of flow and was propelling along, full of trust that I had the energy to sustain my pace to the end. To underpin my ambition, I no longer left a few steps in between us but was breathing straight into Gary's neck. The talking subsided. All I could hear were our steps, the ocean swell crashing against the cliffs underneath us, and the monotonous sounds of the rotors of the wind park we were crossing. After a while, I got even faster, passed Gary and led the way to the last aid station, where Rebecca took over.

I was on a mission. I entered the checkpoint, apologised to the supporters that I couldn't have a chat, and seconds later I was gone again. Even Rebecca had to catch up. Rushing through the dark night, I was one with nature. Not once did we accidently bump into the countless spider webs we had to navigate. They were trapping insects but not us. The experience was much more profound than anything I had experienced before. Never in my life had I felt such a deep connection with nature. We navigated the trail as if we were an integral part of it. I had never felt more present, which was surprising, given my advanced level of sleep deprivation. There was something magical, if not even spiritual, about the experience.

I had been joking that if we finished before sunrise, we could add another five kilometres of running and participate in the Saturday parkrun in Albany. It was one of hundreds of community-organised five-kilometre events held across Australia every weekend, attracting thousands of runners. Rebecca sensed I was semi-serious and offered me a viable alternative: 'We have about five kilometres left to the finish line. Let's pretend it's parkrun, so at least we can feel like we've done it — and we can skip running it later on.' We had heard that Candice, who was in third position chasing me, was running a fantastic race, but luckily was too far behind to catch me. Nevertheless, we got faster and faster. It was our way to celebrate what we'd jointly achieved.

On the final kilometres we hit civilisation and almost sprinted home on a bike path. There it was: the finish arch of the inaugural Delirious W.E.S.T. 200-miler. Rebecca and I ran through it in 68:52 hours to claim second place.

I could not have done it on my own. Shaun's arms caught me, and both Rebecca and Gary joined the hug. I was deeply grateful for their invaluable support. Rebecca had run 90 kilometres with me and Gary another 110 kilometres, which were crazy achievements in themselves. They were not too keen to hug me for too long. Since the first day, they'd been reminding me that I stank, and a shower was long overdue. Gary asked me how I was feeling. To my surprise, I did not feel exhausted. If anyone had told me that the race wasn't over yet, I would have kept running. I just sensed a lightness within me, coming from being connected with something immense.

DAYS FOUR AND FIVE: SEEING THE WORLD FROM A HIGHER PERSPECTIVE

My energy vanished as soon as I got into the car, and soreness set in. My legs told me — unambiguously — not to expect any more cooperation. Out of nowhere, random shooting pain hit throughout my body. Luckily, it was only a 15-minute drive to the accommodation we'd booked for the following days. Trying to get out of the car, my back spasmed, and I could no longer rely on any of my muscles. I had run hundreds of kilometres, and now I couldn't even walk three metres without support. My body seemed to be shutting down, and I started shivering. With Rebecca's help, I made my way to the shower and turned on a hot, steady stream. I soon warmed up.

It was remarkable to witness how the body followed the mind. At the finish line, my body had not reached its limits and could have kept going. It was my mind that shut down first. Yet, while I was in a calm, focused headspace, I was capable of unbelievable things. It was worth remembering what that felt like, to be able to tap into that space in the future. Now, my mind let me know it had done its part. Without a focused mind following a strong purpose, the body struggled; with the lack of direction, it was in all sorts of trouble. My body was no more than a wreck.

After a light meal at around 5 am, I fell asleep on the soft bed. As always after big races, I woke up not long after, drenched in my own sweat. I had barely slept for three hours. After I changed into dry clothes, I silently stole out of the house. Janine, the race medic, had sent a message congratulating me and reiterating the invite to fly over the course. I had some blisters preventing me from moving quickly, but nothing would stop me from taking up her generous offer. I was humbled at how somebody I hadn't seen in years could be so generous. It was the icing on the cake of an already very special week. The crisp morning promised spectacular views, without a single cloud in the sky.

Janine kindly picked me up and dropped me at Denmark airfield, where her husband, Wayne, was waiting to take off with me. I learned that the couple had built the tiny blue two-seater themselves, assembling it over the course of six years. Before I had any time to consider how safe this was going to be, we were already in the air. Wayne was an experienced pilot and manoeuvred a few patches of turbulence smoothly. He showed me the final 210 kilometres of the course between Walpole and Albany, and I gained an appreciation of how much ground we'd covered. The entire flight, I was busy taking photo evidence of the overgrown vegetation, sand dunes and blue beaches.

Only now was the realisation slowly sinking in about how insane our adventure had been. Here we were, on top of the world.

Wayne pointed out Parry Beach underneath us. It was there, after two days of running, I'd finally managed to sleep. In bright daylight and from our bird's eye perspective, nothing was special about the place. Yet, it marked the turning point in my race experience.

I'd finally accepted that I was incapable of changing my circumstances. It was me who had to change fundamentally. Being mentally tough had not gotten me anywhere. Rather than fighting any longer, I trusted I could effectively deal with the lows of the race. The gentleness from my crew and my self-compassion proved to be much more powerful than toughness could ever be. Being in control was an illusion, and I'd experienced how much further trust could get me. The sensation of liberation was profound; a heavy weight had been lifted from my shoulders. Surrendering unlocked the magic. For the remainder of the race, I had been liberated from compulsive reactions and had tapped into a gigantic spaciousness that unlocked secret reserves.

My thoughts were interrupted by Wayne pointing out Shelley Beach — one of the most spectacular beaches in the area. He suggested that we pay it another visit and enjoy a dip in the ocean at some later date. Soon after Shelley Beach, the landing strip of Denmark airport appeared in front of us. Almost an hour had passed when we safely landed on firm ground.

The remainder of the weekend was extremely slow. Gary, Rebecca and I were utterly exhausted and even the simplest activities took much longer than usual. Before sunset, we followed Wayne's suggestion and went back to Shelley Beach. It was a great opportunity to support the exhausted runners still on the course. As they headed into their fourth night, I was in awe of their determination. None of them left any doubt that they would make it to the finish line. A spectator highlighted a key observation about the different level of runners: 'The main difference is that the top runners do what they need to do. The runners further back often forget to drink, eat or attend to a blister until it's too late.' Over such a long race, that level of diligence made all the difference. The good news we had for these inspiring warriors was that from there onward the terrain got significantly easier.

No doubt, I had turned right again. I'd pursued a new path that had scared me and, in so doing, step-changed my view of the world. Through the Delirious W.E.S.T., I got a broader appreciation of what turning right meant. Surrendering to the present moment was beyond what seemed rational or emotionally bearable. Yet, by learning how to relate to the full range of the human experience, I was able to gather my courage to take that scary step. It allowed the Higher Self to take over from the ego.

Decades of running were teaching me not how to win but how to lead a more purposeful life. The new twist to turning right was to not chase the needs that controlled me but be guided by the aspirations that would fulfil me. Several years of ultra running required me to let go of an old identity that had begun to chafe over the years — my identification with success. That was what the metamorphosis of the caterpillar to a butterfly was about — not wasting our energy crawling faster but learning to fly. Widening our perspective was the source of the magic. At any time, different levels of consciousness were waiting to be accessed. It was nothing external but resided within us.

The following afternoon we jointly celebrated an incredible week with everybody involved in the event. Primarily, it was not about performance, but about doing what we thought could not be done. The time between Wednesday morning and Sunday afternoon had been life changing for many of us. Looking into the tired yet satisfied faces and listening to incredible stories confirmed that we'd all battled our inner demons. Each of us had found some extraordinary inner force — a strength that was beyond our imagination. We had risen with the challenge, but it wasn't about some regular, perhaps slow, incremental advances in personal growth.

This was one of those rare quantum leaps, and everyone I spoke to said the same thing. We'd confirmed that we could achieve anything because, for once, we'd set aside the limitations of our minds. The intensity of the challenge had given us an insight into how much more we were capable of, when stripped of everyday certainties.

Every finisher received the 'plugger award' — one thong, with their name engraved. To earn the matching thong in the pair, we'd have to come back and run another 350 kilometres. There were easier ways of acquiring a pair of flippers, but were they as fulfilling? Each one of us was a winner, and therefore it was a nice gesture that no extra trophies were awarded for podium getters. Our achievement did not lie in making the finish line. What distinguished the delirious runners participating in this event was that we had the guts to rock up at the start line.

The time had come to not only travel back home, but also bring turning right to the work context. Originally, Gavin and I had wanted to lift from good to great. Looking back, we had far exceeded that ambition. Over the previous years, I'd learned that acquiring new skills led to being good, and becoming consistent under pressure led to greatness. Working on one's own transformation, however, allowed our innate magic to emerge. The journey had revealed many once-believed truths as nothing other than illusions. Looking within uncovered so much more potential than I would ever have dared to dream about. The key was the courage to step out of the comfort zone — to turn right.

My next mission was to pass on the magic Gavin had ignited in me. How to do that? Surely, it didn't mean making everyone run hundreds of kilometres to access the magic. In essence, challenges in work settings were no different from challenges in a race. The magic resided in the present moment, and accessing it required the ability to choose the appropriate perspective.

I wanted to inspire others and help raise consciousness. Gavin wasn't the only one challenging me about how to make it relevant to a broader audience. I'd shared my thoughts on turning right with my CEO, and his response was similar: 'I understand sports theory, but the key is how you translate it into a work environment — how do you turn right at work?'

SELF CHECK-IN

- When do you find yourself struggling hardest with your ego?
- In what situations do your highest values get challenged?
- How do those challenges make you feel? What thoughts and emotions come up?
- What needs are you trying to fill?
- What power and magic do you find through connecting with nature?

ACT III

INSPIRING THE MAGIC

RAISING CONSCIOUSNESS

*We shall not cease from exploration, and the end
of all our exploring will be to arrive where we started,
and to know the place for the first time.*

—T. S. Eliot

CHAPTER 13

TURNING RIGHT TO LOOK INTO THE PAST

Senior leaders guard their credibility carefully, not wanting to lose face ... Change is scary. Who will I be if I am not this?

—Robert Anderson and William Adams

I had lost contact with the ground under my feet and was completely wet. Slowly, the darkness was lifting. I could taste the salt on my lips. I was floating effortlessly and was at peace with the world. For once, I wasn't striving; I was just enjoying being immersed in nature. Several weeks had passed since the Delirious W.E.S.T. 200-miler and, to fully recover, I had given my body a rest from running. Instead, I spent my mornings water-running at Balmoral Beach, only a few kilometres from where I lived. Less repetitive pounding on hard surfaces would hopefully also give my mind the chance to catch up.

I loved seeing the red fireball coming out of the ocean, far on the horizon beyond the Sydney Harbour entrance, and this morning

I was enjoying another spectacular sunrise. The prediction for the rest of the day was less glorious. The wind had already picked up, and the surf was splashing the salty water into my face. We expected some storms to pass through.

FACING OLD DEMONS

At work, the sunny days had also disappeared. Though I was proud of how we'd shifted the overall culture in the previous two years, and of having built yet another amazing team, recently something had shifted. It was more than just my own professional development slowing down. My team's spirit was eroding, and despite trying all I could, nothing was stopping the downward spiral.

My own team reminded me, daily, that experiencing the magic myself was completely different from passing it on to others. For my entire career, I'd prided myself on supporting my teams in their personal growth journey, fostering rewarding and high-performance environments. Even within the cultural darkness at my previous employer, my team had guarded a beacon of light, staying positive and tapping into their intrinsic motivation to do an amazing job where external recognition was rare. I had left behind a strong team.

In my Sydney office now, cliques had formed; they deeply mistrusted each other and regularly created dramatic scenes. Tears were common, and what was happening reminded me more of a playground than a workplace. Soon, sick leave was on the rise. Our team engagement scores plummeted from the most content to the worst team. All attempts to overcome our issues failed. It felt as if we were blind to a disease and frantically trying to resolve its symptoms.

My biggest frustration was that my analytical brain couldn't figure out where I was going wrong. I even faced my boss's question: 'What if they don't want to become corporate athletes?'

I couldn't point the finger at someone else. I was under no illusion that I was part of the problem in the first place. I was embarrassed that this deterioration of culture — the very aspect of work I was most passionate about — could happen under my leadership.

One morning, I called a meeting with all managers within my team, and we were together for a couple of hours. I was looking to facilitate deep insight, and each of us had a role to play in stepping up. We kept it playful.

I gave the group an empty small milk carton and asked them to keep it up in the air for as long as they could. No catching was allowed, just tapping it to the next person. We had done a similar exercise in the senior leadership team and set a record of around 80 taps before dropping the carton. We'd needed about five attempts until we figured out how best to organise ourselves and collaborate.

But my team hadn't, even after a dozen attempts, gotten past 10 taps. Two observations stood out. Team members didn't communicate with each other, and nobody took ownership. When the milk carton came flying in their direction, most had terror written over their faces. Nobody wanted to be the one who stuffed up. Even less encouraging was what happened in between the rounds. This was a bunch of very smart people yet, despite being organised in a team, they could not get past their individual frustrations. They didn't appear to learn from the experience. Instead, everybody looked in my direction, desperate for me to provide the answer or, even better, release them from their misery.

We kept going, but soon all hope to celebrate a team achievement evaporated. I was most likely the only one with an insight that morning. My team was motivated to avoid failure. Worse was the realisation that I, as their leader, lacked the ability to inspire the magic in them.

I needed fresh air; the room was stuffy and full of negativity. Some team members seemed to be bordering on being toxic, and it felt suffocating to be in their presence. So I left. Yet, I sensed that my discomfort wasn't about them; it was about me. How could I believe that I would be a great coach if I didn't even have what it took to lead a challenging team? I questioned my entire identity as a people leader. Was I any better than the uninspiring executives at my previous job?

I'd signed up with Lisa for her transformation courses, and I could only hope these would teach me what I was missing. This was the perfect case study for taking seemingly hopeless teams on a journey towards magic and high performance. An irritating voice within me suggested that the future of turning right depended on my learning of the lesson.

That's when I connected a few dots — I'd overlooked that I was facing another adaptive challenge. Similar to the race in Christchurch, I treated work as a technical challenge. I wanted my team to change. That was where I went wrong. The solution was not about changing them or teaching them missing skills. What was required was a shift in mindset — and, to start with, my own. I needed to transform first. The irony didn't escape me — I was being asked to undergo the inner work that I had expected from my bosses at my previous job in Melbourne.

I intuitively knew I was on to something, but I had no clue what that actually meant.

It puzzled me how my team would be better at tapping a milk carton if I transformed. How could I possibly be contributing to their poor leadership? I even went a step further and asked myself how I was the problem. I had come such a long way in the previous years through running, but I still hadn't found a way to apply those insights to the work environment. I'd learned to bring light into darkness wearing muddy running shoes. I couldn't seem to access the same magic wearing polished leather shoes. Maybe, this was my opportunity — similar to having Christchurch help me take running to the next level — to fundamentally upgrade my inner game at work?

After several days, I remembered how Walter Pollack, a business coach during my consultant days, had hit the nail on the head. 'Kay, your problem is that your head and your gut aren't talking to each other. You bind your tie and cut off any communication between the two.' Even after Walter's diagnosis more than a decade earlier, I'd stayed true to type: logical, methodical, disciplined. It seemed like an endless journey. Every time I thought I'd overcome the demons of the past, they appeared in a different cloak. Gavin had helped me overcome my urge to be in control from a running perspective. At work, I apparently had more development ahead of me than I was comfortable with.

SIGNING UP TO RE-SIT A FAILED EXAM

While running was suddenly relegated to being secondary to transformation at work, it remained my playground for fun and experimentation. Nowhere else in my life was I thriving as much and feeling as fulfilled. Running was when I got in tune with what added deeper meaning to my existence. Coping with the challenges at work was even harder during these recovery weeks, when I barely did any sports. I was looking forward to ramping up running again soon.

My legs were itching to get back, and my mind was craving more magical experiences. That reminded me to contact Martin Fryer, who, out of nowhere in the final hours of the Delirious race, I'd thought of contacting. I hoped he would turn out to be the source of inspiration I pictured him to be.

Martin and I clicked instantly. A long chat about our perspectives on ultra running proved that, undoubtedly, we were on the same wavelength. Neither of us overestimated the importance of physical fitness. While the actual running training was important, it was only the entry ticket to the game. Being able to tap into the mental side made all the difference. The magic happened when we were connected to something much vaster than ourselves. To become an amazing athlete, one had to train their mental capacity. Martin called it our Spiritual Self, but the term wasn't religious. It only acknowledged that there was more to life than a physical body, which acted on thoughts and emotions. How else could I explain my yearning to find meaning and a home? Surprisingly, I used the term 'Higher Self' myself but still cringed at the word 'spiritual'. Not because I disagreed. More because my analytical side struggled to accept a dimension it could not grasp.

Halfway through the phone call, Martin channelled the conversation to the journey ahead. I shared with him that I was extremely busy with work, yet would like to run another 24-hour race. I was sure that under his guidance I could improve my previous result of 212 kilometres. What I did not know was that Martin was the Australian national coach for the 24-hour event. He had done his homework assessing me and stunned me with his verdict. From my performance at Delirious, he deduced that I was capable of qualifying for the 24-hour world championships. He underpinned Gary's words that the Australian national team was extremely good. They had won the team silver medal a few years ago, and five runners already had secured an A-standard qualifier. That meant that, in order to get selected, I also needed an A-qualifier. I had to let what Martin threw at me sink in — he believed I could run 240 kilometres within 24 hours and make the Australian team. 'Easily,' he added firmly.

Martin was asking me for a 13 per cent improvement on Coburg the previous year. That was insane. He was asking for the impossible. My horrible Christchurch experience instantly came to mind. I had already failed to make an Australian national team once, attempting to qualify for the 100-kilometre world championships. I ended up running 40 minutes slower than a C-qualifier. Now I needed to run an A-qualifier — undoubtedly this must be out of my capacity.

Focusing on a pure outcome goal as a measure of success had never served me well. Therefore, I rejected sharing Martin's enthusiasm. I had contacted him to explore opportunities to improve and take running to another level, not to drop my growth aspirations again and pursue glory. With so much going on in my life, the timing was not ideal anyway. I shared my concerns. Martin was mistaken; I was not the worthy world championships candidate he saw in me. I would not again take on the pressure of a short-term result expectation. My ego was not mature enough to cope with it.

Rejecting his view demonstrated that I didn't have the mental toughness required to go to the highest athletic level. At least, that was my belief, and therefore I expected Martin to drop the idea of targeting the world champs. He surprised me a second time in our call. Martin knew exactly what I was talking about and pointed out that the battle with our demons was an integral part of the journey.

He regularly experienced how difficult it was to drop his own ego. Then, casually, Martin shared that it had taken him until the third day of a 10-day race to liberate himself from his ego's grip. That was when he crossed the threshold to pure awareness. From then onwards, things took care of themselves, and he intuitively knew how to navigate several rough patches on the remaining days.

Martin added that, to get quantum jumps in performance, we needed to surrender and have no expectations. That sounded familiar to me. It wasn't mental toughness or willpower that would get us there. I had experienced in the Delirious race that the trick each runner would face, encoded, was the need to surrender to the circumstances as they were. All that was required was the faith in our intuitive ability to deal with anything coming up.

I couldn't believe it. For the first time in my life I had met another runner who could articulate the magic I was pursuing. Martin was no less of an explorer than I regarded myself to be. The joy of experiencing amazing adventures propelled both of us forward. We were on a quest for self-actualisation.

Martin went on. People like us were both successful and limited because of our thinking minds. We had the discipline it took to succeed, but became limited by our urge to control circumstances and protect ourselves. Our challenge was to get out of our heads and allow things to happen naturally. This was a difficult thing for achievement-oriented people, and so only monumental challenges were big enough and lasted sufficiently long enough to let go of the ego. If I found an easier way, he was eager to learn about it. Silently, I noted that that was exactly the journey I had embarked on with coaching. I was looking for a more practical way. It would take me a while to have something to share.

Martin had convinced me. Attempting to qualify for the world championships was no longer a quest for glory — it would allow me to work with Martin and learn from him. I had just found a new mentor.

Why not prove him right and discover that I was much more capable than I gave myself credit for? He could help me to tap more into my spiritual side. For the first time, my development goals in running and in work were aligned — I wanted to overcome my own reactivity. The skill would be to switch perspective and not operate out of fear, but instead pursue my purpose to inspire the magic. To unlock my challenges at work and in athletics, I had to transform further.

Martin finished our conversation on a rhetorical question. He suspected we were all running away from something. What was it I was running away from? He left me intrigued. I had always pictured myself running towards something: exploring the unknown, searching for meaning, chasing the magic. What if he was right and I was counteracting my own efforts?

Suddenly, I found myself juggling more than ever before. I had three months to get ready for the latest possible qualification event before the 24-hour world championships. I would give my best at the Adelaide 24-hour race to hopefully join the Australian team on their trip to Albi in France. In the mornings, I began getting up at 4 am to train before work. At work, I tried to overcome my team challenges and kept an eye out for in-house opportunities in the area of transformation and coaching. After work and on the weekends, I had to study for my accreditation courses with Lisa. On top of everything, I was travelling regularly between Sydney and Melbourne to see Rebecca. Some days I wondered whether I'd loaded too much on myself.

My daredevil plan was that all areas of change would reinforce each other and fill me with energy. The stakes were high, and my intention was to trust the path. The time had come to work towards integrating work and athletics. Lisa's lessons in the coaching course were surprisingly similar to Martin's wisdom. Whether athlete or leader, one created a competitive advantage by shifting the relationship with the present moment. Secretly, I hoped that transformation through the accreditation journey would have a positive impact on my qualifying race.

DISCONTINUING STORIES FROM THE PAST

The following months of learning the foundations of transformational coaching were challenging. I barely had a free minute. I had entered a new world, in stark contrast to the corporate world I was so familiar with. All my life the values of success, knowledge and decisiveness had been beneficial. To reach my vision of bringing right turns into work, I had to embrace different values, such as patience, compassion, selflessness, authenticity, humility and wisdom. They would help me become literate in how to navigate transformational journeys outside of running.

The underpinning principle was Barrett's insight that businesses didn't have the capability to transform — only people did. To unlock adaptive challenges, leaders had to go through their own transformation. Being a leader myself, I experienced how confronting that journey was. To lift my team out of their misery, I had to overcome my own reactive patterns. I could only take them on the journey if I shifted my own attitude and behaviours. I had been relatively comfortable acknowledging intellectually that I was part of the problem; doing the actual work on myself, however, was a step out of my comfort zone.

The first lesson I learned was profound and simple — meet people where they are, not where I want them to be. This, for me, was a shift in my root perspective. It explained why I was facing the challenge in the first place. I had stretched many team members beyond their capabilities, without adequately supporting them. I needed to progress systemic change at a pace that stimulated my team, rather than broke them. The first step was to build trust; then I had to show compassion for where my team was. With that in mind, I would come to the milk carton game completely differently next time. I wouldn't play back to the team how much better they could be. My role was to help them experience the power of cooperation and teamwork.

Lisa promised I'd experience further shifts during her two residential courses in Perth — the first one in the week leading into my 24-hour qualification race, the second before a potential world championships attendance. Both of those weeks would not only be intense but also come out of my annual leave balance. I trusted they'd be worth my time and energy.

Before my running training moved into the intense preparation phase, Rebecca and I travelled to Christchurch and back to Hagley Park. It was there, three years earlier, that I'd failed to qualify for the world championships. This time, we were there for Rebecca to race and for me to encourage her from the sideline. In the past few years, she'd made lots of sacrifices supporting my running; this was my opportunity to give back. After Rebecca's amazing debut over 100 kilometres in China, she wanted to see how far she'd come.

Her goal was to snatch the New Zealand national title. Getting a world championships qualifier for her country seemed less likely. She needed to run less than 8:30 hours, a 32-minute improvement on her race in China. But we could dream — and our dream scenario was for her to attend the 100-kilometre world championships in the Netherlands and me the 24-hour world championships in France.

It was my turn to hand out the drink bottles. Luckily, Rebecca was much more relaxed about the colour of the drinks than I'd been in that same race, when I lost my temper and had a go at her. From the beginning, Rebecca sat in second position, with the first woman running extremely strongly from the start. A couple of hours in, Rebecca stopped at the toilet, which gave us an opportunity for a quick chat through the closed door. 'She is so far ahead,' Rebecca called out. My internal alarm bells went off — Rebecca was entertaining an unhealthy self-dialogue. I encouraged her not to compare herself with anybody else. 'Don't worry about her. Focus on your own race. You are doing so well.' We still had 75 kilometres to go.

Rebecca got lapped a couple of times and, at one stage, lagged behind the leading woman by five kilometres. As a consequence, she spiralled into a dark spot. At just over halfway, she complained about pain. 'I'm too sore. My legs are aching.' I knew too well how horrible those experiences were. The thinking mind pretended to be on our side, yet created problems and then prevented us from going to where we wanted to go. Even worse was that I could do absolutely nothing to make it better. It looked like Christchurch was not a good location for either of us. History was repeating itself.

With about 40 kilometres to go, Rebecca stopped at the toilet a second time. Something was dangerous about the 60 per cent mark in ultra races, and it was the point most people gave up. The realisation kicked in that the body wanted to stop, and the remaining stretch towards the finish line was often seen as too far to cover. I desperately needed to help Rebecca change her perspective. Dwelling on the pain would only entrench her further in the hole she was digging for herself.

I tried to cheer her up and shared the news that the leading lady had started fading. 'Keep going and you'll catch her.' Rebecca rushed out of the toilet. I could do nothing else but watch the rest of the race play out. As a future coach, I'd have to get used to the fact that I wasn't in control. I could only hope that refocusing her attention worked in this instance. From here, she needed to choose whether to continue on the trajectory she was on or access her innermost strengths.

Rebecca started clawing back a few hundred metres from the leader on every lap. While the leader faded significantly, Rebecca maintained her momentum. Sheer determination was written all over her face. She unlapped herself and, a few laps later, took over the lead. I was in awe, witnessing a textbook demonstration of mental stamina. After 8:15 hours Rebecca won the New Zealand title, having executed the perfect race. Her time was not only an A-qualifier for the next 100-kilometre world championships but also the third-fastest ever over that distance from a New Zealand female. The icing on the cake was that Rebecca was faster than the male champion that year.

None of us had expected such an extraordinary performance. I barely found words to express how amazed I was. Rebecca had officially overtaken me as the fastest 100-kilometre runner in our household.

Her race could have gone as pear-shaped as mine. The difference was that, once it got tough, she chose a different route. She demonstrated how to stay calm, composed and focused under pressure. As seductive as the pain had been, she found a different perspective and tapped into her inner greatness. She deserved to win the title because of her resilience from setbacks, her ability to focus her attention and, eventually, her capacity to raise her consciousness beyond the dichotomy of success and failure. Travelling back to Christchurch gave me the inspiration I needed to round out my own race preparation. If I needed any reminder, the message was clear; it was all in the mind.

GETTING READY FOR A BIG TOTAL

From the beginning, Martin and I agreed that I needed more of a mentor guiding me than a coach prescribing me what to do. I was relieved that we had so quickly built a trust-based mentoring relationship. But with just over two months remaining before the race in Adelaide, time was not on our side. Our plan was simple: focus on developing the inner game, supplemented by an appropriate training plan.

Daily meditation featured very highly on my priority list. For Martin, it was a non-negotiable. A focused mind was paramount, so this barely surprised me. In order to achieve a big total mileage during 24 hours of running, I had to let go of attachment to the result. More and more, I could see how coaching and running were intertwined; equanimity was my biggest challenge for the race. Missing composure in the face of adversity was also the reason I struggled with my team at work.

Running training itself changed very little. Learning by playing and having fun was key, particularly at this elite level. The only major tweak was adding fast walking sessions to my repertoire, which just made sense. How could I walk regularly during the competition without practising that element specifically in training? Rebecca mocked me for the awkward movement of race-walking, recommending I train before the sun came up so none of our friends would see me. I couldn't have cared less and was happy that it did not take long before I was walking fast enough to overtake slow runners.

Martin was equally as busy as I was, and we were both comfortable with only a handful of meaningful check-ins on the way. In one of the early chats, I mentioned to him how surprised I was to be juggling everything I had going on pretty well. In running specifically, it felt as if I was absorbing the high training load better than ever before. My body was barely sore, and I was not as tired as in previous preparation phases. Martin probed me to explain my observation. I was unsure, but suggested it was because I had no energy left to engage in draining interactions. Martin offered a different explanation. 'It's your mind.'

At the end of the training cycle, Martin and I discussed race strategy. Upfront, he revealed he was going to attend the Adelaide race and could help out Rebecca with crewing. Primarily, he wanted to watch me in action.

Being able to count on his mental support during the race was a comfort. He began talking about logistics, and then put on his serious voice. Instead of a straightforward message, he went into a long-winded outline about how much experience he had coaching great runners. I should not underestimate his capacity to know what these runners were capable of. That was not news to me — it was the reason I'd contacted him in the first place. What shocked me was his prediction. 'Kay, you'll easily run 240 kilometres. An A-qualifier is not difficult for you. I think you can run 250 kilometres and wouldn't be surprised if you ran 260.'

A wave of panic instantly took hold of me. We were talking outcomes again. While it was well-intended encouragement, Martin had just dumped high expectations on me. I could never meet them. The bureaucrat in me instantly translated Martin's words into, 'Anything less than 240 kilometres is failure.'

I took a deep breath and thanked Martin for his kind words. I then made the choice to take them as they were intended, as pure encouragement. Otherwise, they weren't going to change anything. My intention stayed the same: surrender to the race and do my best moment to moment. The result would take care of itself. It would be whatever it would be.

SELF CHECK-IN

- What is your biggest (personal and/or business) challenge?
- Why is it a challenge for you?
- How are you part of the problem with your biggest challenge?

CHAPTER 14

TURNING RIGHT TO LOOK INTO THE FUTURE

You can use a challenge to awaken you, or you can allow it to pull you into even deeper sleep.

—Eckhart Tolle

Race week was my most important week in years. I not only had the chance to qualify for the world champs, but was also attending the first of Lisa's accreditation courses in Perth. A week with a high mental toll, involving interstate travel and time zone shifts, along with a disruption in routine, was perhaps far from the perfect lead-in to an important race.

Getting to Adelaide by Friday afternoon would be stressful. The race started on Saturday morning, and I could only hope that nothing went wrong. I'd have to leave the course early to catch the last flight to Adelaide for the 24-hour race, but I wasn't prepared to sacrifice my professional development or a potential trip to France with the Australian national team. Only with hindsight would I see whether attending the course in Perth was going to be my downfall or a blessing in disguise.

WRESTLING WITH ANCIENT BEASTS

Lisa's course 'Facilitating Transformation through Values' — a globally renowned facilitator accreditation program — was focused on leveraging the power of our values and purpose. I was hoping to learn the basics of coaching as well as how to be a facilitator of business transformation. I wanted to move into facilitating meaningful personal shifts for leaders and helping their organisations become thriving cultures. Yet I understood that my own reactive tendencies would be a complication in taking others on an inspirational leadership journey. We practised getting a higher perspective when we became caught up in our own drama — instead of staying in the 'dance' we stepped onto the 'balcony' to become aware of what was going on in our internal world and see the bigger picture. I understood that when hijacked by their emotions, nobody could be effective in what they were doing. This was true in sports, in business and certainly in coaching.

What made the week challenging was the work on our reactive patterns. Before the workshop, we'd been asked to seek 360-degree feedback by interviewing our bosses, peers and members of our teams. We made sense of this feedback during the workshop, and I was thrilled to get positive call-outs that included empowering others, having a high level of care and challenging others to take steps they'd never dared to before. Some mentioned that I celebrated positivity, that I was quirky and, possibly my favourite, that I was the opposite of vanilla.

Of course, the encouraging feedback was pleasing, but we were really here to focus on the aspects to improve on — and I had a list that seemed to never end. I could be judgemental, impatient and too task-orientated. These traits, in turn, overpowered my ability to be empathetic; one colleague encouraged me to be more vulnerable and share my emotions more. Another pointed out how confronting, even pig-headed I could be when frustrated.

It emerged that dropping a plan and allowing things to emerge without needing to control wasn't my forte. Far too often, I was hiding behind my intellect, creating unnecessary distance with colleagues to protect myself. Some conceded that I'd become less 'black and white' over the years but believed I should do even more work on my agility when stuck. It dawned on me that I had to discover a completely different approach to dealing with conflict and setbacks at work. Another colleague questioned how I would take cynical people on a transformational journey, especially if they seemed uninterested in any change. She challenged me to not stick to the easy route and write people off.

What was extremely confronting was to realise the extent to which I was still on autopilot. I had hugely underestimated my reactivity. Not for the first time did I feel the urge to just run away. How much easier would it be to stay in the world I was familiar with? Yet, I had to face my discomfort. If I ever wanted to become an effective coach, running away wasn't an option.

In the world of sports, I knew what it took to turn right. When triggered, it was my choice to purposefully respond — to let go of my default mechanisms — rather than to react automatically. At work, I still struggled to overcome the reactive patterns that were holding me back. The formula for transformation in the corporate world was the same as in ultra running: from upset to awareness to choice. I just had not learned how to apply that formula in the business context.

Throughout the course, I grew more and more aware of how often I protected myself through emotionally withdrawing or grasping control. In those moments, fear took over from my purpose; motivation not to fail pushed aside motivation to succeed. The basic theory was simple; the reality, however, was much more disturbing. The issue was not understanding what happened, but standing tall when emotion tried to overwhelm me in moments my fear of being exposed was triggered.

During the week in Perth, I had plenty of opportunities to familiarise myself with mindless reactions to seemingly trivial triggers. On the last morning, we were asked to take a few minutes and draw a picture. I couldn't even recall what the image was supposed to represent. Before we even received the full instructions, I went into panic mode. I got hot and started sweating instantly. I did not want to do it. Deep-rooted aversion surfaced. My inner monologue was firing along at an incredible speed, focused on how much I hated anything to do with drawings and paintings. I couldn't do it, and I wouldn't do it. Nobody could force me to. Why was I here and how could I escape? Maybe I could disappear to the airport early?

To my embarrassment, I noticed everybody staring at me throwing a tantrum. The puzzled expressions on their faces only grew when I pathetically tried to withdraw from the exercise. From the outside, my disproportionate reaction was not comprehensible. What was wrong with asking for a simple drawing? Anything would be acceptable. Nobody expected a Picasso.

The maximum I was capable of giving was to colour in like a preschool kid. Since the mediocre marks in primary school, I'd hated arts with a passion. One of my colleagues had asked me recently why I needed to be good at everything I did. At the time, it seemed like a strange question. Yet, at that moment in the workshop, I could see how bad being awful at something made me feel. My emotions were going berserk. My resistance was so solid that I couldn't do anything productive for a few minutes. When my strong wish to run away eventually settled, I scribbled something onto the flipchart.

To my surprise, Lisa didn't challenge me on what had happened, and I took this as an invitation to go deeper on my own. A deep-rooted fear had clearly overwhelmed me. We had worked with fears and upsets during the entire week. In retrospect I could see that, once run by fear, all I wanted to do was to reduce the internal conflict I felt. Running away was a tempting option. The trick was to stay present, go into the centre of the contraction and just sit with the emotion. If I resisted the urge to follow the usual storyline, I would learn more about the nature of the fear. Doing so would allow me to shift upsets into setup for growth. Reactivity always had some underlying limiting beliefs, and typically these were assumptions created in our early childhood. I wasn't clear what I believed that very moment to make me so distressed.

I'd felt as if I could rely only on myself and not trust anybody. What was I protecting myself from? I doubted that it was the ancient fear of getting laughed at because of a clumsy drawing. My fear went deeper than loss of self-esteem. The final revelation was missing. I left Perth feeling I'd disturbed an ancient vicious beast within me, but the feral creature had withdrawn again into darkness before I could recognise its nature. Surely, it guarded the answers to many of my questions. For now, I was glad it had settled again because I needed my full focus for the upcoming race.

I left the course with the confidence I was on to something big. I felt like I was approaching another threshold, one where new opportunities were waiting. Every time I replaced reactivity with responsiveness in the past, I experienced immense performance jumps. I was curious how the race would play out and was quietly confident that I might even benefit from the course in Perth. While I got little sleep leading into the race, at least I was distracted and not worrying about what to expect. During the week, I'd been too busy to get nervous. Now, I was too exhausted to get stressed.

Rebecca was waiting for me at the Adelaide airport. It was already late when we arrived at our accommodation, within walking-distance of the park where the event would be held. To get race-ready, I needed three things: a 15-minute shuffle to freshen up my legs after the flight, a big bowl of pasta for dinner to top up the carb reserves and as much sleep as I could get. It was the last opportunity for any Australian runner to get their name on the board; the last race before team selection closed. My second attempt to make it onto an Australian national team could highly likely be no better than the first. However, Rebecca had role-modelled in Christchurch what it took to change the narrative.

RETAKING THE EXAM

Martin was already at the start line in the morning and gave me a big hug. He introduced me to Matt Eckford — a long-standing member of the Australian 24-hour team. He'd already qualified, yet was still racing with me. Unfortunately, I had no time to ask for any last-minute advice from a seasoned world championships runner.

It was 10 am when we were sent onto the 2.2-kilometre loop — our new home until the following morning. The air was crisp, and the race conditions appeared perfect. But we hadn't even completed our first lap or had time to properly warm up when the conditions changed dramatically. The heavens opened up, and the gravel path became muddy. The downpour soaked our clothes, and puddles formed quickly. I barely had the capacity to worry about the rain, however, because I was busy trying to get my heartrate monitor, strapped around my chest, to work. But it wasn't picking up a signal. According to my heartrate data, I was dead.

My strategy had been to use the heartrate information to avoid over-pacing and so not build up detrimental levels of lactic acid. But I quickly gave up on that plan, took off the faulty strap and dropped it with Rebecca and Martin. They could see already that I wasn't happy. Multiple early warning signs were emerging that we were in for a very long 24 hours.

I was aware that my immediate task was to work on a good rhythm and lift my spirit, regardless of the conditions. My intuition was being asked to step up. Many familiar faces were along the course, including David from Coast to Kosci and his mother. I decided to start having fun with anybody I knew and making new friends along the way. A few hours into the race, everything was going better. I wasn't too fast or too slow, was walking for a few hundred metres each lap, and regularly consuming drinks, bananas or mashed potatoes. What I didn't manage was to switch off my thinking mind.

While I was having fun on the course, I became serious when I approached my support crew. Interacting with them felt, inexplicably, like hard work. I had to concentrate to get things right. At one of the drink stops, I missed the bottle and knocked it out of Rebecca's hand. Was I getting impatient? No doubt I was tense, if not even grumpy. My interactions with Martin and Rebecca were polar opposites of how I treated everybody else on the course, instead mirroring how I was treating myself. It was still before sunset and my legs already were getting heavy. I was on track to run 240 kilometres, but there was no margin for error. It took me a few more laps to notice what was happening: the bureaucrat had crept back into the driver's seat and was now running the show.

I had to let go — easier said than done. Rationally, I understood that my thoughts were counterproductive. But I couldn't switch them off. A continual internal newsfeed commented on my every step. For the first time since my high school years, I tried running with music. I listened to Spanish songs and, for an hour, this took me to a happy place and improved my spirits. Then, the trouble was back again. It was close to midnight when I approached the critical point in any performance — the juncture where success and failure diverged.

While I got sucked deeper and deeper into the dark world of my head, a spectator suddenly ran a few metres next to me. He introduced himself and said we had a joint friend in Melbourne. Later, I learned that he was an Australian representative in the ultra distance trail world championships. His encouraging and kind words came just in time. Fate must have noticed that I needed a double-shot of stimulation to keep me going. Not even 100 metres later, Mick Thwaites, another amazing Australian representative, also offered words to reinvigorate me. Desperate for relief, I shouted back that I couldn't let go of my ego. I just caught what Mick responded with, because I'd passed him already, and the simplicity of his response was striking. 'Just drop your ego.'

There was little to add. I just had to run for the sake of running. The crucial question I asked myself was, 'Who do I want to be?' Instantly, the answer bounced back to me: I would fight like

Shackleton in Antarctica and explore my limits. This time, no bureaucrat would hold me back, regardless of the outcome. The ghosts who were haunting me disappeared the very moment I called them by their name. I was determined and walked straight into them, and direct confrontation revealed how hollow their threats were.

When I passed my support crew, Martin nervously called out that I was fading too much. I had to pick up my pace to make the national team. His instructions were simple: run a few laps at a slightly faster pace. During that surge, I caught up with Matt. He had lapped me multiple times and was on track for a stellar performance beyond 250 kilometres. For the next hour, I fed off his momentum. He had slowed down slightly, and we were now running at a similar pace. A playful back and forth started — I was faster than him, but he never walked. Therefore, he caught me in my walking breaks. Once he did, I ran away again. It kept me focused. Even more importantly, my inner explorer had taken over the rudder.

I had no buffer at all for the final hours. Only if I maintained my speed with no further fade would I make it. One toilet stop too many could make all the difference. The pressure was on. This was a race, and I kept fighting. Self-preservation would certainly not get me on the team. I had to give everything to make it through the darkness of the night. My only hope was to still be in a promising position at daybreak. With a final rush to the finish gun, I might have a chance — but this was touch and go. Martin was pacing up and down the sideline like a caged tiger, probably wishing he could run for me. Yet, I had to fight my own battle.

In the past, I had made some great runs look easy. This race was different; I was working hard. At least I kept my composure. Lap by lap, I did what had to be done. At no point did I over-deliver. Finally, the seemingly eternal night was over. The birds woke up and filled the morning air with their chatter, and the first light appeared like a promise of relief over the horizon. Out of the twilight, I recognised Mick again. After some sleep, he'd come back to the track to watch us finish, and he shouted, 'We want you on the team.' That was all I needed. I knew what I had to do and, full of faith, responded, 'I'll make it.'

From one instance to the next, it was like a veil had been lifted. I could see clearly. Suddenly everything made sense. My greatest fear was to not belong. I was desperate to be part of the Australian national team. It was not so much of a self-esteem issue but one of finding a home. Mick's encouraging words made me feel so good. For once, I didn't feel rejected but welcomed to a team who wanted me on board.

In the last three hours, I would do anything to make it. Mick's earlier encouragement to drop my ego had a similar effect — less because it was the right thing to say and more because it was he who said it. The playful interaction between Matt and I, running away and getting chased, was equally helpful. All of those instances had made the difference.

While the sun was coming up over Adelaide, my mind took me back to Perth and to wanting to run away during the course, because I'd been asked to draw a picture. This was the missing piece of the puzzle I couldn't figure out at the time — in that situation, I'd also been run by my fear of not belonging. If I wasn't capable of a decent drawing, I believed I wouldn't be accepted. I'd be excluded from the group.

But I had a protection mechanism of running away before I got thrown out. Seeing I preferred distance in uncomfortable situations and highly valued staying in control, this was not a surprising impulse. Of course, with the clarity of daylight, my tantrum looked like an irrational response. I was never facing any real risk of being excluded. But that wasn't how brains worked. Subconscious beliefs could be overpowering and feel real.

As I thought about the origins of this deep-rooted fear, I completed another lap and passed my support crew. Martin interrupted my introspective investigations and called out to remind me no time could be wasted. According to his calculations, I wasn't fast enough. If any skill were to come in handy right now, it was my ability to reach a set goal. Even my own exhaustion couldn't prevent me from realising how nervous Martin had become. The A-qualifier was slipping away, and I had to step up and run faster. Only, I had nothing left. Getting stressed about it was the worst thing I could do now. I had to trust myself. To avoid any further toilet breaks, I reduced my fluid intake, acknowledging I would have to hold on to my discomfort until after the run. Anybody following my progress was biting their nails.

With one hour to go, it didn't look good, and Martin wanted to see a final surge in pace à la Delirious. I would have loved to, but I couldn't. I was giving everything I had and could not run any quicker. I counted down the minutes, feeling like I was in a bad dream, running without making up any ground. The last few laps got crazy. Spectators had returned and were making a hell of a noise. Finally, the finish horn tooted and it was over. I almost collapsed. My own rough calculations told me I had just done it. But could I trust the maths of a sleep-deprived, exhausted runner? I had to wait for the official measurement of the partial lap I had finished on. Every metre counted, and I needed each single one of them.

Rebecca ran towards me and helped me stay upright. This was the toughest race I had ever done. Even 68 hours of running over trails had not been this exhausting. The race director approached us with his measurement wheel and brought the great news: 240 kilometres and 341 metres. That was 0.1 per cent above the required target. We had pulled off an A-qualifier and, together with Matt, who had run almost 13 kilometres further, I would travel to the world championships in France.

FACING GRIM PREDICTIONS

The crucial difference from Christchurch was that I had embraced the painful emotions. My ego had me in its grip but I had, eventually, managed to switch off my autopilot. I chose my destiny. This achievement had the names of two amazing mentors written next to it: Martin and Lisa. I wouldn't have been capable of pulling off this race without their guidance, and without their understanding of how to overcome the limitations of my mind. Their mentorship had unlocked a 13 per cent performance improvement since my previous 24-hour race — and all in just over a year.

That evening, Martin, Rebecca and I celebrated our team achievement in the local pub. Although it was only a few hundred metres from our accommodation, we had to take the rental car. My legs were so sore, I hardly managed to walk to the car. All three of us were content and excited that we would jointly travel to France soon. I thanked my crew for sacrificing their sleep and keeping me on track. That must have been the prompt Martin had been waiting for to share some feedback with me: while the race result was something I should be proud of, how I had treated my crew was unacceptable. My interactions with him and Rebecca had been far from world class, and I'd need to rethink my approach. Knocking bottles out of Rebecca's hand wasn't necessary and wouldn't happen if I was more present and cheerful. The version of me he'd seen over the last 24 hours wasn't up to the standard required for world championships.

Hearing those harsh words was painful. I had been on a high till Martin pulled me back to earth. I suppressed my first impulse to keep up the impression of being flawless. Instead of denying any need for improvement, I was going to own the criticism. I got the message.

The situation reminded me of my qualification race in Christchurch when I had a go at Rebecca because she hadn't given me the right coloured drink bottle. How embarrassing that I still hadn't learned my lesson to be respectful to my support team. How easy was it to justify my actions by pointing to the result or blaming it on the immense pressure? I'd underestimated its negative impact on the wider team, and the costs were too high. I had observed this common pattern in others, condemning their behaviour in many boardroom meetings. By holding a mirror in front of me, Martin reminded me that transformation had to start with myself. And this was much more confronting than pointing out other people's shortcomings.

The open question was around how much energy I'd wasted in this race. Maybe a different approach could lead to new, unknown possibilities. So much more was possible. Martin was clear: my ego wasn't welcome to travel with the team to France. No question, a different Kay needed to rock up at the world championships.

I was at the edge of another right turn, integrating demons from the past. The emotional cost of keeping my reactive patterns alive was just too high. I had seen that a lot of great qualities and strengths originated in those patterns. Now, however, was the time to free those strengths from their reactive structure. What once had served me was now limiting me. If I could expand my consciousness, the sky was the limit. More right turns would get me there.

The good news was that it was up to me. The bad news was that I was short on time. I was facing three demanding situations simultaneously: to transform at work, to get accredited for my future career and to prepare for the world championships. The pressure wasn't easing off.

I didn't sleep well after the race. As per usual, I woke up in a puddle of sweat in the middle of the night. Also, my body was full of aches and pains. We got up early to fly back home and, sitting in the plane flying high over the clouds, I wondered where my fear of not belonging originated from. Typically, these kinds of fears were relicts from early childhood memories. I couldn't remember any particular instance from that far in the past, but instead an episode from my last year at high school popped up.

A few days before my final oral exam, I had a major blow-up with my mother, because I'd been too self-absorbed to organise a considered Mother's Day present. I was consumed by my final exams and preparing for my first-ever marathon. My idea of painting the ugly garden door as a present didn't resonate at all with Mum and instead brought a frosty climate into our house. Another ice age seemed to have come over us. After a short and sharp emotional eruption, full of anger and self-righteousness, my mother stopped talking to me for days.

I had to ignore the cold climate and concentrate on graduating from school. When I came home from the final exam with the news that I'd not only been given full marks but also snatched the best high school diploma of the entire year, my mother's heart opened again. At the time it happened, I could not see what I recognised now for the first time. When I stuffed up, I was on my own. Perfect results, on the flipside, had the power to heal any wounds. Output was the prerequisite for being worthy. I had to get somewhere to be somebody.

The plane landed hard, and my contemplations were put on hold. The more urgent and practical concern was how to make it to the luggage belt in some sort of reasonable time. I could barely walk, and we feared the suitcases would be long gone. Well and truly, I had given everything I had in the race. Our concerns disappeared when one of the beeping electro carts drove past in the long airport corridor and picked up Rebecca and me. Sitting on the cart, I had time to check my emails and saw an email from my mother in Germany. We must have been thinking of each other at the same time. Her message included a response to a short race update I'd sent the night before and, overall, was disturbing.

Mum didn't congratulate me, or even acknowledge the extraordinary effort of the race. Not in the slightest was she interested in me running at the world championships. Success had always been paramount to her, but apparently the rules of the game were about to change again. I got frustrated because, again, I could see the ever-repeating pattern that my mum became erratic when I was in a relationship, although she would deny it. With one of my first girlfriends, she had introduced a curfew by which I had to be home; with another partner, my monthly allowance was cancelled. The timing of the stories resurfacing from my childhood felt like more than a coincidence. I wondered what they wanted to teach me about myself.

The email was a weird accumulation of questions — why was I doing what I was doing, and why did I expect her recognition? In the past, my mother had encouraged my inner journey through running.

Now she urged me to recognise that I was lost in life. I couldn't figure out my mother's motives this time for withholding her warmth, but I was disappointed to see that even now, when I was grown-up and independent, she didn't accept how I was leading my life. To her, I was still the little boy she, the grown-up, couldn't trust. I rarely had major disagreements with my mother, but when they happened, I was often annoyed at her passive-aggressive behaviour, always hinting but never articulating precisely what the issue was. Most alarming was a part of the email that read almost like an oracle of what lay ahead: 'Flights of fancy must be grounded. He who flies high falls deep, sometimes very deep.'

My mother was alluding to Icarus who, in Greek mythology, flew too close to the sun with disastrous results. In the story, Icarus's father gives him wings he has made, held together by wax, and warns him about flying too close to the sun. Icarus ignores these warnings and, as he flies high in the sky, the wax melts, the wings fall apart and he crashes to his death.

Did my mother want to take away my wings to protect me? She had always loved me more than anything, had shielded me from my father as much as she could and ensured I stayed strong. Yet, this message didn't come across as protection. To me, it was a manifestation of fear. Fear of a mother who was afraid of losing her child, of being left behind.

I'd worked hard on myself for years to trade in my fears for the pursuit of purpose. Now, I was being confronted with her fears. The question it sparked was how our fears were related. I had never questioned my mother's role in the genesis of my own fears.

SELF CHECK-IN

- In what circumstances do you become caught in your own drama and react disproportionally?

- Can you identify some of the beliefs that hold you back in life?

CHAPTER 15

TURNING RIGHT TO GET READY FOR THE WORLDS

> *When he liberates that strength from its reactive structure ... [he] is no longer in a compulsive relationship to that strength—offering it in exchange for validation and security.*
>
> —Robert Anderson

I woke up before the alarm. It wasn't completely dark anymore, and sunshine leaked through the curtains. A Saturday morning, and I wished I didn't have to leave the comfort of the warm bed. I was tired from work, interstate travels, studying for the final week of accreditation in Perth and preparing for the world championships. There just weren't enough hours in the day. The irony of my situation was that, just at the time when I officially became part of the Australian national team, running was no longer my highest priority in life. I couldn't give it my undivided attention, because my agenda had been taken over by trying to bring the magic to work.

Reducing the race in Adelaide to its success component would have been easy. I'd stepped up to be one of the top ultra runners in Australia. But I could feel that this achievement was secondary. Much more important was that I was familiarising myself with this new world, the magical world — the world where anything was possible. In this magical world, the focus of attention wasn't dollars, kilometres or minutes. It was very different from the world I'd grown up in, and it had taken me years to figure out its rules. What mattered most was the energy and the intent one brought to every moment. In this new territory, great achievements morphed into extraordinary experiences, leading to personal growth and joy.

Repeatedly, I'd accessed this magical world through running. What was missing, though, was being able to access it at work and share my experience with others. I could feel that now my time had come to step up and take businesses, teams and individuals on the journey to also benefit from that magical world. I had learned that the entry pass to this world was to raise consciousness — and to do that, one had to turn right.

Both Lisa and Martin had — in their own way — pointed out that in the pursuit of my dreams at work, in running, and even in life in general, I couldn't take my ego with me. They asked me to operate across the different levels of consciousness, showing vulnerability and courage, pursuing meaning and trusting the power of cooperating. The goalposts, the measures of what mattered, had not just shifted; pursuing the magic was a completely different game. To unleash something extraordinary within me, I had to restructure my inner landscape. How I related to the present moment was more crucial than what I achieved. My next growth edge wasn't *doing* but *being*.

The need to belong and perform was holding me back, and my old patterns of protecting and controlling would keep me stuck and increasingly frustrated, until I fully transformed the underlying limiting beliefs. The race in Adelaide had indicated that new, unknown possibilities would emerge once I released my strengths — such as challenging the status quo and trusting my intuition — from their fear-based reactive structures.

RUNNING FROM THE HEART

The most important practice I could do at the beginning of these busy days was to meditate. Had I cut out the daily meditation sessions in the past months, I would have saved time. I would also have sacrificed the most important hour of my day. I practised slowing down in an environment that tempted me to accelerate.

I needed to break the anxiety of all the thoughts reeling through my mind. I got up and, after a short meditation, headed to the training camp Martin had organised. There, I finally met all the other Australian runners in the national team. Our nickname was 'the Emus' — the Australian men's rugby union team were the Wallabies, the women's netball team were the Diamonds, and we, we were the Emus. It would be a weekend to meet, bond and strengthen our team culture. With 15 runners — six females and nine males — ours was the biggest Australian team ever selected for its ability to shine on the big stage. And I was one of the few newbies on the team.

I could sense a rising feeling of inadequacy. Several of our extremely strong team had already run at the world championships when Australia claimed the team silver medal. One member, Barry Loveday, was the all-time second-fastest Australian over the 24-hour format, with only the legendary Yiannis Kouros faster than him. Yiannis even held the world record with an astonishing track distance of 303.506 kilometres in 24 hours. Nobody on the world horizon even got close to that mark. As I had seen in the *Yiannis Kouros — Forever running* documentary, he was a master in taking over his body with his mind. It was no surprise that Yiannis had seen the transcendence of self as the backbone of his performances. I longed to take a page out of his book.

Martin described us as the best Australian team he'd seen. Certainly, a portion of luck would be involved, because we didn't know how the other nations would perform. However, Martin thought that if we managed to achieve consistently great totals, the podium was within reach. The prospect of any of us standing on that podium receiving a medal was thrilling. And with that ambition came immense responsibility for each of us.

The team's dreams and the attendant pressure brought back a memory of being at boarding school in Scotland as a 16 year old. The boarders lived in different houses, which regularly competed against each other at various disciplines. In the annual House Music competition, points were awarded for three performances: a choir, an orchestra and a solo. My team had high hopes of winning and, eager to contribute, I volunteered to play the solo piano piece. I loved Robert Schumann's 'Dreaming' from his famous suite *Scenes from Childhood*. I'd played it in public several times before, and I was delighted I could contribute when we were one of the favourites for the trophy.

As I sat down at the piano on the huge stage, with the entire school present, hundreds of eyes were staring at me. I felt tiny. I was nervous, and my hands shook wildly. I couldn't calm down. I was so distressed I couldn't connect to the piano. Any other day, I could have played with my eyes shut. That day, I failed miserably.

Everybody heard the wrong tones coming out of the instrument. Desperate to put everybody out of their misery, first and foremost myself, I rushed through the embarrassing performance. It was as if this music competition was really about getting to the end of the piece in record time. All I wanted was to hide in shame, preferably deep in the ground. Even the huge stage wasn't big enough for me to get lost in. I stuffed up in front of everybody, and received the fewest points out of all performances that year.

For days, I could not look any of the boys from my house in the eyes. I'd let my team down — badly. I'd played the piano since primary school. That day, however, would turn out to be my farewell performance to my music career.

Now, decades later, I faced the risk of history repeating itself. I might be older, might have grown, but so had the stakes. Instead of representing a group at school, I'd been selected to represent the entire country. It wasn't the possibility of failure I was afraid of, but the possibility of being ashamed.

While messing things up so badly was painful, I had come to terms with failure being an integral part of challenging myself. At the championships, I was afraid of something much more powerful than failing. I was terrified of shame. The cold, rough pain that had overtaken me in Perth when asked to draw a picture was something I never wanted to feel again. I never again wanted to not feel worthy of being a member of the group. I knew the feeling of not belonging, all too well. I understood what it felt like to not have a home.

As a kid, I'd felt the cold horror of being ashamed — a lot. Ashamed of the neighbours hearing my father's rage through the open windows — and even when windows were closed, such was the force of his maniacal ranting. Ashamed of him losing control in front of strangers in public places. (Many routine supermarket trips ended with an outburst from him.) Ashamed when he shouted at a friend of mine who happened to be at my house to play. Ashamed of the possibility somebody would find out that my father beat me. Ashamed when it happened, and he chased me down the stairs when my mother's best friends were visiting, witnessing. My guilt about my father's behaviour made no sense, and it confused me a great deal. I knew, rationally, it had nothing to do with me; it was his inability to regulate his temper. But that was not what it felt like when I was a kid. All I'd wanted to do was disappear into the ground.

The ultimate shame, though, had nothing to do with my father; this was about my behaviour. Until the age of 13, to my shame, I had regularly wet the bed at night. It only stopped shortly after the embarrassing incident at the school camp.

The word 'shame' was the answer to one of Martin's first questions to me. What was I running away from? The answer came spontaneously, and it had to do with recognising and trying to escape the pain of my childhood. It explained everything I was dealing with — my fear of vulnerability, my urge for control, my high success rate in anything I touched, and my lack of trust in myself and others. As a kid, I believed I had to be flawless in any activity to secure my spot. Love was never generously shared in our household, either from my father or my mother. Love had to be earned. Although I had grown up, emotionally, I still carried that burdensome belief like a shadow. Love was conditional. It was running my life, invisibly.

I had lost track that I was with the Australian national team, listening to an important lecture from our coach. Martin must have noticed that I wasn't present. He mentioned this in the group and asked me to focus on the workshop. The theme had progressed from team goals to values and mindset. Nobody underestimated how much the race required us to dig deep. That was what an elite level demanded.

Yet Martin put an unexpected spin on our approach. He did not need us to commit to being mentally tough. Toughening up and armouring ourselves further was unnecessary; instead, we had to let go and be vulnerable. He encouraged us to run with not only guts but also grace and gratitude. Great performances happened when we were running from our heart. We should soak in the atmosphere and surrender to the race, get out of our minds and access a state of being, with no expectations. We should run out of love, not fear.

Asking us to run from the heart wasn't usual coaching talk. Martin addressed the group and, in an emotional speech, talked of the world he pictured. It was a realm where joy and gratitude replaced the more common goals of competitiveness and success. That way we would create a space that allowed quantum jumps in its expansiveness. I looked around the room for reactions and saw that Martin's words resonated. He continued and added that probably many of us weren't primarily fascinated by ultra distance running because we were good at it, but because we sensed that, at its core, it was about understanding the meaning of life. Deep down, I knew what he was referring to.

My takeaway from the training camp was that there was no need to fear failure. The more vicious enemy we might face was our fear of greatness. I appreciated that nobody placed expectations on me, given that I was new on the team — nobody apart from Martin, who had already told me that I was capable of so much more. According to him, I just needed to release what was within me. How much more would I be capable of without my old stories holding me back? The world championships were the perfect opportunity to find out.

WORRYING AT NIGHT

Soon after the training camp, I headed for a second time to Perth, seeking to pass all required tests for the accreditation in executive coaching. For a week, we were evaluated on modules we were expected to be au fait with by then. Simultaneously, the second part of the training program served our development and deepened our personal transformational journey. My ability to facilitate business transformation and help leaders progress with their development work depended on my own maturation as a leader. By now, I could see how my reactive patterns were holding me back when trying to upgrade the culture of my team. When triggered, I defaulted to problem solving, emotionally distanced myself, and exerted control to try to ensure favourable outcomes. Relationships suffered as a consequence of me focusing on tasks. To transform my team, I had to overcome these reactive patterns. The same was essential to becoming a credible coach and facilitator of transformation.

The second day in Perth had ended, and I was frustrated. Intellectually, I could see what was happening. I even recognised the 'mother of all fears' driving my habits and patterns: the fear of not belonging. I strongly identified with results, because these were my vehicle to find a home and be connected. I defined myself externally and, therefore, was strongly affected by others' impressions of me, as well as my own fears. I desperately wanted to make the shift away from needing external validation to defining myself from within. But my entire identity was at stake. Who was I without the results that guaranteed me acceptance?

What frustrated me, however, was that understanding didn't help me in the slightest. My intellect and impatience got in the way of finding a resolution to my frustration. I was exhausted from the intense days and collapsed into bed for much-needed recovery. The best I could do was to get some decent sleep to be fit for the next day of evaluations.

At 11:45 pm I was wide awake again. After barely any sleep, I was worried. I worried about accreditation, about the world championships and about getting back to sleep. Instead of continuing my worries, I got out of bed, put on my running clothes and entered the black night. It was witching hour. Tuesday was about to conclude and hump day had not yet begun. Yet, going for runs in the middle of the night was uplifting, with something intriguing about them.

Apart from a police car patrolling the area, the streets were deserted. While Perth was dreaming, I was running along the Indian Ocean, listening intently for what the crashing surf had to tell. My mind took me to Adelaide, remembering how Mick had made all the difference by calling out that he wanted me on the national team. Driven by the determination to represent Australia, I secured an A-qualifier by the narrowest margin. Next, I heard my mother, as if she were present. Her questions were harsh. 'Why do you want to represent Australia? When you lived in Spain, you wanted to be Spanish. Now, you think you are an Aussie. Ha, ha; you are none of them.' I sensed my heart rate increasing. The line between memories and imagination had blurred. I reminded myself to refocus on the sound of the ocean.

A few instances later, my inner eye was drawn to my parents' kitchen table. It was the old furniture we'd had in the '80s, the time when I went to primary school. As per most days at lunch, the conversation revolved around the tough morning my mother was having at school. (In Germany, school starts earlier and finishes at lunchtime.) She was a school teacher and invariably brought home unresolved conflicts with misbehaving students, their arrogant parents or her tedious colleagues. Her solution was to teach people a lesson. Rebellious students received worse marks than they deserved and colleagues had better watch their backs. I could conjure her usual statement: 'Wait until they pass by my garden gate. Then, I'll get them back.' While my father reacted to conflict by becoming aggressive, my mother's solution was to get into a position of power and punish people when they least expected it.

Conversations with my mother became an almost daily lecture, reminding me who I had to be in order to deserve her love. The extremes of her reactivity were visible after the rare visits of my mother's sister and mother, my aunty and granny. As regular as clockwork, these gatherings always ended in blow-ups. Typically, my mum would then punish my aunty and granny by not speaking to them for months, cutting us off from the rest of the family. The broken family bonds healed slowly, and would be ripped open again shortly after healing anyway.

I became masterful at avoiding my mum's passive-aggressive behaviour. My mother's impulses were barely more predictable than those of my dad, but at least I'd figured out who I needed to be in order to not provoke her. Also, as I delivered to the high standards of her expectations, I managed to secure my standing as her favourite child. My sister was far too unorganised to be as lovable; those were the rules we all played by. I got into trouble rarely, and my punishment was my mother's cold, silent wrath. Those instances were painful, and it always seemed like an eternity before her warmth came back.

CONNECTING WITH THE HEART

As I was thinking this on my night run, I suddenly noticed how far from home I was. I'd run more than 20 kilometres along the coast. If I wanted to get any sleep before another big day, I had to turn around immediately. Running back towards my accommodation, I no longer had to battle a headwind. Almost effortlessly, I glided along the coastline so I could get a few hours' sleep.

I'd found the last piece of the puzzle. My fear of not belonging didn't have its origin in my relationship with my father but with my mother. My father's overt aggression seemed the more obvious, and so had drawn all my attention. But it mainly served to help me stay blind to the conditional love my mother had on offer.

I was dependent on my mother's love, because I could never rely on anything like it from my father. She was my role model and, as a consequence, I had become more like her. Already in primary school, I'd taken on her ways of dealing with conflict. When I had a major argument with my best friend Laura that summer day, I settled my anger by kicking her out of my life and never talking to her again. My mother had done a fantastic job of preventing me becoming like my aggressive father. However, instead of Dad's open rage, I'd adopted Mum's passive-aggressiveness.

I must have been terrified that not performing to her expectations would leave me abandoned. It was an incalculable risk, and one too big to take. Surely, I could secure her love through becoming like her? She successfully role-modelled protecting herself, and so I armoured my heart and hid within my intellect. I was carrying old beliefs — 'I'm on my own', 'The world is hostile', 'I can't trust anyone', 'I have to be successful'. I learned to be independent, solve the most difficult problems and become successful at anything I tackled. The downsides were control, mistrust and lack of empathy.

I'd developed highly effective coping mechanisms to deal with my environment at home. From my father's treatment of me, I realised that staying small was dangerous. I learned that everybody out there wanted to get me, so I learned to be tough. Particularly memorable was the instance in my late adolescence when I finally stood up for my mother and myself and put an end to my father's aggressions. From then onwards, I was no longer his victim, and I managed to propel myself forward and escape to a more rewarding life. While that belief brought success, the price it demanded was exhaustion, frustration and emptiness.

My mother taught me that wanting to be loved was not safe. Everything in human dynamics and connection had its price, and love's price — vulnerability — was too steep. Passive-aggressive repercussions, resulting in isolation, were the punishment for overstepping the narrow boundaries. In my solitude, I developed a detached, observing mind, with a reputation for independence. Surrounded by closed hearts while growing up, I had never learned how to open mine. Distancing myself by escaping into my thinking mind and avoiding feeling emotions made it difficult to trust anybody, let alone love them.

Now I sensed that the time was ripe to move on from my childhood stories. The crucial question was who did I want to be now? What new values were emerging that wanted to be lived more fully? I embraced the silence in between the waves. I could feel that I was onto something big. Suddenly, I imagined my mother and my father in front of me, both looking at me calmly. My mother spoke. 'You belong to us. You always have. We love you.' My father nodded, and I could feel tears of joy welling up. Unconditional love at last.

The answer to my feelings of rejection, the pain of not belonging was, I now understood, compassion — compassion for my parents, compassion for others and compassion for myself. It was the antidote to my reactivity. Demonising either of my parents was inappropriate and would keep me stuck. They had their own childhood wounds but, no doubt, always loved me. It was not about forgetting anything or pushing the pain away. Things were shifting, and I could forgive all of us without holding a grudge.

When I reviewed the old stories, looking at them in a different light, their meaning changed. My parents' intention was never to harm me. They did the best they could with the tools they had. Focusing on the aggressive side of my father was lopsided and meant I ignored his caring side. He was as crucial to who I became as my mother had been. I had developed many strengths to counteract his actions, and his strong determination had also become my salvation.

When my mother was pregnant with me, I hid in her womb for as long as I could. Perhaps I was trying to avoid seeing light on this earth. Two weeks after my due date, there was still no sign of me. At the time, we lived in Romania, a socialist country, and rules governing a first-time pregnancy dictated that the doctor in charge wouldn't perform a caesarean section, even for such an overdue pregnancy. (Two weeks is the maximum time doctors and midwives usually allow a pregnancy to be overdue.) My father, impatient and mostly worried, worked out a way to bribe the doctor. He bought two bottles of vodka on the Saturday, and they seem to have done the trick because, before sunrise on Sunday, I was delivered via surgery. To everyone's shock, the umbilical cord was wrapped around my neck, and it's likely that I would not have survived a natural birth. Without Dad, I could have been disabled, if not dead.

After three hours of running, I arrived back at my accommodation. I'd run only a few hundred metres short of a complete marathon. I stopped my watch, contently calling it a night. Nothing more was needed. No fear would run me anymore; not even the fear of missing out on a marathon because of some lousy few hundred metres. In those three hours, I'd gained so many valuable insights about myself. It was time to allow the old stories that I'd told myself to drop away. No longer would I constrain myself by what happened when I was a kid, and nor would I let somebody else, even people as central as my parents, define who I had to be. I would, from then on, be the author of my life.

Back in bed after a shower, despite being tired, even exhausted, I couldn't sleep. The excitement kept me awake. For the first time in my life, I had run from the heart. I had truly grasped what Martin meant when he had brought our attention to that term. Now I'd experienced what it was like; I'd felt the power it had.

All day, I radiated energy in spite of being very sleep deprived after excessively exercising at night. It was remarkable what could happen when I didn't invest all my effort in unnecessary discipline and willpower. All the participants finished the transformational week in Perth with the accreditation in our pockets. 'From the heart' was now the path forward, not only for the world championships but also for my leadership development. What I had been missing was a focus on relationships, compassion and, first and foremost, unconditional love. Focusing on tasks had gotten me far; focusing on relationships could unlock a whole new level.

The following weeks flew past. At the end of October, Rebecca and I landed in Toulouse and had a few days to acclimatise before the big race in the nearby city of Albi. We did some sightseeing and, happily, were able to meet my German uncle who was there to cheer me on. Kurt had been very excited and said he wasn't going to miss the opportunity to be part of the biggest event in my life.

On the day before the race, we had a full schedule: a series of team briefings, the official opening ceremony for all teams, inspection of the crewing tent and race loop and doing whatever else we needed to get race-ready. I'd watched many large and impressive opening ceremonies of international events on TV, and now, though I couldn't believe it, I was part of one myself. Me, in the middle of around 400 athletes and their support crews as we took over the streets of Albi. It was like a massive school camp, only this time I didn't feel like an outsider.

On race morning, I woke up well before the alarm. The race would give me a meaningful indication of the extent to which I'd left my old self behind. We hadn't come to collect souvenirs; we had come to run from the heart.

SELF CHECK-IN

- What are you running away from?
- What causes do you believe in? Why are they so important to you?
- What is the biggest challenge you would like to overcome at the moment?

CHAPTER 16

TURNING RIGHT WITH THE REST OF THE WORLD

When the heart opens a little, you start to have intuition; and when it opens even further, you get inspiration ... When the heart is completely open, it can receive divine revelation.

—John Demartini, 2002

I was at the start line, surrounded by the best runners in the world, waiting for the gun to go off. I was proudly wearing the Australian uniform and soaking up the exciting atmosphere. We were expecting a hot autumn day with no cloud cover whatsoever. I was reminded of the tough race conditions in Wuhan, where many athletes did not finish. Our 1.5-kilometre loop started on the tartan track of the athletics stadium and led us around the sporting complex. Next to me was Camille Herron from the United States, who had announced her target was to smash the women's world record. I was unlikely to write history myself, but I was confident that everything would work out nicely. My race intention was to connect and trust myself.

IMMERSING IN THE MYSTERY OF THE WORLDS

Seconds later, my confidence took a hit. Just before the start gun went off, my GPS watch connected to the satellite. I remembered having switched off that functionality, because allowing it meant the battery would die well before the end of the race. Something had gone wrong. Bang! The start gun announced a mad rush around the first bend. I had no time to fix the issue; we were all on our way. Runners left, right and centre were passing me, while I had my eyes on my watch.

For about 30 minutes I multitasked. Still clicking buttons on my watch, I also searched for rhythm and the appropriate pace. Every time I thought I had figured it out, the GPS function came back on again. Ironically, I was suffering from too much connectivity.

To my surprise, the situation didn't upset me. I was fully present and just curious why it didn't switch off. I remembered Gavin's advice in Christchurch: drop the watch and just run. To hell with the technology. This early curve ball was not going to affect my race. I was not going to let my fear of not being in control run me. This was an invite to trust my intuition.

I turned off the watch completely and knew, then, the distraction had been a blessing in disguise. I probably needed the chaos so that I'd surrender to the present moment. Had everything been perfect from the beginning, I might have gone on autopilot, which had its own risks. Instead, I chose the route of less thinking, less worrying and more trusting in my intuition. Anyway, we were shown our splits and position on the oversized stadium screen every lap. All I had to do was run and regularly interrupt that with strategic walking breaks.

I was embracing Martin's encouraging words from our training camp — run with gratitude. I was grateful to wear the green and gold

Australian outfit and was most appreciative of all the highs and lows that had gotten me here. Without the pains of Christchurch, I might not have found resolution for a faulty watch. I had learned how to navigate without a tracking device. With trust alone, I would find my way.

My past challenges invariably shaped me to become who I am, and I felt a healthy mix of pride and humility. I had worked hard to get here, and now I was going to enjoy the fruits of my labour. Every time I passed the Australian tent, I got a massive cheer. I returned the favour by having some fun with the crew. The same happened on the course each time I bumped into teammates. Even my interactions with many international runners were uplifting. I met plenty of familiar faces from previous races. Although I was a newbie at this level, I did not feel like a stranger. This was where I belonged. It was a very different experience from Adelaide.

I must have gotten carried away with my enthusiasm. After an hour, Martin held up a sign with the unambiguous message to reduce our speed. The heat was building up, and smart race tactics would pay off. I followed the instruction, yet noticed that most other runners seemed to be less concerned. Out of 200 male competitors, I dropped to 102nd position — one of the slowest Aussie runners. After experiencing the high did-not-finish rate at the elite race in China, however, I was very comfortable trusting this conservative strategy. Just because I was surrounded by elite runners did not mean that everybody was 'running like a wise woman'.

At no point in the race was I close to boredom. I was fully present and felt more like a witness observing the race unfold. And a lot of exciting action kept me entertained. Camille was setting a ridiculous speed in the pursuit of her own world record. She lapped me every

45 minutes — until the 'poo incident'. The afternoon sun was burning down on us when, once again, Camille rushed past. I noticed that her shorts were not clean anymore, and realised her digestion was out of control. Next time, I could smell her before I saw her. She was a mess. Yet, she was on a mission and showed no sign of taking a break to put on clean shorts or even give her legs a wipe.

For a moment, I felt ashamed for her. As a kid, I had been terrified that people would discover I wet my bed at night. Pooing oneself during bright daylight in front of the entire world was a completely different ballgame. It seemed incomprehensible to me that Camille chose to ignore the embarrassment. Didn't she want to uphold her dignity? Yet, I realised it was not for me to judge. My brief self-righteousness was no better than the reactions I had always feared from others, in the terrifying scenario of them uncovering my secret. I did not need to project my relationship with shame onto her. Compassion was more appropriate than condemnation.

Maybe that was what the other kids had done when I'd woken up in a wet bed during school camp. For weeks and months, I had been afraid to face the ultimate embarrassment. It felt like an eternity before I was confident that I had guarded my secret. I'd been wrong. The boys had known all along. Years later, my best friend told me what had happened.

I had been the first boy to fall asleep in the dormitory. Therefore, I was the prime target for a practical joke, and the other kids dipped my hands into containers with warm water. The well-known reaction to that stimulus was that I would wee myself — and I did not disappoint. I still could not comprehend why they went through all that effort to then keep it to themselves. Maybe it was compassion. Now it was my turn to pass that on to Camille.

I didn't wish her — or anyone, for that matter — to go through such an embarrassing situation. While Camille radiated pure determination, I could rest assured a fragile human side resided underneath the chase for a world record. She was a lovely lady, and I felt sorry for what had happened. The runner in me was also concerned that her digestive issues would cost her a new world record. We had more than 12 hours to go, and Camille no longer lapped me. Rumours after the race reported that she put on clean clothes shortly after, due to an intervention from race officials. At first, the US team resisted calling her in, but some fine-print rule stated that runners' uniforms had to be clean.

The best I could do was concentrate on my own race. By the time night spread its cloak over Albi, I was one of the strongest runners in the field. I had learned to make the night my friend, and it was my time to shine. No more ice bandanas were required to keep me cool. Running in the surreal floodlight of the sporting complex, I gradually climbed up the classification. As expected, the early quick pace took its toll on a lot of runners. Many started walking; some appeared so dour they could have been on a long death march. The prevailing strategy was to walk once tired. I did the opposite; I walked from the beginning in order not to get tired. It had payed off. Now, I was ploughing through the field. I was curious how far my legs would carry me before getting tired but, for the moment, I was flying.

CLAIMING MY PLACE

After midnight, the leader board puzzled me. Although I had regularly overtaken people, I had dropped a position. It did not make sense and looked like a lap had not been counted. In spite of my lack of sleep, I backed my judgement. Not being able to rely on my watch was one thing. Dealing with an untrustworthy timing system was unacceptable at world championships. I got angry.

I could sense a similar self-righteousness arising as I had felt during the poo incident. I was running well, because I wasn't thinking. Getting upset and moving into problem-solving mode had the potential to destroy my race. But I wasn't going to accept anybody stealing laps off me.

When I next passed the Australian tent, I called out to Rebecca to ask Martin to investigate the matter. I had not thought this through but intuitively chosen to drop control. We were one team, and neither I nor Rebecca had the capacity to deal with this matter. To get it off my mind, I trusted my team and sought collaboration. Martin was experienced in timing matters and dealing with race officials. It was a question of balance: making things happen or letting things happen. Whatever he would achieve on my behalf, I was going to accept.

I instantly felt better and kept running freely. Soon after, I saw Martin at the timing tent. Within half an hour, my running total was reflecting the correct number of laps. I was grateful for his support and content that I had not been feeding my negative thoughts and getting stuck. A downwards spiral could easily have left me in a dark mental spot, where I did not want to end up. The incident confirmed that I could trust my intuition and find adequate solutions without having to think. It gave me another boost, propelling me towards sunrise and the last few hours of running.

No longer was I worried about the classification. I was in a deep meditative state of pure awareness and joy, beyond any concerns. My creativity levels where heightened, and I could rely on my intuition.

The few loyal spectators who had stayed overnight gave me a lot of energy. Even my uncle sacrificed his sleep and kept cheering me on. Every lap, the playful interactions with Rebecca and the rest of the Australian crew were reinvigorating me. I was in a state of pure performance and fully present. No battles with my ego and full focus. My body was calm, and I felt not a single muscle doing any unnecessary shifts. When a muscle was not required, it relaxed, which made running and walking light and smooth.

This was 'running from the heart' at its best. I had finally dropped my usual judgements about how the world should be. I was aligned with the laws of nature and, for once, not opposed to them, because I accepted everything as it was. As a consequence, I was in a vulnerable state. The paradox was that the vulnerability made me invincible. I felt no fear. I was just present in the middle of the mystery. I was in a state beyond what my intellectual mind could ever grasp. Logically, it did not make sense, but I experienced it to be true. Trusting and being connected kept me safe.

The best I could do was not think at all. Because I was not thinking, no thoughts had any power over me. Mind and body were in harmony, and I kept up the rhythm I was in, while most people around me were deteriorating significantly. Unfortunately, most of my Australian teammates had slowed down, and all I could do was try to reenergise everybody I was passing.

I waited for my own fatigue to set in and to only be able to run significantly slower in the second half of the race. That was the usual pattern of the past and common for such long runs. Yet, what confused me was that the fade did not start. While I had run the first half only marginally faster than in Adelaide, I was now on track for a much bigger total. The different mindset was manifesting itself. At this pace, 250 kilometres was realistic, and potentially even more.

With daybreak, life came back to the course. We could smell fresh croissants being baked nearby. Runners who had withdrawn into their tents overnight were filling the track again. Those who had gone out too fast or become too tired to continue had taken a rest, while only those who kept going for the full 24 hours had a realistic chance at a top position. After a good night's sleep, returning spectators had the energy to carry us to the finish gun with their rowdy and welcome encouragements. It was peak traffic, and we still had enough time to influence who would receive medals. A crazy chase for some extra distance started between all teams.

The stadium announcer proclaimed that Camille Herron was just about to beat the female world record. Overnight, I'd barely crossed paths with her. We had been running at similar speeds at opposite sides of the track. Now, with the elation of setting a new world record, she stormed past me. I felt honoured to be part of such a historic moment. I tried to keep up with her, but she was gunning it. I increased my pace until I felt at breaking point.

SPREADING MY WINGS TO FLY

Felix, a top runner of the German national team, caught up with me and encouraged me to run with him. It was like hopping onto a plane and feeding off his momentum. The year prior, I'd had the privilege of witnessing him run a spectacular 24-hour race in Australia, totalling a mind-boggling 260 kilometres and still looking fresh in the final hours of the race. This time though, he had struggled throughout the night and stayed well below his possibilities. With only minutes of the race left, all the struggles were forgotten, and he took on the selfless challenge to get the best out of me. I tucked into his wind shade and followed his strides. By now, I could hardly speak, so heavy was my breathing. Walking breaks were relicts of the past; this was a race to the finish.

The sun flooded the course in glorious morning light, and we were chasing our long shadows. Felix must have done some quick calculations in his brain and shouted out to me, 'You can break 260 kilometres. Let's run faster and do it!' Fear grabbed me. Instantly. For the first time in the race, I was terrified. I didn't want to try anything I might fail at. My personal best was 240 kilometres and I was very happy with running significantly better than 250 kilometres. Without even knowing what mileage I was tracking towards, I responded, 'I can't do that. That's out of my league.' The bureaucrat was back, pushing the 'self-preservation' button.

For the second time in the race, I saw Gavin in front of my inner eye. He looked at me calmly and asked why I was limiting myself again. He was right. Why was I here? Not for magnificence but to surpass the limits of my mind. The result itself did not matter. What mattered was my state of mind. It was the bureaucrat who was afraid of new heights. His fear was to lose his wings when too close to the sun and crash. The tragedy appeared inevitable and just a matter of time. My mum's voice of reason was pulling me back to earth, protecting me from falling. The explorer did not know those fears. That was the fundamental difference between the two selves — one was indifferent to any altitude, the other was obsessed by height, yet suffered from vertigo. When the bureaucrat was in charge, the next fall was never far away. The game changer was letting the explorer take over.

A tempting inner voice whispered that nobody would see my weakness. Another voice countered it: hiding from my shadow by giving in to darkness would never work. I had to face it and be the light I wanted to see. It was my choice to follow the devil on my shoulder or listen to the angel.

I accelerated. I was here to give my best and, even more so, put an end to the old self-limiting story I kept telling myself. I had mastered GPS issues and missing laps, and even had fun with the team while I dropped my usual control. Why clip my wings in the dying minutes of the race? All I had to do was to back myself and run. The result would be whatever I was capable of. Maybe 260 kilometres, maybe less. I hung on to Felix for as long as I could. He left me for the last couple of laps to soak in the atmosphere on his own. That was fair enough; I was already deeply grateful for his unexpected help. With him taking off at an incredible speed, I also spread my wings to fly. *Look, Mum, I'm flying!*

My body was flooded with sensations. I was expansive, light, slightly tingly in my arms, connected within my body, held by the surroundings, buzzing in my head. I had a pleasant form of a headache and felt somewhat boundless. I was hovering through space. The experience went hand in hand with a quiet, spacious, empty, silent, present mind, which was not judging anything. It only acknowledged whatever I observed. My sense of self had vanished, and I could not tell who was moving my legs. The sense of inactivity was not passivity, but more of an effortless effort. Any action happened through leaning into uncertainty, almost relaxing into it.

A profound happiness emerged. It was the joy of the present moment. I experienced an immense amount of clarity, yet no questions required answering. All concepts and theoretical ideas had evaporated. No superfluous expectations got in the way. The weight of everyday life had been lifted from my shoulders to allow the unusual experience. As a consequence, everything fell into place. The very nature of the peak experience was beyond the logic and rules of life as I knew it. Yet, while it was happening, it was apparent that there was no mystery to it. This was much more than a fleeting emotion. It was a state of being. How great life could be when I left behind all self-protection and control.

The final five minutes were counted down, and I was sprinting. At no time in the race had I been this fast. I tried to finish as close to the Australian tent as possible. The reward would be less walking 'home' afterwards. I even passed the Australian tent and, only a few seconds later, the sound of the finish horn set an end to the race.

I let go of the marker I had been given so that the accurate total distance could be measured. At the same time every muscle in my body let go as well. Luckily, a kind member of the New Zealand team offered me a chair to sit on; I would have crashed, otherwise. I was in front of their tent, and Rebecca came to hug me and give me water and warm clothes. But first we took a photo of me — proof that I was there, sitting blissfully in my chair, smiling into the camera, holding up the Australian flag behind me. What a race.

What followed looked very much like a penguin parade. A flock of clumsy, flightless runners hobbled to the hotel buses. Despite so many of us being barely capable of walking, I was on cloud nine. Our Australian male team had finished in fifth spot, missing the podium. Yet, we had nothing to be unhappy about.

It had been a strong year with amazing results from other countries. To make the team podium next time, we would need to come back even stronger. And our women's team finished in a respectable 11th position. Each one of us had fought their own battle, and together we had supported each other to give our all.

I still couldn't believe what had happened. Martin brought me the great news that I'd finished 11th male, covering a distance of 259.67 kilometres. He had predicted that I could pull off such a run, when I had no reason to believe him, and when it had appeared impossible. I had barely reduced my speed in the second half and not only pulled off the biggest total of an Australian at any world championships but also in any 24-hour race outside of Australia. I got dizzy listening to the long list of statistics Martin was throwing at me.

The final one was that by 189 metres I had passed another amazing runner to secure the spot of all-time fourth-fastest Australian. Was Martin proud to be the co-author of that achievement? Perhaps there was, as well as pride, a sad part for him. My ranking meant that his dropped to fifth-fastest in the all-time ranking. But for me, though they were all great numbers, none could capture the essence of my run — I had run from my heart.

One of the other runners asked why I couldn't squeeze in another 330 metres to crack the 260-kilometre mark. I was content knowing that I had left nothing on the table. The next milestone was just another arbitrary one; it only appealed to my inner bureaucrat. I had experienced over and over again that no success whatsoever was enough to quench the ego's thirst. The secret of the previous 24 hours was that I had brought light to moments where darkness would have been the easier choice.

REFLECTING OVER BREAKFAST

When I opened my eyes, bright light was finding its way through the closed curtains. The sun was getting up, and so was I after a decent night's sleep. My towel and spare clothes were still folded up next to my bed. For the first time after a major race, the bed was dry, and I hadn't had feverish sweats in the middle of the night. When I got up, I noticed my ankles weren't even swollen. I could walk to the bathroom without having to propel myself, somehow using my arms as props. I wasn't dreaming. A missing toenail and a big blister confirmed it. This was a different world I had woken up in.

I wanted to test my legs further, so I slowly walked down three levels of stairs. My muscles were certainly complaining, but holding up and less stiff than expected. Downstairs, half of our team was already sitting around a big round table. My appetite was huge, and a generous breakfast buffet was waiting for us in the hotel restaurant. I tucked into fresh fruit, crunchy baguettes with cheese, divine croissants and a big mug of hot chocolate. I didn't need any more sports drinks, bananas, salted chips or instant mashed potatoes.

For the next hour, I was asked the same set of questions dozens of times: How was I feeling, and what was my secret? 'Elated' summed up my state of mind. I was still imbued with a strong sensation of having tapped into something immense. I felt a very real inner peace, which was neither deflated from the physical exhaustion nor inflated by the unexpected achievement of the race. I was even comfortably aware of its fleeting nature.

Explaining the quantum leap in my performance was more difficult, but not because I didn't understand. On the contrary, I was very clear, but I struggled to put the mystery into words anybody could understand. How could I convey something so liminal? A transformational shift had happened in my awareness. People focused on the jump in capability and, thus, missed the miracle — I had let go of an old identity that had become restrictive and had made room for a wider perspective. No longer was I trying to hush away problems and discomfort through external solutions; I had learned how to nurture that inner voice — my intuition. The much simpler answer I gave was that I had nailed the inner game.

Regardless, people kept asking about particular running sessions I'd done in my preparation. I didn't want to appear too esoteric, or even 'crazy', yet many of those who were asking me how I did it seemed to miss the essence of what I tried to convey. It was not a matter of *doing* but one of *being*. I did not focus on missing skills to unlock seemingly unsolvable dilemmas. I figured out who I needed to be.

Every adaptive challenge invited us to raise our consciousness and morph into somebody who could hold the increased tension this chaotic world brought with it. Too much of our effort was concentrated in developing horizontally. Everything changed through vertical development. My default had shifted from being motivated to avoid failure towards being motivated to succeed.

To get there was a matter of turning right. I had over-extended my strengths until they had become my weaknesses: relying on my intellect, maintaining emotional distance, believing that success was the solution for everything. To get me unstuck, I needed disruptions, needed to get challenged, deal with setbacks and overcome confusion. Those activities, those achievements, allowed me to embrace a new set of more powerful values: compassion, connection and trust. As a consequence, my model of who I was started to become fragile and gradually fell away.

My biggest surprise was how much energy I had freed up by letting go of my reactive patterns. The shift in consciousness had allowed me to run almost 20 kilometres further than in Adelaide three months prior. The new mindset was driven by purpose instead of fuelled by fears, and led to much better outcomes at a fraction of the energy required.

Already, this soon after the race, the temptation to just focus on the race result arose. I could recognise a repeating pattern. Letting go of my ego needs, such as the need for success or belonging, resulted in magical performances. Nonetheless, reducing the ego in order to become successful was never sustainable. The ego was too strong and cunning to not eventually claim any success. Given the slimmest opportunity, it resurrected and came back, strengthened by every achievement. Encountering the magic made no difference; it too could be claimed by the ego.

My inner bureaucrat's role was to defend me and keep me safe. His strength ebbed and flowed. I became more reactive when the inner tension seemed unbearable. Yet, treating the bureaucrat as my enemy and fighting him was bound to end in catastrophe. Divisiveness was his preferred weapon, and he had mastered it better than anybody else. So I was inadequately armed to turn against him. It was as if I could not escape the wide reach of his administration.

In the world champs, though, I had experienced that this conclusion wasn't true; my inner adventurer was getting stronger. What if the journey was not about rejecting the bureaucrat but about accepting him? While he wanted to take over in pressure situations, I brought awareness to those instances. The absurdity was that carefully listening to what he had to say, while staying present, took away all his power to undermine.

Maybe the purpose of all my challenges was not to attract more light? Maybe it was to get comfortable with the darkness? Why not accept all my selves as integral parts of my identity? Over the years, I had been desperate to accumulate a toolkit that better equipped me in dealing with the darkness. I was fighting an uphill battle. The ultimate prize that came from challenging myself by turning right was not more power. With rising consciousness, I could be in the presence of darkness without getting absorbed by it.

It became more apparent that the concept of the ego was hollow in the first place. It based its existence on my insecurities of who I thought I was. It was nothing else than an inflated sense of self, legitimising its role in my desire to fight my fears by assuming control and distancing me from others. Every time I liberated myself from limiting beliefs and their underlying fears, the inner bureaucrat had less to do, therefore allowing made more room for the explorer to thrive. With presence, patience and love, a path could be found to set the ego free. It seemed I had nothing and nobody to fight.

That was the big-ticket item of the entire adventure — the liberation from my out-of-control mind. My quest for the magic had started out as a self-improvement project but morphed into an upgrade of my identity. The running journey helped me learn how to surrender and no longer identify myself with success. The coaching journey took me a level deeper, revealing I would not be free unless I let go of all external validation to keep my self-worth alive, including my need for belonging.

The paradox of letting go was that it led to gaining control of our destinies. Looking ahead, it created the space to follow my purpose and explore where the mysterious calling would lead me. What was

I meant to do in this life? I sensed an unlived life was waiting for me, to be filled with meaning. It waited at my doorstep, and I accessed it by turning right at my garden gate.

INSPIRING THE MAGIC

Rebecca and I had to say goodbye to the rest of the team. My uncle Kurt picked us up to spend the following week in his holiday house near Bordeaux. I was sad to have missed saying farewell to Martin. He'd had to depart at the crack of dawn and kindly sent me a message. As I read from it, I realised I was not the only one in a reflective mode:

> *It has been such a delight to work with you. Your enthusiasm, dedication, lust for learning and sheer hard work ethic have combined to give you an achievement that very few people understand the difficulty in achieving. Your race was a textbook example of self-transcendence. As nothing, and no-one, you got out of the way of yourself and shone brightly for every single hour. 130/129.7 split — C'est incroyable!*

The week with Kurt passed far too quickly. I traded in running for eating my way through French delicacies and making a dent in my uncle's wine cellar. Inevitably, our holiday came to an end, and the reality of getting back to work loomed.

Within days, we were back on the long flight to Australia. I was crammed into a narrow economy seat and flew thousands of metres somewhere above Asia, yet I felt utterly grounded. My perspective had changed. For the first time in years, I looked forward to getting back to work. The first green shoots of transformational shifts at work were emerging. They gave me comfort that choosing a different career path was not running away from anything, but an expression of pursuing my purpose. Plenty of scary junctions were ahead of me in setting up my own business and guiding transformational journeys.

I knew that I no longer needed to run ridiculous kilometres to access the magic. Anybody had the ability to bring magic to their challenges. There was no 'thing' to learn; the magic happened when we were present. Running was merely one possible avenue I'd encountered to become present. Plenty of other routes were available, most of them less taxing than running. Before the world championships, Richard Lowe, one of my direct reports, had encountered his pathway to his innate magic. After months of struggling with my own reactivity in dealing with my team, a story from his weekend gave me hope that we were at a turning point.

Richard, from England, loved playing soccer and played in a local club. The club was facing its most important match of the regular season: the battle between first and second for the top spot on the ladder. Until the closing minutes of the game, all signs indicated that both teams would split the points. A draw seemed inevitable.

That all changed when Richard's team was given a penalty. Every player on his team was jubilant that they now had the chance to win, and so take a huge step towards the premiership. Meanwhile, the referee was waiting for somebody to take the penalty. Everybody looked at each other, desperately hoping that somebody else would take responsibility.

That was the moment when what we had talked about for months clicked for Richard — be motivated to win, not motivated to avoid failure. It was no longer a theoretical construct; he experienced what it meant. With no further thoughts, he took charge and stepped forward with the ball in his hands. Richard looked at me, proud as punch, waiting for my reaction. I was impatient to hear the end of the story and asked him whether he scored. His response was, 'It did not even matter. What mattered was that I dared to take the shot.'

I was speechless. I'd been through months of not getting anywhere with my team, in a repetitive cycle of painful interactions. Even after acknowledging that I had to meet my team where they were at, not where I wanted them to be, I could not see the fruits of our labour for weeks. Unexpectedly and out of nowhere, one of them had turned right. Richard confirmed that the magic happened when we had the courage to tap into our innate greatness.

Richard clearly had the right skills to manoeuvre the upcoming junctions and break out of the cycle of repetitive reactivity. An inner warmth filled me. Even more remarkable was that Richard had not focused on the result. Wasn't it ironic that for years I'd wanted to bring the magic to other people, only to find out that those people ended up being the ones who accelerated my own transformation? My team had made me a better corporate athlete.

After a long pause, Richard added, 'Yes, I scored! And we won. I still cannot believe that you, a German guy, has taught me, an English fellow, how to score penalties.'

SELF CHECK-IN

- What do you sense is your contribution in this world?
- What unlived life is waiting for you to be filled with meaning?

EPILOGUE

NAVIGATING OUR TURNS AHEAD

Sometimes you don't want to face or acknowledge it, and sometimes you're frightened to death of it, but the reality is that you know what you're truly here for.

—John Demartini

The sun kept shining for a few months after the world championships. First, I received two prestigious awards, crowning my 24-hour race as the Australian Ultra Performance of the Year. Then, I left my job in Sydney to set up my own business. The energy to help leaders upgrade their inner game and inspire the magic within work environments carried me forward.

Then I was catapulted out of my comfort zone. Lightning struck, seemingly out of nowhere, and the shock pushed me off a cliff into ice-cold water. The coronavirus ended my illusion of being able to stay in comfortable waters.

We were all facing the same adaptive challenge across the globe — how to respond to an invisible virus. The pandemic brought more complexity and chaos than most of us were prepared for. The rush to supermarkets for excessive buying of toilet paper was only the relatively harmless beginning; very quickly, the situation escalated beyond the healthcare sector. Record unemployment numbers, tumbling share prices and peaceful demonstrations turning into warlike scenes filled the news. Worldwide, all of us began to realise that COVID-19 had implications far beyond Wuhan.

SEEING THE PERFECTION

Creating my new business Turning Right was risky. I was leaving a secure job to make a living with a company that had barely been launched and was under threat before I had even found my first client. The thought occurred that I could give up and, at least, fail fast.

Or, I could surrender — let go of my urge to control, tap into my intuition and trust the process. My business was about transformation, building resilience and embracing challenges as the pathway to our highest aspirations. Ramping up during the outbreak of a global pandemic had not been my dream scenario, but wasn't it actually perfect? To nurture Turning Right through its infancy, I was asked to model turning right. COVID-19 had raised the stakes and, overnight, I found myself in the middle of another mystery run. This time, it wasn't Corey's unexpected moves I had to keep up with. It was the rapid disruptions the pandemic threw at us.

The business needed my full attention, and not having to worry about the next running-related challenge helped. The future of ultramarathon races was as uncertain as everything else. My dream to qualify for the 100-kilometre world championships in the Netherlands, the race Rebecca had already qualified for, were shattered just when I was fitter than ever before. First, my qualification race was cancelled and then the world champs. Even the next 24-hour world championships in Romania in May 2021, an event I had already qualified for, looked less likely as time progressed. But who could predict what state the world would be in by then?

Most unexpectedly, Coast to Kosci resurrected in the midst of the pandemic, and my dream of running 240 kilometres from the beach to Australia's highest mountain was about to come true. However, 222 kilometres into the race, yet another curveball led to a surprising twist. I was running in third position, only 18 kilometres off the finish line, when my support crew and I made the toughest team decision we had ever had to make — to withdraw from the race and leave finishing Coast to Kosci for another year. While I hadn't given in to the severe stomach issues I had endured for the previous seven hours of the race, my state was too fragile to continue in the freezing gale-force mountain wind on the final ascent to the summit. Prioritising safety was the right choice, and turning right had given me the ability to make such painful decisions even in an exhausted and sleep-deprived state. I realised how far I had come since my experience in Christchurch; I no longer regarded not finishing a race as an attack on my identity; neither success nor failure defined who I was.

I run because of my love for running and, from that perspective, Coast to Kosci was an amazing experience.

When I had crewed for David three years prior, the race director Paul had pointed out that I was capable of finishing the race but that it was possible it would take more than one attempt. How right he had been. My journey to reach the summit will continue.

I have a clear long-term vision — bring light to darkness, and create thriving environments. We all come to a point where playing small no longer satisfies us, and where the familiar path isn't any easier than taking a scary turn into unknown territory. At that juncture, we'll all fight our internal battles with, on the one level, a seductive inner voice suggesting that the misery we know is far better than the terror of facing the unexpected. On another level, the voice may ask what the cost is if we don't have the courage to live out our vision. When was the last time we asked ourselves what happened to our earlier dreams when we grew up? It could be tempting to relegate our dreams to mere childishness and brush them away. But it might be even more childish to desperately cling to predictability — even when it doesn't fulfil us.

It helps to remind ourselves that what got us here and was successful in the past often prevents us from reaching our aspirations for the future. Deep inside, we know that when we challenge ourselves, we make fascinating discoveries of who we really are and what fulfils us. Through our biggest challenges we transform — similar to the transition caterpillars undergo when they turn into butterflies. The ability to fly unlocks possibilities that could not even be imagined when the focus lay on crawling faster. The game fundamentally changes; we develop the capacity to see things we couldn't imagine and allow ourselves to shine brightly.

CHOOSING LIFE'S DIRECTION

For so many of us, the most rewarding moments in our lives arise when we're immersed in challenging activities in line with our purpose. Instead of dreaming about what life could look like, we choose its direction. This means learning to lift ourselves, and changing from the passive position of being the object — something that is being acted on and done to — and stepping up to act as the subject, or the agent, where we are choosing how to respond. No doubt, stepping up from being the antagonist in our lives to becoming the author of our destinies is scary.

Instead of running in the Australian uniform in 2020, I ran my first inspirational online keynote session. We were in our first lockdown, and I didn't want to wait any longer to test whether my dream would withstand a reality check. A simple approach — rapid prototyping — had already made the difference for Big Red Run, allowing me to not get bogged down in overthinking. It helped bypass my internal critic in times when innovation and agility were paramount. My topic, 'Acquiring a mindset where anything is possible', attracted 60 participants, mainly managers, from various countries. I wanted to share my fascination for magical experiences, which had reappeared at an intersection where I had habitually turned left. I wanted to pass on the fire Gavin Freeman had lit in me during 'Inspiring the Magic'.

Reading their faces on the tiny tiles on my laptop was almost impossible. Yet, from the emerging discussion, I sensed they shared a craving to become the masters of their own destinies. To no longer confine their innate greatness but dare to pursue their biggest dreams.

With the drive came the curiosity. How could we ever meet such high aspirations? The answer was simple, yet far from easy — do something different from our default; turn right and break out of the repetitiveness in our lives. From there, sustained focus and deliberate practice is required, supported by skilful guidance. Anybody wanting to live their life more authentically shouldn't wait for other people's approval to become great. We have that magic within us.

How our stories continue depends on the turns we take. Our big visions and dreams hinge on us raising our consciousness. The risk of having rising power with an absence of the accompanying surge in consciousness can be seen in the global leadership crisis we are all currently living through. Every moment we have the choice of how we respond. What the world needs most are conscious leaders, dedicated to creating environments where people thrive and contribute to the sustainable wellbeing of the ecosystems we operate in. Leaders who, in doing so, share and extend positive values and purpose.

Leadership development starts with each one of us. If we want to improve all aspects of our lives, we need to mature as leaders and human beings. An inward journey is needed to liberate us from our fears and any preconceived ideas of our own limitations. We need to look beyond what we believe to be true. How often do we limit ourselves to what is 'realistic' and only do 'what makes sense'? It can help to ask ourselves, 'How could we lead our lives? How can we master the moments that matter?'

When we blindly trust in our ability to anticipate the future, we can pretend to know what will happen. However, our knowledge is anchored in the past and, therefore, limited. So are our thoughts. When we stop being run by past experiences that were limiting, we tap into an astonishing source of energy within us and seemingly insoluble challenges evaporate.

We are all capable of leaving a legacy consistent with our highest aspirations. But reading books about adventures is no substitute for setting sail on one's own quest. If we want to be surprised by life, we need to surprise ourselves. Through transformation we will morph into who we need to become to bridge the gap from the safe and, mostly, unlived life to what the world demands of us.

On that journey, we will be reminded of the lesson I learned from reading about a little boy who overcame his cancer — we are capable of anything we put our minds to.

Each moment you and I are taking an important step, we're making a choice — stay safe, solid and dulled, or move, taking a step into something new. Morphing into something or someone new only takes a simple step in a new direction. When we have the courage to explore unknown paths, we unlock the magic we are capable of.

I believe we all have an unlived life, waiting to be explored. Welcome to the journey.

ACKNOWLEDGEMENTS

My heartfelt thanks go to my publisher Lesley Williams and my editors Shelley Kenigsberg and Charlotte Duff, who challenged me to lift *Turning Right — Inspire the Magic* to the next level. While I'd worked and believed in the book from the beginning, something is magical about having people who see and support what you want to bring to light. The team at Major Street Publishing, including Hannah Beaumont, Tess McCabe, Kerry Milin and Will Allen, have been outstanding.

I am particularly grateful to Dion Leonard. First, he challenged me to bring out my best racing against him in the Delirious W.E.S.T. 200-miler. Then, his guidance, challenge and support for this book have been second to none. Dion's generosity has been overwhelming; I am humbled to call such an amazing champion my friend.

Without Gavin Freeman's and Corey's enthusiasm and skilful guidance, it's unlikely I would ever have turned right at my garden gate in Albert Park. I can never thank Gavin enough for challenging me to trust my intuition as well as role-modelling how the magic unfolds when we do so. I am still in awe of Corey's courage to ignore the unwritten rule I had been living by and dare to turn right. At the time, it might have seemed like an irrelevant choice of direction; however, since then, it has had a profound impact on how I live my life.

I am deeply grateful for Rebecca's love and support, through which our journey has become a real team experience. Thanks for countless sleepless nights crewing for me, sharing my passion for extreme challenges and encouraging me to turn right even beyond work and running.

Gary Mullin's guidance and friendship has lifted my joy for running and how I train to the next level. Nothing is more important than a mentor I can trust, whatever my current challenge is. Thanks as well to TRT (Track Road Trail), the running community who adopted me in Sydney and with whom I shared numerous runs of many kilometres, with a special shout-out to Joe and Michelle. I would also like to express my gratitude to my running buddies in Melbourne — those from the Crosbie Crew and South Melbourne Athletics Club.

I wouldn't be the person I am today without Martin Fryer's mentoring. Martin has helped me tap into a deep well within me and introduced me to 'running from the heart'. Thank you for all the backing from the Australian Ultra Runners Association and from my fellow 'Emus' — my mates in the Australian 24-hour ultra running team. I am also grateful for the extensive support from Sophia and Mark Navin, Tegan Heywood, Michael Brierley, Dion Finocchiaro and Andrew Hoare, who've all helped me prevent, and overcome, injuries.

As for the professional part of turning right, Harald Fanderl and Dario Giarrizzo helped me accelerate the transition from a corporate leader to founder of my own business, Turning Right. Thanks to Lisa and Malcolm Doig, I have taken many more right turns to leave behind more of my urge to control and protect myself. Thanks to their fabulous team and the inspiring leaders who form the FTV (Facilitating Transformation through Values) community.

Special thanks go to my parents and sister. They have helped me become who I am today. I am grateful that, from an early age, I have been taught how to embrace the values of courage, integrity and personal growth. I would also like to share my gratitude with Aunty Imi and Uncle Kurt, who leave no doubt that they are always there for me.

Many more unsung heroes have helped me find my path of turning right in sports, at work and in life. Thank you to all of you for sharing and helping this journey.

ABOUT THE AUTHOR

Dr Kay Bretz, a 42-year-old German-Australian, lives in Melbourne, Australia, with his partner, Rebecca. Kay is a corporate leader, elite athlete and explorer. Since childhood, he has felt the urge to explore the world. He spent a year in a Scottish boarding school, followed by three years at the University of Seville, Spain. After his master's degree in International Business, he took what he would now call a right turn, and received a Doctorate in European Law. He has more than 15 years of corporate leadership experience across the globe as an Associate Principal at McKinsey & Company and as a member of senior leadership teams in the buying functions at major Australian grocery and liquor retailers.

Kay moved to Australia in 2011 where, in 2014, he turned right at his garden gate. Over the next five years, he transformed from a hobby marathon runner to a world-class ultramarathon runner. In 2019, he joined the 'Emus', the Australian national team of 24-hour runners.

His current right turn is to establish Turning Right, the business he founded in 2020 with the vision of working with individuals and organisations to inspire the magic. Kay is dedicated to helping them thrive, without the need to run crazy distances. He focuses on keynote speaking, executive coaching and tailored transformation programs to lead teams to exceptional performance and organisations to establishing inspiring cultures.

CONTACT US

To find out how to follow Kay Bretz on social media or get in contact with him, please visit www.turningright.com. There, you will also find more information on how his business Turning Right could help your personal transformation or that of your team and organisation.

REFERENCES

Anderson, R. J. (2020). *Leadership Circle Profile Certification: Manual*. Version 2020.02. Sydney, New South Wales: The Leadership Circle LLC.

Anderson, R. J. & Adams W. A. (2016). *Mastering leadership: An integrated framework for breakthrough performances and extraordinary business results*. Hoboken, New Jersey: John Wiley & Sons.

Barrett, R. (2006). *Building a values-driven organization: A whole system approach to cultural transformation*. London, Taylor & Francis.

Barrett, R. (2009). 'From Maslow to Barrett: A brief overview of the origins of the seven levels of consciousness model'. Waynesville, North Carolina: Barrett Values Centre.

Castaneda, C. (1969). *The teachings of Don Juan: A Yaqui way of knowledge*. Third California paperback edition 2008. Berkeley, California: University of California Press.

Chambliss, D. F. (1989). 'The mundanity of excellence: An ethnographic report on stratification and Olympic swimmers'. *Sociological Theory*, 7 (1), 70-86.

Csikszentmihalyi, M. (1990). *Flow: The psychology of optimal experience*. New York, New York: Harper and Row.

Demartini, J. F. (2002). *The breakthrough experience: A revolutionary new approach to personal transformation*. Alexandria, New South Wales: Hay House.

Eliot, T. S. (1943). *Four quartets:* 'Little Gidding'. San Diego, California: Harcourt.

Frankl, V. E. (1959). *Man's search for meaning: The classic tribute to hope from the Holocaust*. United Kingdom, Rider.

Frost, R. (1916). *Mountain interval*. New York, New York: Henry Holt.

Freeman, G. (2008). *The Business Olympian: Overcoming hurdles in today's business environment*. Chatswood, New South Wales: New Holland.

Giannakakis, E. (2004). *Yiannis Kouros — Forever running*. Available via YouTube, uploaded by blazremic, April 20, 2013, www.youtube.com/watch?v=l7UzmKxe3Xk&t=128s.

Harford, T. (2016). *Messy: How to be creative and resilient in a tidy-minded world*. London: Little, Brown.

Heschel, A. J. (1955). *God in search of man: A philosophy of Judaism*. Philadelphia, Pennsylvania: Jewish Publication Society.

Kabat-Zinn, J. (2013). *Full catastrophe living: Using the wisdom of your body and mind to face stress, pain, and illness*. New York, New York: Bantam Books.

Leonard, D. (2017). *Finding Gobi: The true story of a little dog and an incredible journey*. London: HarperCollins Publishers.

Mipham, S. (2012). *Running with the mind of meditation: Lessons for training body and mind.* New York, New York: Harmony Books.

Mitchell, S. (1990). *Parables and portraits.* Pymble, New South Wales: HarperCollins Publishers.

Shackleton, E. (1911). *The heart of the Antarctic.* London: Heinemann.

Stefansson, V. (1913). *My life with the Eskimo.* Reprinted London 2020: Arcadia Press.

Tolle, E. (1999). *The power of now: A guide to spiritual enlightenment.* London: Hodder & Stoughton.

Watts, A. (1954). *The wisdom of insecurity: A message for an age of anxiety.* Milsons Point, New South Wales: Rider.

Wilson, L. & Wilson, H. (1998). *Play to win! Choosing growth over fear in work and life.* Austin, Texas: Bard Press.

Wise, A. (1997). *The high-performance mind: Mastering brainwaves for insight, healing, and creativity.* New York, New York: Taschen/Penguin.

Young, S. (2016). *The science of enlightenment: How meditation works.* Boulder, Colorado: Sounds True.

INDEX

100-kilometre championships 117, 121-133
24-hour world championships viii, 121, 218-221, 263-274
—qualification 234-240

Adams, William 3, 213
Adelaide 229, 234, 238
Albany 173, 199, 205
Albert Park 16-18
Albi 221, 260, 267
ambition 133
Amundsen, Roald 135
Anderson, Robert 3, 213, 247
Antarctica 135
Apollo Bay 66
Argentina 135
Auschwitz 147
Australian Ultra Performance of the Year viii, 283
Australian Ultra Runners Association 116, 172, 292

autopilot 25, 147
Balmoral Beach 213
Barrett, Richard 181-183, 198, 222
Beach Road 17, 24
belonging 238, 242, 254, 257, 258-259
Berlin 28-29
Berlin marathon 3, 29-31
Bibbulmun Track vii, 172, 192
Big Red 86, 92
Big Red Run 41-42, 82-107
Billet, David 156, 159-163, 235
Birdsville 69, 73, 74, 75, 78, 83, 104
Birdsville Hotel 42, 78, 104
blisters 83-84, 88
Blue Mountains 119
Bogan Run 184-185
Bordeaux 279

boredom 62
Boyce, Rob 116
Brandenburg Gate 3, 30
Brazil 135
Brierley, Michael 153
Brisbane 73, 74, 106, 107
Broken Hill 159
Brownhill, Dr Adam 73, 88
bursitis 118
Burt, Candice 186, 191, 193, 199, 203
Business Olympian, The 11, 22
Buzz 161

cancer 145
Castaneda, Carlos 127
Chambliss, Daniel 57, 65, 67-68
Charleville 74
Charlotte Pass 161
childhood xi-xiv, 40-41, 48-51, 93, 111-112, 113, 151-152, 250-252, 255-259, 266
China 153, 167, 185
Christchurch 117, 127, 223
Coast to Kosci 115, 116, 139, 146, 159-163, 169, 285
Coburg 62, 64, 163, 165

Cologne 50, 113, 146
Columbus, Christopher 144
compassion 259, 266
complacency 67
Corey 15-25, 43, 59-61, 66, 67
Corporate Evolution 179
COVID-19 283-284
Crosbie Crew 22
Csikszentmihalyi, Mihaly 95
culture, work 5-6, 32, 109-110, 141, 177, 214-216
cynicism 69

Dandenong Ranges 22, 61
Delirious W.E.S.T. vii-viii, 174-176, 184-209
—preparation 57-71
—travel to 73-78
Demartini, John 263, 283
Denmark (WA) 200, 205-206
diabetes 42, 82
discipline 24-25, 69
Doig, Lisa 179-184, 223, 230, 233, 240, 248
Doig, Malcolm, 179
Donovan, Greg 75
Dykes, Gene 186

Eckford, Matt 234, 237, 240
Eden 169

Index

ego 139, 168, 182-183, 189-193, 198, 219-220, 241, 277-278
Elephant Island 136
Elephant Trail Race 165
Eliot, T.S. 211
Emus, the 249
Endurance 136
Every, Paul 163, 167, 169, 172, 185, 285
excellence 57, 67-69

failure 45
Fairweather, Simon 7
Falklands, the 135
Fanderl, Harald 178-179
fear 9, 43-48, 136-137, 233, 244
Felix 270
Finding Gobi ix, 185
flow 95-96
football 41
France 221
Frankl, Viktor 147, 170
Freeman, Gavin 7-16, 20, 22, 24-37, 40-41, 58-59, 64-68, 115, 123-124, 128
Frost, Robert 1

Fryer, Martin 202, 218-222, 226-228, 234-241, 250, 252-253, 265, 268, 274, 279
Fuxian Lake 153

Galapagos 135
gear 75
Germany 3, 4, 28
gibber plains 85
Gobi Desert ix, 185
Great Australian Bight vii
Great Ocean Road 66

Hagley Park 121, 223
Harford, Tim 17
Herron, Camille 263, 265-267, 270

Icarus 244
Inspiring the Magic course 4, 6-11, 32, 287
intuition xv, 13, 26, 90, 105, 137
Ironman 40

Janine 187, 205
Joe 166, 167-168

Kabat-Zinn, Jon 55, 141, 150
Kaesler, Shaun 173, 175, 184-186, 190, 204
Kimetto, Dennis 34

Kouros, Yiannis 250
Kurt 260, 279

Laura 113, 257
Leonard, Dion ix, 185-186, 191, 193, 196, 199, 202
love 252, 253, 257-258
Loveday, Barry 249
Lowe, Richard 280-281
Lysterfield Park 20, 22, 25, 43

Machu Picchu 135
marathons 48-51
Maslow 182
McKinsey xiv, 4, 178
meditation 29, 63, 149-151, 153, 226, 249
Melbourne 4, 21, 51, 66, 69, 109
Melbourne marathon 118
Men's Health 50
mental toughness 219-220
Merchants Guild, The 13, 24, 33, 64
Mitchell, Stephen xi
Monash University 64, 66
Monkey Rock 200
Mount Everest 186

Mount Kosciuszko 115, 139, 185
Mount Solitary Ultra 146
Mullins, Gary 116-121, 185, 191, 194-197, 200-204
mystery runs 14-25

Natalie 77, 103
New South Wales 115, 139
New Zealand 273
Northcliffe 173, 184, 189
nutrition 64

Old Shatterhand 93
Olympians 68
Olympic Park 61
Olympics 7-9

Paralympics 7
parkrun 203
Parry Beach 196, 206
Patagonia 135
Perth 180, 223, 229, 232-234, 254, 260
Peru 135
Pollack, Walter 217
Port Macquarie 165
Port Melbourne 18
pressure 91

Queensland 109
Quilpie 74, 78

Rebecca 61-62, 107, 122, 124, 128, 135, 166-168, 194-206, 223-227, 239-243
respect 241
Romania 186, 259, 285
rugby 41

sand running 53, 57
school xi-xii, 41, 45, 93, 113, 242, 250-251, 257
Schumann, Nils 7
Scotland 41, 45, 250
Scott, Robert Falcon 135
Shackleton, Sir Ernest 135-139, 189
Shelley Beach 206
Simpson Desert 42, 86, 94
Sisyphus xi
Six Foot Track Marathon 119-120
sleep
—deprivation 160-161, 193-198
—strategy 186
snakes 59-60, 192, 201
soccer 41, 280-281

South Georgia 135
South Melbourne Athletics 22
South Pole 135
Spain 116
St Kilda 18
Stefansson, Vilhjalmur 73
Sven 49-51
Sydney 141, 176, 214, 283
Sydney Harbour 213

talent 69
tall poppy syndrome 15
The Rocky Horror Picture Show 196
thought stoppage 27, 84, 123
Thwaites, Mick 236, 238, 255
Tolle, Eckhart 229
Toowoomba 74
Toulouse 260
training
—heat 70
—mental 7, 11, 14, 218
—plan 12-14, 58, 81
—running 14-19, 70, 117-120, 146, 226
Transylvanian Saxony 186
triathlons 40
Triple Crown 185, 186

Turning Right (business) 284
Twofold Bay 115, 169

ultra running ix, 41, 218
uncertainty 25-26

Vespucci, Amerigo 144
vulnerability 3, 43, 52, 231, 248, 252-253, 258, 269

Walpole 194, 205
Walpole Motel 193
Wayne 205-206
Weaver, Diane 163, 172, 185

Western Australia vii, 172, 180
William Bay 197
Wilson, Hersch 39
Wilson, Larry 39
Windorah 74
Winnetou 93
Wise, Anna 175
World War II 147
Wuhan 167, 284

Young, Shinzen 81

zero gravity flotation tanks 64-65

We hope you enjoy reading this book. We'd love you to post a review on social media or your favourite bookseller site. Please include the hashtag #majorstreetpublishing.

Major Street Publishing specialises in business, leadership, personal finance and motivational non-fiction books. If you'd like to receive regular updates about new Major Street books, email info@majorstreet.com.au and ask to be added to our mailing list.

Visit majorstreet.com.au to find out more about our books and authors.

We'd love you to follow us on social media.

- linkedin.com/company/major-street-publishing
- facebook.com/MajorStreetPublishing
- instagram.com/majorstreetpublishing
- @MajorStreetPub